THE CANADIAN MIND

Merry Christmas,
Maxx!

Love,
Mum & Dad
xo

THE
CANADIAN
MIND

Essays on Writers and Thinkers

Andy Lamey

**SUTHERLAND
HOUSE**

Toronto, 2023

Sutherland House
416 Moore Ave., Suite 205
Toronto, ON M4G 1C9

First edition, October 2023

If you are interested in inviting one of our authors to a live event or
media appearance, please contact sranasinghe@sutherlandhousebooks.com
and visit our website at sutherlandhousebooks.com for more
information about our authors and their schedules.

We acknowledge the support of the Government of Canada.

Manufactured in Canada
Cover designed by Lena Yang
Library and Archives Canada Cataloguing in Publication

Title: The Canadian mind : essays on writers and thinkers / Andy Lamey.
Names: Lamey, Andy, author.
Description: Includes index.
Identifiers: Canadiana (print) 20230458270 | Canadiana (ebook) 20230458289 |
ISBN 9781990823343   (softcover) | ISBN 9781990823398 (EPUB)
Subjects: LCSH: Canadian literature—20th century—History and criticism. |
LCSH: Canadian literature—21st century—History and criticism. |
CSH: Canadian literature (English)—20th century—History and criticism. |
CSH: Canadian literature (English)—21st century—History and criticism.
Classification: LCC PS8071.4 .L36 2023 | DDC C810.9/0054—dc23

ISBN 978-1-990823-34-3
eBook 978-1-990823-39-8

Lawrence Lamey
1939–2022

TABLE OF CONTENTS

INTRODUCTION: LITERARY
NATIONALISM RIDES AGAIN

Chapter One of this book was originally published as a magazine article. It characterized Margaret Atwood's then-recent *Strange Things: The Malevolent North in Canadian Literature* as attempting to pass off a false version of Canada's literary history. At the time, *The Globe and Mail* had a section that summarized newsstand reading of possible interest. The author of a squib about my piece disagreed with its thesis but softened the blow by writing, "Lamey's passion for his subject is exciting, his iconoclasm brave."

This remark pleased my ego (the obvious reason for quoting it here), but also puzzled me. I saw myself as making an argument rather than coming at my topic with any degree of emotion. The *Globe* writer's offhand remark forced me to admit that I did have feelings about the cultural nationalism that informed Atwood's approach. Unlike debates about the literatures of other countries, there was something personal at stake for me in this debate. It bothered me that Atwood and other nationalist critics seemed to praise mediocre works because their authors were Canadian. I felt slightly used as a Canadian reader.

To admit these feelings, however, was to admit that part of my motivation was due to a sense of national belonging. There was therefore something paradoxical about the position my article defended. On the one hand, most of the arguments it made challenged the idea that nationality had an important role to play in understanding or experiencing literature. On a deeper level, nationality was the reason I took enough interest in cultural nationalism to work up a critique of it in the first place. Even though I wasn't a cultural nationalist, I approached the world of letters as a nationalist in my own way.

This book is the result of that realization. Each chapter focuses on a different Canadian writer. In this way, it employs Canadianness as an organizing principle, much as works by cultural nationalists did. But where old-fashioned nationalists often approached works of Canadian fiction determined to find one set of symbols that would unlock them all, my approach ranges over both fiction and non-fiction and is animated by curiosity. Can we learn anything by examining a group of writers and thinkers who have nothing in common save a connection to Canada?

I believe we can. Take the debate around Joseph Boyden that occurred after he was revealed not to be indigenous. In writing my chapter on *The Orenda*, I was struck by how similar critics who accused Boyden of "cultural appropriation" are to old-fashioned cultural nationalists. To be sure, the latter group failed to consider indigenous perspectives, as by celebrating authors who were literal settlers. But anti-appropriators share with cultural nationalists a tendency to resist acknowledging just how naturally artistic influence crosses political and cultural boundaries. Proponents of both approaches view authors essentially as spokespersons for one particular aspect of their identities—even if one identity is Canadian, the other indigenous. In this way, the cultural appropriation debate combines a new concern with indigenous subjects with an older, identity-based approach to literature that, in Canada, runs straight through the nationalist generation of the 1960s and 1970s.

Nationalists of Atwood's generation wanted Canadian literature to embody Canadian "distinctiveness." If we take this to mean a particular message or theme that is the unique hallmark of Canadian fiction and poetry, it is unlikely to exist. But if we widen our concern from literature to writing more broadly, there is a branch of Canadian letters that does offer a distinct lesson. This is the political philosophy that came to prominence in Canada in the 1990s. The two best-known philosophers in this regard are Will Kymlicka and Charles Taylor, each of whom is also the subject of a following chapter. Kymlicka, in particular, has become a globally influential thinker in part because his political philosophy is informed by Canada's experience as the home of three national communities: English, French, and indigenous. Examining his work alongside Canadian fiction and criticism reveals it to possess its own form of Canadian distinctiveness, even if it is not quite the kind that cultural nationalists were looking for.

Juxtaposing chapters on different subjects highlights other connections that are easy to miss. Dany Laferrière's engagement with Quebec nationalism of the 1960s and 1970s reveals it to have noticeable similarities to that which gripped English Canada during the same period. David Frum's failure to adequately reckon with torture highlights how Boyden's novel stumbles over a similar problem. Mavis Gallant's discussion of French history sheds light on how "Vichy Republicans" became a label for collaborators with Donald Trump, Frum's central subject. The discussion of Kymlicka's rise during the 1990s, finally, has bearing on Steven Henighan's discussion of that decade and why it was a more positive time than Henighan allows. But several chapters also point out that fiction writers are not the final word on how they should be read. We can find meaning in a literary text beyond those the author intended. It will therefore not be surprising if something similar proves true of works of criticism, and readers find connections beyond those of which I am aware.

If I had to give my approach a label, it would be "minimalist nationalism," to distinguish it from previous forms. My final chapter aims to bring to light Gallant's concerns with fascism and related subjects. One such subject is the propensity for nationalism to generate pleasing but false narratives about the past through the invention of tradition and other means. Gallant's immediate concern may be France after World War II, but the tendencies she portrays are universal. If this book is an exercise in literary nationalism, I hope it is a nationalism that can be worn lightly enough to take heed of Gallant's depiction of nationalism as a source of exclusion and self-deception when it is allowed to go too far.

In more than one chapter, I am campaigning to improve a book or author's reputation in English Canada. This is most obvious when making the case for still reading *The Orenda* after Boyden's exposé or lamenting how many of Laferriere's recent books have not been translated into English, despite his ascension to the Académie Français. But in a less obvious way, this is also true of my discussion of Gallant, who in Canada is loved more by writers than readers. Indeed, in the chapter on Gallant, like those on Metcalf and Kymlicka, I am writing about writers who have shaped my adult consciousness. I am trying to communicate, however imperfectly, a sense of gratitude and admiration.

Books written during cultural nationalism's heyday sought to convince the reader that Canada had produced literature worth reading. I take for granted the value of not only Canadian fiction, but criticism, history and philosophy. The important task now is to evaluate Canadian writing and give some sense of what its signature developments have been. My title is intended to reflect this view of Canada as a generator of culture and ideas mature enough to be worth approaching in a spirit of discrimination. Hence my focus on writers who have already achieved prominence, as opposed to up-and-coming new voices. Of course, no single work can do justice to the vast output of the last 50 years. But I hope this book still helps to explain central debates that have defined Canadian life during this time, particular as they involve literature, politics and the intersections where they meet.

CHAPTER 1

THE WACOUSTA SYNDROME

By 1951, Borges had enough. Argentina had given rise to a wave of literary nationalism, and he felt concerned enough to break from his habit of avoiding political comment to deliver a lecture that now survives as "The Argentine Writer and Tradition." In that speech, Borges argued that nationalist critics had subjected native works to the literary equivalent of quarantine. They viewed Argentine literature as a thing apart, uncontaminated by any influence from Spain or Europe or elsewhere, and saw it as being constituted by a wholly indigenous literary "tradition." Borges charged that the nationalists, in their rush to portray indigenous works, such as those of the gaucho poets, as untouched by foreign influences, were distorting Argentina's literary history. In their eyes the supreme task of Argentine writers was to celebrate "local color," which meant the flora and fauna of the countryside and the speech of people who lived there. Borges believed, by contrast, in the cosmopolitan nature of literary influence, in its ability to pollinate across national borders and through the ages. In his view a writer could range beyond obviously Argentinian subjects and still remain a perfectly Argentinian writer. And so he called on Argentine writers to take the

1

whole of the Western tradition as the quarry for their imagination and never settle for second best. "If we surrender ourselves to that voluntary dream which is artistic creation, we shall be Argentine and we shall also be good or tolerable writers."

The extent to which Borges's idea resonates today depends in part on where you grew up. Literary nationalism is hardly unique to Argentina. In the twentieth century Australia was the site of a similar debate. And back before the United States was any kind of superpower, Emerson articulated a similar worry when he told his fellow New Englanders that "we have listened too long to the courtly muses of Europe. The spirit of the American freeman is already suspected to be timid, imitative, tame." Literary nationalism usually takes root in societies that are anxious about the influence of a foreign power. Often it has been part of a nation's developing self-confidence, particularly in former colonies. But usually it is the sort of thing a country grows out of. Critics can go on lionizing depictions of "local color" only for so long before Borgesian calls to maturity are sounded.

In our day, it is the culture of the United States that casts a great shadow, and this unprecedented influence has given rise to another generation of literary nationalists in yet another place. That place is English-speaking Canada, the recent history of which Borges's strictures still have bearing on. In Canada, we have sometimes been forced to choose between how we feel about our country and how we feel about good books. The literary criticism of Margaret Atwood has a lot to do with how Canadians came to be faced with this unenviable choice. But this is a story about cultural memory, and so it is important to start at the beginning.

English Canada had its share of problems in the 1960s and the early 1970s, but on the whole, things were much sunnier than they were in the United States. Instead of a divisive foreign war, a demoralizing scandal at the highest levels of political office, or a spate of crushing assassinations, the country was awash in a celebratory nationalism. It had an economic component, but mostly it was about what its advocates called cultural nationalism, as they urged people to "read Canadian," to "Canadianize" university curricula and faculties, and to lobby for state-sponsored arts and cultural patronage. This baby-boomer phenomenon was in large part a healthy rejection of the belief of the previous generation that nothing of cultural significance could be produced domestically; and, unlike some nationalisms, the majority of these cultural nationalists evinced a genuine respect for pluralism. Less admirable, however, was a self-righteous attitude toward a certain other country. This attitude was common also to previous waves of national celebration, and it was best expressed by the turn of the century journalist Andrew Macphail, who, looking back on the "Canada First" nationalist movement of the nineteenth century, lamented that "for a generation we have been the thank-Gods of America. We were not like those republicans and sinners... who lived to the southward, with whom it was dangerous for simple-minded people like ourselves to have any truck or trade."

This traditional suspicion of the United States helps explain why cultural nationalism in Canada was primarily a left-of-center movement. And the 1960s version was unique in the degree to which it saw literature as an accessory to nationhood. Canada would not be a real country, it was argued, unless English Canada could be shown to have a unique cultural identity. Canadian books had to be read through the prism of this quest for a national character. At the center of this movement was a group of writers in Toronto, and at the center of the group was Margaret Atwood.

She was already a prominent poet and novelist. *Survival: A Thematic Guide to Canadian Literature,* her first book of literary criticism, which appeared in 1972, is the founding text of this school. Unlike, say, Lionel Trilling's engagement with literature as "the human activity that takes the fullest and most precise account of variousness, possibility, complexity and difficulty," Atwood read with a different concern in mind. It was victimhood. Eschewing any evaluation of "'good writing' or 'good style' or 'literary excellence,'" she began with the consideration that "Canada is a collective victim" and came up with a four-part taxonomy of "victim positions" ("Position one: To deny the fact that you are a victim.... Position four: To be a Creative nonvictim").

Atwood proceeded to impose this template on Canadian books. *Survival* is composed of chapters about victimized immigrants, victimized families, victimized animals—victimized everything. At the end, Atwood included a list of "starting points for those who would like to know more about their own culture." In something of a first for a work of literary criticism, the premier text recommended here is the Yellow Pages. "If these are carefully studied," Atwood instructed, "they will often tell you about things available in the community which you never suspected." To this day, the average English Canadian literary work can expect to sell less than a thousand copies. *Survival* would eventually sell over 80,000 copies. It would be difficult to overestimate its influence.

The nature of that influence can be illustrated by examining Atwood's discussion of a forgotten Canadian poem of 1856, called "The St. Lawrence and the Saguenay," by Charles Sangster.

4

Here Nature holds her Carnival of Isles.
Steeped in warm sunlight all the merry day,
Each nodding tree and floating greenwood smiles,
And moss-crowned monsters move in grim array.
All night the Fisher spears his finny prey;
The piney flambeaux reddening the deep.
Past the dim shores, or up some mimic bay:
Like grotesque banditti they boldly sweep
Upon the startled prey, and stab them while they sleep.

Piney flambeaux? Grotesque banditti? It is hard not to agree with the pre-nationalist critic who called this effort of this second-rate Spenser "diffuse, vague, and ridiculously inflated in diction." Atwood herself notes an inconsistency between the poem's picture of nature as a carnival and its picture of nature as a monster's lair. Revealingly, however, she goes on to remark that "in any other country this kind of unexplained inconsistency of image might just be bad poetry; here it's bad poetry *plus*, and the plus is the doubtless unintended revelation of a split attitude [toward nature]." The poem is not being read, in other words, from the standpoint of its success as a poem. Atwood is writing apologetically, from the standpoint of local color and national need. This political and cultural extenuation is applied exclusively to native works. If the poem were not Canadian, the Canadian reader would be free to judge it as art, uncomplicated by an appeal to her patriotism.

This type of reading was long popular among English Canadian critics. Throughout the 1970s and into the 1980s, one finds nationalists declaring that "I repeat once again that the mainstream of Canadian literature has nothing to do with literary merit;

it is a matter of sphere of consciousness" or that "only a consciously nationalist criticism will provide a convincing rationale for making Canadian literature a separate field of academic inquiry." One critic seriously proposed that Canadian short-story writing is "the development of the Letter to the Editor as a specialized literary form."

The cause of this lack of faith in the ability of Canadian writers to work in conventional literary terms is complicated, but it is bound up with an anxiety about national identity. Canadian books in English must set English Canada apart, and if that involved celebrating "bad poetry," well, that was a price to be paid in service to the nation. It was in this context that a work of criticism such as *Canadian Literature: Surrender or Revolution* could demonize artistic development. In discussing Canadian poets who admitted to American influence, Robin Mathews, its author, made clear the consequences of this "rejection of the Canadian tradition": "At one level they have found in US poetry the liberation and the new directions—on a purely technical level—that they have sought. On another level they have been absorbed by the powerful rhetoric the US has broadcast about itself. That rhetoric invites an annexationist response in Canadians."

This link between stylistic innovation and treason has its roots in the perennial nationalist dream of an organic literature, wholly indigenous, uncontaminated by the alien. That such a literary development is neither realistic nor desirable should be obvious to anyone who has had their imagination captured by a foreign work. And it is not even a particularly patriotic dream, as John Metcalf has admirably observed. He writes movingly of reading as a "private and wayward pleasure," free of anxiety about national identity;

and in his important book *What Is a Canadian Literature?*, which appeared in 1988, he challenges a critic who called for fiction "rooted in local soil." "The division he is trying to create between 'international modernism' and fiction 'rooted in local soil' is an entirely false division," Metcalf wrote. "It would be difficult to imagine a book more rooted in local soil than Joyce's *Ulysses*.... Did Alice Munro's use of the tools of 'international modernism' somehow weaken the rootedness of her vision of Jubilee [a fictional setting in Munro's *Lives of Girls and Women*]?" But this is the voice of a dissenter.

Atwood is not responsible for every nationalist excess, but she has made her own contribution. In 1973, in an article defending *Survival*—it had been charged with not being nationalistic *enough*—Atwood made a strange remark:

> Other literatures *do* have "victims:" but we have to consider the relationship between victim and society. For instance, in *Hard Times*, the working class is a victim within an otherwise non-victim society: in American literature, those who fail do so by dropping out of a society where success is the norm. The thing about Canadian victims is that they tend to be representative of the society. In *As for Me and My House* [a prairie novel by Sinclair Ross that appeared in 1941], everyone else in the book is failing too. Victims the most like Canadians are to be found in the literature of other "emerging nations" or former and present colonies (or, as someone suggested, the literature of the Holocaust) and I think it would be useful to do a study on this.

Canadian victims and Holocaust victims? In *Survival*, Atwood said, about the patterns of victimization that she discussed, that "these key patterns, taken together, constitute the shape of Canadian literature insofar as it is a *Canadian* literature, and that shape is the reflection of a national habit of mind." The literature of the Holocaust presumably resembles the literature of Canada, then, because of a similar "habit of mind."

The poverty of this analysis is plain. Still, it is necessary to understand how it is that Atwood and the nationalists let their identity-anxiety push them to such lengths, and in this connection mention needs to be made of Northrop Frye. Atwood studied with Frye, and her critical method of looking for "patterns" owes a debt to his taxonomy of literary myths and structures. To be sure, Frye's writing about Canadian literature includes repeated, honorable calls to accept "international" standards, and he made one such call at the height of the nationalist fervor, when the country needed to hear it most. Still, as Edmund Wilson pointed out in *O Canada*, critics of the 1950s were "uncertain of themselves. They are inclined either to overpraise Canadian books or to be afraid to praise them," and he singled out Frye as guilty of the former, due to his decade-long policy of reviewing domestic poetry, as Frye put it, "in Canadian proportions [not in world proportions].... I have for the most part discussed Canadian poets as though no other contemporary poetry were available for Canadian readers."

Frye was a learned and perceptive critic. To read of him nearly breaking down in tears while teaching Milton is to know that he was, before anything else, a friend of literature. But on this question the giant stumbled. He is a multitude, he contradicts himself.

And that someone of his stature would read Canadian writing through a nationalist filter surely provided Atwood's generation with an influential precedent.

But Frye came before, and what comes after is also important. *Survival* met with a lot of severe criticism, and it no longer has the status it once did. The important thing now is to understand what it can be like to grow up in the wake of a nationalist literary generation. The influence of the cultural nationalists in English Canada was spread largely through the schools and the universities. To be instructed that one's identity is that of a victim, to be tested on it in class, is an alienating, demoralizing experience. You walk away from it with an unnatural aversion to books written by the people with whom you share a home. This can take a long time to overcome.

Strange Things is made up of four lectures on Canadian literature that Atwood delivered at Oxford in 1991, four years before the book was published. Overseas interest in Canadian writing as a literature is uncommon, and so a certain level of responsibility comes with delivering lectures such as these. *Strange Things* is something of an event. It provides an ideal opportunity to reflect on, and gain distance from, the excesses of the past. Atwood, in one way, does this. She once defended her exclusion of immigrant writers from *Survival* by stating that "it seems to me dangerous to talk about 'Canadian' patterns of sensibility in the work of people who entered and/or entered and left the country at a developmentally late stage in their lives." Now, in her new book, she is willing to discuss some immigrant female writers, even though "none of these women grew up in Canada; but then, neither did a lot of people who have written about the country." This inclusion is to be welcomed. There is less didacticism than in her previous criticism, and she is loose enough to joke that "surely the search for the Canadian identity is like a dog chasing its own tail." The lectures themselves are quite funny.

But these winning qualities are in the service of a misguided project. "These lectures depart from the position," Atwood writes early on,

> that, although in every culture many stories are told, only some are told and retold, and that these recurring stories bear examining. If such stories were parts of a symphony you'd call them leitmotifs, if they were personality traits you'd call them obsessions, and if it were your parents telling them at the dinner-table during your adolescence you'd call them boring. But, in literature, they hold a curious fascination both for those who tell them and for those who hear them; they are handed down and reworked...

Sounds pretty anodyne. Atwood is arguing for the existence of a certain Canadian literary tradition and implying that the works in that tradition are significant and have an audience in Canada, if not quite a massive one. This is an interesting, uplifting argument. The problems begin when you take a closer look at the works that Atwood is positing and praising.

In her first lecture, about the folkloric and literary representations of the Franklin expedition, a doomed nineteenth-century effort to find the Northwest Passage, she discussed an out-of-print novel called *Perpetual Motion*, which appeared in 1982. It appears again in her third lecture, which treats the literary representations of the Wendigo, a cannibalistic monster from indigenous legend. That the author of that novel, Graeme Gibson, was her partner may or may not have influenced Atwood's decision to discuss it, but she does not disclose this relationship to her foreign audience. More importantly, her focus on this novel is idiosyncratic when considered from the standpoint of literary reality in Canada. Indeed, of the twenty novels that Atwood mentions, a quarter are obscure and out-of-print. As is the only play she quotes from. Likewise the only book of literary sketches that she discusses. I don't mean to suggest that artistic achievement is synonymous with popularity. Critics must sometimes make the case for a neglected work. But portraying minor and obscure works as central to a society's literature is something else. Such sleight of hand deserves to be challenged on several grounds.

The first concerns the portrait of Canadian writing with which Atwood leaves her audience. Consider her lecture on the Wendigo, where she cobbles together a mix of fiction, poetry, and non-fiction, leaning heavily on unrewarding works such as William Henry Drummond's little-read 1901 poem "The Windigo." Atwood patiently quotes Drummond demonstrating his flair for a French-Canadian accent, in a passage describing a cruel logging-gang foreman:

Beeg feller, always watchin' on hees leetle weasel eye,
De gang dey can't do not'ing but he see dem purty quick,
Wit' hees 'Hi dere, w'at you doin?' ev'ry tam he's passin' by
An' de bad word he was usin', wall! It often mak' me sick.

An' he carry silver w'issle wit' de chain aroun' hees neck
For fear he mebbe los'it, and ev'rybody say

11

He mus' buy it from de devil w'en he's passin' on Kebeck
But if it's true dat story, I dunno how moche he pay.

Such risible stuff is typical of Canadian literature in Atwood's mind
alone. But it will not reward genuine criticism, so she must content
herself with interpretation on the order of "the bad thing that
happens to [the foreman]... is a direct result of the bad thing he
himself has been doing to someone else." Were Atwood presenting
the material in this lecture as the subject of her own eccentric
enthusiasm (which is what it is), it might have a certain charm. But
she holds it up as something more, as when she declares that "one
of the first laws of late twentieth-century Canadian literature being
that he who scorns Native beliefs will come to a sticky end." One of
the first laws about contemporary Canadian writing, in fact, is that
the majority of it is not about Indigenous people or their beliefs.

Atwood's resort to distorting claims is a consequence of her
decision to expound on local color—sorry, "the malevolent
North"—and thus to exclude completely "the literature of urban life."
As in Argentina, literary nationalism fosters a false image of Canada
as a fundamentally rural country. And even so, Atwood cannot make
her theme into a coherent whole, and must instead spend most of
her energies on plot summaries, with a few generalities thrown
in for good measure. ("For Ethel Wilson, as for Gwen MacEwen,
the mind of the observing individual helps to determine what is
observed.") The result is an unilluminating presentation of both
Canadian literature and the society that produced it.

There is also the more serious matter of her standards of selection.
What criteria must a work meet before Atwood will promote it into
an object of Canadian fascination? Consider one of the books to

which she kindles. John Richardson's *Wacousta: or The Prophecy: A Tale of the Canadas*, a melodramatic romance novel, was first published in London in 1832. It was popular in England, and in the following year a publisher in Philadelphia brought out an American edition. There were no international copyright laws for books at the time, and the pirating of foreign work was common. This happened to *Wacousta*. The American title was changed to make it not a tale of the Canadas, but of "Detroit and Michillimackinac." It was reissued again in 1833 in two volumes, not the original three. This second pirated edition, according to Richardson's biographer, was "abridged by some 15,000 words, changing plot, character, style, philosophy, setting–almost every aspect of the novel."

It is an open question to what degree this edition, heavily edited for an American audience, can still be considered Canadian literature. In the United States, it was highly popular, reprinted, and even made into a play (not by Richardson). But it never had the same response in Canada. Richardson bitterly lamented his Canadian failure in his memoirs, noting that "not more than one twentieth of the Canadian people were aware of the existence of the book, and of the twentieth not one third cared a straw whether the author was a Canadian or a Turk." On the differences between his popularity in Canada and in the United States, Richardson would go so far as to refer to "the vast difference of the reception I had invariably met with by the *reading* Americans, and the *non-reading* Canadians."

Richardson's efforts to find a Canadian publisher for *Wacousta* were futile. In 1868, sixteen years after his death and coinciding with the introduction of Canadian copyright law, the abridged, pirated edition was finally published in Montreal. The spelling was changed, and the end of the title was now simply "An Indian Tale."

There is no evidence that it was particularly popular, and by the turn of the century, a Canadian newspaper would report that *Wacousta* "is now out of print, and copies of it are now practically unobtainable." *Wacousta* was reprinted in Canada a few times after that, but not until fifty years after Richardson's death, which made the book public domain.

The nationalists of the 1920s dubbed *Wacousta* one of the "master works of Canadian authors," but the masterwork could not find an audience, and by the 1930s it was again out of print. After that, what little attention Richardson received was unambiguous. "Wrote abominably," was how one critic put it in 1954. As late as 1961 it is possible to find a critic, who speaking of Canadian writing as a whole, declares that "the worst (which we therefore here ignore) was in the popular historical romance of Richardson, Kirby, and Sir Gilbert Parker and the sentimental novel of local colour." These judgments echo nineteenth-century critical estimates of Richardson's work. In 1881, the historian J. C. Dent flatly asserted that "it is difficult to understand how any writer possessed of true critical sagacity could have found anything in them to admire." *Appleton's Cyclopedia of American Biography* struck a similar note: "His novels are deficient in interest and his histories are inaccurate." By the 1960s, *Wacousta*, like almost everything Richardson wrote, had disappeared from view.

Then something happened. In 1967, under the editorship of literary academic Carl F. Klinck, a nationalist press brought out a new edition of *Wacousta*. Nationalist writers could now grant the book and its author a ferocious welcome. "An internationally famous romance, whose appeal has lasted down to the present day." "Seminal." "Fresh and exciting." Richardson provided "the foundation stone of Canadian literature to which Canadian writers may look back for guidance." *Wacousta* was "at the centre of the Canadian imagination." And an appropriate quantity of critical apparatus was conferred upon the sudden "father of Canadian literature." There was a biography of Richardson called *The Canadian Don Quixote: The Life and Works of Major John Richardson, Canada's First Novelist*. A book of criticism, *The Wacousta Syndrome*, would allege, inevitably, that his work sheds light on "Canadian culture as a whole." Someone who is allowed to teach the young at Royal Military College has gone so far as to write a book that "explores Richardson's influence on James Reaney, Alice Munro, Robertson Davies," and other writers. Leaving aside the profound differences between Munro and Davies, it is almost certainly false that Richardson had any "influence" on them, as everything he wrote would have been almost impossible to find until they were well into their careers.

John Metcalf has properly described this type of nationalistic tampering with the literary past as the manufacture of "the new ancestors." Of course, no corresponding interest in Richardson exists in England or the United States, where he had his original audiences. That is because the only claim that can be made on behalf of *Wacousta* is that it was "the first major novel written by a writer born in this country," a claim that is more accurately understood to mean *Wacousta* is a major novel *because* it is the first novel by a writer born in Canada.

This spinning of the literary past is not unique to *Wacousta*, but this case is special in one way. In an act that nicely illustrates the nationalist concern with "teachability," the Klinck reprint of the edited American version was still further abridged, in 1967, by another 26,000 words. This left not only a terrible book but an incoherent terrible book. Even a nationalist critic has admitted that

15

"now, with over 40,000 words cut, it is no longer possible to even follow the plot of Richardson's novel."

It is this broken, sorry thing that finds its way into Atwood's bibliography. She cannot bring herself to quote from it, but I cannot restrain myself. The following two sentences describe life in the garrison of Detroit in 1763:

> The officers never ventured out unless escorted by a portion of their men, who although appearing to be dispersed among the warriors, still kept sufficiently together to be enabled, in a moment of energy, to afford succor, not only to each other, but to their superiors. On these occasions, as a further security against surprise, the troops left within were instructed to be in readiness, at a moments warning, to render assistance, if necessary, to their companions, who seldom on any occasion ventured out of reach of the cannon of the fort, the gate of which was hermetically closed, while supernumerary sentinels were posted along the ramparts, with a view to give the alarm if anything extraordinary was observed to occur without.

This passage is typical. *Wacousta* is full of wordy, dead passages. In larger doses it is simply unpleasant to read. For her part, in trying to make a point about whites "going Indian," that is, rejecting their own society and trying to pass as indigenous (which is one of the many, many things that happens in *Wacousta*), Atwood treats the book as a serious literary document, and says of it and another book that "two essentially nineteenth-century writers illustrate the enormous popular appeal of this idea." She asserts about the novel that "it was phenomenally popular, both in Canada and the

United States, until at least the mid-1930s." Here, and elsewhere, Atwood is reading Canada's literary past through a nationalist prism. And nowhere in her book does she acknowledge that even after all such efforts to rehabilitate the book, few Canadians have even heard of *Wacousta*, let alone read it.

Instead, Atwood goes on to tell us that "*Wacousta* was recently given a resurrection, in the form of a play called *Wacousta!*" By mentioning this little-known work, Atwood can give *Wacousta* and her reading of Canadian literary history the appearance of normalcy: It looks like she is merely checking off items in an unremarkable, orthodox tradition. This is not the case. The author of *Wacousta!*, James Reaney, has characterized his engagement with the original work in this way: "Although I had the rare privilege of reading *Wacousta* in its three-volume original English edition, I was unmoved and unexcited.... I couldn't seem to read this Gothic epic romance. There is a certain amount of skill needed to read it beside the normal suspension of disbelief." This is not artistic inspiration in the normal sense. This is a patriot admitting that he has given lingering attention to a book that he finds unreadable. Perhaps this extra-artistic motivation is why Reaney's version was itself unsuccessful. (Patricia Ludwick, who was in the play, observed about *Wacousta!* that, unless performed in "rural areas" or before children, "it is simply laughable.")

There are other areas, notably in her lecture on Canadian women writers, in which Atwood lets her nationalism color her account of the past. She divides women writers into two "waves." The first wave was made up of nineteenth-century pioneers, "and the 'second wave,' women of the twentieth century who followed these first women and either built upon, wrote about or contrasted their own lives with those of their predecessors." Atwood has herself written poetry about a nineteenth-century female settler, but she is again inventing a tradition when she generalizes in this way.

Atwood claims that the women writers of the nineteenth century inaugurate "three patterns: the tourist, the coper, and something we might call 'dismayed,'" each reacting to her surroundings according to her model. Consider her evidence for the "pattern" of the coper. This is the only one of her patterns that she tries to substantiate. Her evidence consists entirely of detecting it in two twentieth-century works. Of the first, she simply asserts that "it's the Catharine Parr Traill model—the practical coper—that Joyce Marshall uses for the female protagonist of her story 'The Old Woman,'" but she offers no proof that Marshall had Traill in mind as a model or that Traill provided any meaningful influence. Atwood's second reference is to Margaret Laurence's *The Diviners* (1974). She, Atwood, quotes a passage in which a fictional character muses about how much she is unlike Traill.

In the end, Atwood never establishes that Traill served as anyone's "literary ancestress." This is unsurprising, perhaps, when you turn to the work by Traill that Atwood has in mind. "Traill's book, *The Canadian Settler's Guide*, is a practical how-to book for prospective immigrants. She concentrates on coping–recipes, furnishings, and making the best of it." In Argentina, at least, they only wanted to canonize bad poetry. It is a little difficult to argue with someone who is willing to lecture on the literary influence of a work that is, in large measure, a cookbook. (Although, in fairness, the sections on tasty jams are quite good.)

There are ten pages in *Strange Things* that should be taken very seriously. They occur at the end of Atwood's discussion of the

Franklin expedition, where she finally makes a case for the attraction that genuine artists have felt toward the quest for the Northwest Passage. Atwood is good when she gets to the poets Gwendolyn MacEwen and Al Purdy, the novelist Mordecai Richler, and the singer-songwriter Stan Rogers. And yet, it is important to remember that most of their work was done after 1960. It is only from that point on that we can safely talk about the beginning of a Canadian literature or literary tradition. The sad (and liberating) truth is that, with few exceptions, most earlier Canadian writing, especially pre–World War II efforts, is of merely historical interest.

After 1960, things change. After 1960, the books teem with immigrants, streetcars, and restaurants at closing time: This does not make them un-Canadian; it makes them true to how we live. After 1960, there appear many fine writers, Alice Munro and Mavis Gallant chief among them, with large, well-deserved reputations inside and outside Canada. Serious examinations of Canadian literature must repair to this era, to our own time, within which Atwood's better work, such as *The Handmaid's Tale*, is appropriately included. Which is why, in attempting to pass off a literary tradition of which few Canadian readers or writers have heard, Atwood is reduced to citing *The Book of Woodcraft*, and to giving John Richardson more space than Munro or Gallant. Perhaps it is because so many of the nationalists grew up in the 1950s, before English Canada had a real literature, that they can permit themselves to hold Canadian work to a lower standard, including in how well it reflects Canada as it really is.

"The famous Canadian problem of identity may seem a rationalized, self-pitying or made up problem to those who have never had to meet it, or never understood that it was there to be met," wrote Northrop Frye. "But it is with human beings as with birds: the creative instinct has a great deal to do with the assertion of territorial rights." This, too, resonates. And it helps explain why Canadian literary criticism was for so long a receptacle of political anxiety and why an anachronistic book such as Atwood's *Strange Things* can still be written. Culturally speaking, there is a danger in living next to, and sharing a language with, a country as powerful as the United States; but this is not a danger that makes us victims. We must own up, instead, to the fact that people in our place, like people in every place, have to read and think and write as best they can. Neither power nor powerlessness exempts us from the duty to be honest with ourselves. In voluntary dreams begin responsibilities.

CHAPTER 2

THE BLACK BOOK
OF CANADA

The written history of Canada begins in medieval Icelandic sagas that recount Norse seafarers being blown off course and making landfall on a distant shore they named Vinland. The Norse were impressed by Vinland and its bounty, but were no match for its inhabitants. "Good land have we reached, and fat is it about the paunch," was the description of Thorvald Eriksson, who is also described as being killed by an arrow shot by a "skraeling," as the Norse came to call the various indigenous peoples they met.

Many tellings of Canadian history skip over its fascinating Norse prologue. The appeal of *Rise to Greatness*, by contrast, with its ambitious subtitle and stunning length, is completeness. Here at last, its heft silently suggests, will be the story of Canada in all its vastness and terror and glory, right down to the Vikings. If Conrad Black (my former employer) is its author, this is not immediately implausible. Black has written biographies of historical figures such as Maurice Duplessis and Franklin Roosevelt. After his high-profile fraud conviction, later pardoned by Donald Trump, his writing showed concern for African-Americans and other groups over-represented in the US justice system, demonstrating a capability for empathic identification that, if applied to the past, can be a powerful tool of understanding.

Rise to Greatness lives up to this foreshadowing in its early chapters on New France and colonial Canada. Black writes sympathetically about establishing a French Catholic society in North America and brings to life subjects such as explorer Samuel de Champlain, who converted to Catholicism, and Guy Carleton, who protected the rights of Catholics as Governor of Quebec. As Black's story unfolds, however, a second theme soon crowds out the minor interest in Catholicism.

This theme recalls a view in the international relations field known as realism, which sees international affairs as an amoral struggle for power among states. Realism downplays the influence of international law or moral norms on foreign affairs. Where the Catholic tradition looks to Thomas Aquinas and the New Testament, realism draws on Hobbes and Machiavelli. Black makes too many moral judgments to be a pure realist, but his approach to history shares with realism an intense preoccupation with the prerogatives of power, statecraft, and foreign relations. Power is understood narrowly, as something concentrated in the hands of a small group of politicians. Hence the book's tight focus on elite decision makers, particularly prime ministers, to the exclusion of mass movements, moral reformers, ordinary Canadians—everything else.

Given this approach, when Black calls Quebec's Cardinal Villeneuve a "cunning and unsentimental observer," it is high praise. Conversely, when he characterizes Louis Riel as lacking "the tactical sense to try to entice the United States to do some of his bidding and frighten the British," it is a damning criticism, marking Riel as a feckless leader.

Black's approach has some high moments. The portraits of Macdonald and Laurier are gripping, even inspiring. Black shows us the morning of Canada, when bold leaders could indeed do great things, such as create a new confederation or people the Prairies through a daring plan of mass immigration. Black's recounting of Trudeau's battles with René Lévesque is also compelling. Whatever Trudeau's flaws, Black suggests, in his greatest hour he kept Canada together, and this outweighs all else.

But these moments are too rare in this long book. Black's view of national history as the history of the 1 percent, to paraphrase the Occupy movement, would be inadequate anywhere, but is especially ill-suited to the history of Canada.

Canada has achieved much of its influence through means other than force of will. In 1973, Australian immigration minister Al Grassby discovered official multiculturalism on a trip to Canada and brought the idea back to Australia. Canada's Charter of Rights and Freedoms has influenced laws in Eastern Europe, South Africa, Israel, and Hong Kong. The Supreme Court of Canada now exerts a leading influence on courts around the world, surpassing its US counterpart, because "Canada, unlike the United States, is seen as reflecting an emerging international consensus rather than existing as an outlier," in the words of US legal academic Frederick Schauer. Canadian experience as crystallized in the Clarity Act holds that secession requires democratic affirmation in response to a clear question, an idea recently endorsed in Scotland.

These examples highlight Canada's role as a generator of new norms embraced by outside observers. This power-by-example cannot be reduced to a great personage pounding a negotiating table or calling in an air strike, and so is devalued by Black's approach, which fails to tell the full story of Canada's "greatness."

It also fails to explain Canada's leaders, who, like leaders everywhere, are shaped by their society. Take William Lyon Mackenzie King, not only a wartime prime minister but the longest serving, and so someone Black's approach would presumably fit. In fact, Black struggles to make sense of King, who believed that he could communicate with dead relatives, historical figures, even his dead pets. This aspect of King was influenced by the spiritualism movement, which peaked in the late nineteenth and early twentieth centuries, and acquired influence in part because it allowed women an influential role when this was often denied them. Black ignores King's historical context and labels him "complicated," "strange," and an "eccentric mystic." This misleadingly suggests King's spiritualism was just a personal quirk, when it was also a product of Canadian society.

King sometimes consulted Kingston fortune-teller Rachel Bleaney. Bleaney thus exerted a kind of power over King, but not the kind that wins many elections or wars, and so Black scants it. This typifies not only Black's take on spiritualism but also the temperance and labor movements, feminism, the Quiet Revolution—every social trend that originated outside parliament. In their place, the book contains exhausting detail on European and American leaders out of proportion to their influence on Canada, often one senses because Black has written about them before (Roosevelt) or has a personal interest in them (Cardinal Richelieu). The result is an undisciplined narrative that spends more time describing the dimensions of British naval guns before World War I than the Winnipeg General Strike.

On the rare occasions when disadvantaged groups are discussed, it is often in an obnoxious way. An early decision by Laurier concerned "'a gentleman's agreement' limiting Japanese immigration to Canada of unskilled labour to four hundred people per year. It was a good but modest start on sovereignty." Japanese laborers are unlikely to have considered it good, but no matter. Black remarks of the nineteenth-century United States that "there was only an economic reason for slavery in the South, where African and Caribbean workers were more productive in agriculture than Caucasians, being more adapted to tropical weather." Black fails to engage the complex debate on the economics of slavery and instead relies on a crass racial generalization. The Meech Lake Accord died in the legislatures of Manitoba, where Elijah Harper blocked it, and Newfoundland, where leaders of both major parties had promised a free vote it could not pass. "It was absurd that such a measure would be derailed by one legislator in Manitoba and parliamentary niceties among the Newfies." Important matters are decided in Quebec and Ontario. Mere "Newfies" should know their place.

Rise to Greatness is particularly disappointing in regard to Canada's native peoples. It was because the natives beat off the Norse that Columbus could later be credited for making contact with North America. "If it had not been for the Native Americans," US author Jared Diamond has noted, "Vinland might have undergone a population explosion, the Norse might have spread over North America," and Icelandic would be the primary language of North America. The native defeat of the Norse was a military victory of the kind Black's approach purports to emphasize, but Black gives them no credit for their influence on world affairs. Their culture he characterizes as "Stone Age," ignoring how indigenous tools, such as kayaks and snowshoes, gave them an edge over Europeans in adapting to Canada's environment.

Inevitably, there are factual errors. Riel did try to have the United States do his bidding. In a meeting with President Grant, he proposed that the United States fund an assault on Manitoba in exchange for which Riel would govern Manitoba in a manner beholden to US interests. Black endorses the canard that some of the 911 terrorists entered the United States through Canada. There is a full-page map that identifies a large island off the coast of Canada as Newfoundland. The exotic terrain in question is in fact Cape Breton. (Say what you want about Newfoundlanders, but they can usually identify the major landmasses of Atlantic Canada.)

Rise to Greatness ultimately dashes one's hope for empathy and completeness. It does however bring one historical lesson home. Our skraeling land is a graveyard not only of lost seafarers, but ill-prepared historians as well.

***

This review of Black's book, particularly as it touched on indigenous issues, prompted two very divergent reactions. The first was that of Hayden King, a prominent indigenous intellectual who at the time directed the Center on Indigenous Governance at what was then called Ryerson University, now known as Toronto Metropolitan University. "Thank god the reviewer comes to our defence," King remarked sarcastically on Twitter. "What's worse," King went on to ask, "Black calling Native people stone age, or the reviewer listing accomplishments as snowshoes and kayaks?"

I felt misunderstood by King's criticism. I did not use snowshoes and kayaks as generic examples of native accomplishments. It was rather to show a problem with Black's use of "Stone Age." The so-called three-age system (Stone Age, Bronze Age, and Iron Age) arose in the nineteenth century, when it was used to demarcate the history of Europe and the Mediterranean according

26

to how people in different periods made tools and artifacts. Such an approach was often taken to suggest that tools were all that really mattered, and so a later period was always better than a previous one, as it had all the old tools and more.

Most archaeologists now reject this method, preferring to note that a later period can be better in some ways while worse in others (anyone who got married or received a promotion during the COVID-19 quarantine will know what this is like). Black only makes things worse by using "Stone Age" as a term of cross-cultural comparison. This usage fails to acknowledge that indigenous people had inventions of their own that Europeans lacked. Black wants to rank pre-contact indigenous society as lower, period, than its European counterpart, based on its tools and artifacts, when this is not a judgment that the archaeological record actually supports. I don't see how pointing to snowshoes and kayaks in this context suggests that these achievements are all that can be said of pre-contact native people (as we will see in Chapter Five, they also had innovative forms of government). The point was to show that Black's argument fails even by its own standard.

King and I had a cordial Twitter exchange about his criticisms, in which he expressed reservations about non-natives writing about indigenous history. He did however acknowledge that, compared to my review, "Black is obviously worse." I was grateful for this. There's no point in non-native writers pointing out the problems with Black's approach if we are inevitably going to be grouped with him.

I recalled my exchange with King and my review when I later read about *Clearing the Plains: Disease, Politics of Starvation and the Loss of Aboriginal Life* (2013), by James Daschuk. Daschuk's acclaimed book, which won the Aboriginal History Prize, among other awards, documents how nineteenth-century Canadian governments encouraged famine among indigenous peoples in order to gain final control of the Prairies. Daschuk's research has contributed to a high-profile and at times contentious debate over re-evaluating the legacy of John A. MacDonald, who withheld rations and preferred to see food stockpiles rot rather than feed starving native people begging at the gates of Canadian forts.

Daschuck shows that non-native writers can make important contributions to indigenous history. On a more personal level, however, his work made me cringe at this sentence from my review: "Black shows us the morning of Canada, when bold leaders could indeed do great things, such as create a new confederation or people the Prairies through a daring plan of mass immigration." Laurier's immigration plan was only possible because MacDonald first cleared the plains. Narratives of Canada's founding that downplay or ignore this are a form of propaganda. By positively repeating Black's verdict on Canada's early prime ministers, I spread a vicious falsehood, which I regret.

The other noteworthy reaction to my review was that of Black himself. In a *National Post* article titled "A word of reply to my critics," Black commented on his negative reviews, including mine. "Seriously absurd pretexts for taking issue with this book have surfaced. I was unacceptably dismissive of Mackenzie King's spirituality (I wasn't, though I did represent some manifestations of it as odd)," Black wrote. "I failed to recognize that if the Canadian first nations had not repulsed the Vikings, there would be 300 million people speaking Icelandic in North America today (I think not)."

Readers can decide for themselves how well Black rebuts my criticisms. Readers can equally decide what to make of the fact that the "Stone Age" label reappears in his reply. As does the remark, "John A. Macdonald really was a great statesman."

CHAPTER 3

THE IMPORTANCE OF BEING METCALF

John Metcalf's name was once at the top of Canada's literary blacklist. In 1989, Metcalf and another writer, Leon Rooke, coedited *The Second Macmillan Anthology.* The collection included a section called "Position Papers," in which writers outlined their aesthetic principles. The section had been Rooke's idea, and in the introduction he divulged that more than one writer he approached had turned him down, "out of firm disagreement with John Metcalf for his variety of stands on assorted issues related to art and society." Metcalf felt betrayed by Rooke's disclosure, and the two writers were temporarily estranged. Writing about the affair in his memoirs, however, Metcalf acknowledged that the ill-will directed against him was real. "I did not doubt that what Leon was reporting was accurate. As [Leon's wife] Connie Rooke said to me about this time, 'You have *no idea* how many enemies you've got out there.'" The enmity once directed at Metcalf is worth revisiting, not only for what it says about Canada's literary history, but Metcalf's changing place within it. Where he was once a literary pariah, Metcalf today appears closer to a prophet.

There are many reasons why we might prefer not to look back at Canada during the early 1980s. Joe Clark's Prime Ministership was fresh in public memory, leg warmers were cool, and the Canadian Air Farce was on television *and* radio. In hindsight, however, the period was important for a shift that was taking place in how the country's literature was received. That shift was one that Metcalf hastened along in his 1982 essay collection *Kicking Against the Pricks*.

The change in question concerned cultural nationalism. A benign version of this doctrine holds that people should be able to see their own experiences reflected in art. On this reasonable view, it was a negative fact of Canadian life that up until the 1960s there were comparatively few works of fiction set here and even fewer taught in Canadian schools, where the curriculum focused on British and then also American works. English Canada went through its own Quiet Revolution in the late 1960s and 1970s as the boomer generation affirmed the value of Canadian art and culture. To this day, many theater companies, small presses, and Canadian-studies programs trace their origins to this period of cultural ferment.

The cultural nationalism that was ascendant in Canada in the long 1970s was necessary and valuable. It also had blind spots and excesses. Mordecai Richler captured them by recounting a conversation with Mavis Gallant, who had lived in Europe for years before returning to Canada in the 1970s for a university reading tour. "She had been astonished by the hostility of Canadian cultural nationalists who demanded to know why she wrote stories about damn foreigners and why she continued to live abroad, as if that were an act of treachery."

Gallant was born to Canadian parents and spent most of her formative years in Canada, but among some cultural nationalists this was not enough to establish her as a Canadian writer. Along with expatriots, nationalist critics also had limited interest in immigrant authors. In place of both, they lionized writers of traditional settler stock. Typical in this regard were works such as Atwood's *Survival* and Mathews' *Canadian Literature.* Atwood justified her lack of interest in immigrant fiction on the grounds that it was "dangerous to talk about 'Canadian' patterns of sensibility in the work of people who entered and/or entered-and-left the country at a developmentally late stage in their lives." Mathews' differences with Atwood included being slightly more open to immigrant literature, but like Atwood his primary goal was to argue for a uniquely Canadian literary tradition, one that celebrated musty nineteenth-century authors such as John Richardson, Susanna Moodie, and Charles G. D. Roberts. If these writers received more measured assessments from outside critics, Mathews retorted that this was the result of colonialism. "If the foreign critics are described properly, they almost always have to be called 'cultural imperialists.'"

Metcalf was Canada's first major critic of 1970s nationalism. To be sure, there had been essays by other authors challenging the nationalist *zeitgeist. Kicking Against the Pricks*, however, was the first book to argue against it at length. As Metcalf continued his argument in later works, particularly *What Is a Canadian Literature?* (1988) and *Freedom From Culture: Selected Essays 1982–92* (1994), offering an alternative to literary nationalism became his abiding theme.

Metcalf argued that 1970s-style nationalists advanced a narrow and blinkered view of Canadian literature. As he put it in a 1987 magazine article, "for more than a decade, I have been arguing that the experience of immigrants both here *and* in their countries of origin must inevitably form a large and fascinating part of Canadian literature yet to be written." He also criticized nationalists for inventing Canadian literary traditions. Not only did their sweeping claims for the influence of antiquarian works crumble when subjected to historical investigation, they failed to acknowledge the inevitable influence of international literature on Canadian writers. One critic, for example, argued that Alice Munro was influenced by In The Village of Viger, an obscure nineteenth-century Canadian story cycle. When Metcalf asked Munro whether this was true, she wryly replied, "Tell them that the book that influenced me was Winesburg, Ohio," referencing Sherwood Anderson's famous work, which was published in New York.

Metcalf sought to replace the nationalist hunt for uniquely Canadian themes and traditions with an emphasis on style. In explaining his preferred approach, Metcalf has often noted that it derives from twentieth-century British critic Cyril Connolly. Connolly believed that literary criticism should focus on individual passages in isolation from the rest of the works in which they appear. As Connolly put it, "An expert should be able to tell a carpet by one skein of it; a vintage by rinsing a glassful round his mouth." Metcalf has called this sentence his Damascus Road experience. As he wrote in Freedom From Culture, "This sentence changed the way I thought and felt about prose. As the sentence grew in my mind, the implications and ramifications continued to amaze me."

Perhaps the most fundamental ramification Metcalf drew was a distinction between writing that we experience and writing that we understand. Literary texts do not just convey information and ideas. They also occasion an emotional experience in the reader. This is what distinguishes them from philosophical treatises, workplace memos, and other writing. Non-literary prose speaks to us from the neck up, whereas literature engages the whole self. Applying this idea to cultural nationalism, Metcalf charged that its proponents were insufficiently attentive to the status of literature as something we experience, which resulted in their celebrating emotionally dead antiquarian works simply because they were Canadian.

A second conclusion that Metcalf drew was that prose should be read with the intensity normally associated with poetry. He is fond of Randall Jarrell's description of the novel as "a prose narrative of some length that has something wrong with it." Short stories, by contrast, are more likely to survive the intense sentence-by-sentence scrutiny that Metcalf favors. In keeping with this, Metcalf has long argued that stories are the best writing Canada has produced. In particular, he has long championed Alice Munro and Mavis Gallant as our two greatest writers. They are followed closely in Metcalf's estimation by Norman Levine and Clark Blaise, who Metcalf argues, are underappreciated by the general public (though not by their fellow writers).

Bringing this approach to bear on Canadian literature caused Metcalf to posit the mid-twentieth century as a fundamental dividing line. Different works cite different dates, but the point Metcalf has most often cited is 1960. Prior to this time, Canadian literature was distinguished in the main by a lack of formal innovation. There are exceptions here and there, and Metcalf does not dispute that literary works can be important on non-aesthetic grounds; *Uncle Tom's Cabin,* for example, is important for encouraging abolitionism. But after 1960, when modernism finally arrives in Canada, everything changes. Writing from 1960 onward is artistically innovative and resonant. Nationalist critics who spurned this work to lovingly paw over nineteenth-century works were committing the literary equivalent of necrophilia.

Writers sympathetic to cultural nationalism probably would not have wanted to appear in the 1989 book Metcalf coedited with Rooke. But Metcalf's brief against cultural nationalism only goes so far in explaining his unpopularity. To fully understand his blacklisting requires noting two further aspects of his writings during the 1980s and 1990s: one political, the other more personal.

Metcalf has for decades called for the abolition of the Canada Council. He argued that subsidies given to writers and publishers distorted the country's literary output. Government subsidies were distributed to particular regions, demographic groups, or along other lines Metcalf considered anti-literary. More than anything, he argued, subsidy resulted in a literature that did not have to connect with readers who appreciated it enough to pay for it. As he put it in *Kicking Against the Pricks*, "Our present 'culture' is a subsidized and legislated culture; it must become, however narrowly, a possession of real people." Metcalf's objection to subsidizing creative labor put him deeply at odds with many of his fellow writers, which was bad enough. That he advanced his campaign against the council in high-profile forums, including a pamphlet published by the right-wing Fraser Institute, only worsened his already bad odor.

Finally, there is Metcalf's writing style, which has been well described by retired University of Toronto English Professor Sam Solecki: "Agree or disagree with it, you must admit that it's better written, more energetic, more various in its effects, more witty, more provocative, and simply more interesting than almost anything written on Canadian literature within the academy." There is great passion and personality in everything Metcalf writes, and this makes his criticism memorable and vivid in two opposing but equally central modes.

Metcalf's generous mode is on display in his affectionate portraits of Canadian writers he admires. It also informs poignant essays he has written on autobiographical subjects, such as his experience growing up as a bookish boy in post-war Britain or taking his daughter to see the slaughter of a pig in rural Ontario. He is at his most profoundly affirmative on the topic of fine prose, whether it is by an established master such as Munro or one of the many young writers he has published in his capacity as a literary press editor. In these passages Metcalf has no enemies, only a deep and transformative capacity for admiration.

Metcalf's destructive mode is evident in the many passages in his criticism that assume an oppositional stance. It comes to the fore when he is writing about the Canada Council, cultural nationalists, the modern university, and many other subjects of which he disapproves. Particularly when he is engaged in a struggle for critical authority, as when dispatching a critic whose views he considers pernicious, Metcalf can be scathing and insulting.

These passages are often witty and entertaining. In *Freedom From Culture*, for example, Metcalf responds to a defense of the Canada Council offered by a now-forgotten journalist. While Metcalf addresses her argument in detail, the most memorable moment comes when he turns his attention to how the author identified herself. "[She] was described in the by-line as 'a Toronto writer and the author of *A Woman and Catholicism: My Break With the Roman Catholic Church*.' The comic immodesty of this title reminded me of Spike Milligan's memoirs of his World War II career as a private and lance corporal. His book was called *Hitler: My Part in His Downfall*."

At other times, Metcalf's negative mode is less entertaining and suggests an attitude of sneering superiority. This is particularly true of the passages in his anti-nationalist trilogy that bemoan the low sales and other indignities of being a writer in Canada. In *Kicking Against the Pricks*, for example, Metcalf complains about the fate of an anthology he edited. "Squat, unblinking, ready to engulf and absorb it leaving not a trace, sits the vast warty toad of Canadian taste." Elsewhere in the book he laments that "Canada remains so very much the land of Anne Murray, *Anne of Green Gables*, and Toller Cranston."

Bitter passages such as these gave rise to the view that Metcalf was anti-Canadian. This perception was not fair. As Metcalf also wrote in *Kicking Against the Pricks*, "While I would describe myself as an ardent Canadian nationalist, I have little time for narrow nationalist concerns *in literature*." It was, however, easy to lose sight of Metcalf's positive attitude toward Canada amid the many passages complaining about the deformities of Canadian taste. This, together with the fulsome stream of insults that Metcalf's books direct at prominent writers, journalists, and academics, whom Metcalf always took the trouble to name, only reinforced Metcalf's pariah status among his literary peers.

Today, with the benefit of hindsight, it is possible to come to a more nuanced view of Metcalf's legacy. Seeing its importance requires looking past his cranky passages. It may not have been clear to his critics at the time, but during the 1980s, Metcalf took grief for defending ideas that would later be widely accepted.

This is least true of Metcalf's writing on the Canada Council. His view of the institution as a pernicious force is hard to square with his view that Canadian literature dramatically improved around 1960, three years after the Council was established. His argument that a paying audience is the sole factor that sustains quality literature would also seem to overlook how paying audiences can fail to appreciate contemporary works that posterity later recognizes as masterpieces, as famously happened with *Moby-Dick*. A carefully administered subsidy program seems a more realistic guard against this problem than the revolution in literary taste that Metcalf calls for.

On the topic of immigrant writing, however, Metcalf was ahead of his time. The nationalist generation had a narrow view of what counted as Canadian, which Metcalf was right to challenge. Metcalf was also prophetic in making an issue of the nationalist generation's lack of interest in aesthetic questions. Canadian writers of the generation that immediately followed the boomers often satirized the view of Canadian literature as something to be read out of a grim sense of obligation. In his 1996 novel *Chump Change*, for example, Toronto writer David Eddie has his protagonist scan the nationalities of the authors on an older character's bookshelf: "heavy on the Brits…along with a sprinkling of Europeans and Americans, and a fairly heavy medicinal dose of Canadian writers." Douglas Coupland clearly spoke for more than one member of Generation X when he told a 1991 interviewer, "there's such a problem in Canada with duty reads, and there's no such thing as a duty read in the States."

For Canadian readers such as myself who came of age in the aftermath of the boomers, one of the most liberating effects of reading Metcalf is to destroy the medicinal view of Canadian literature. If Metcalf has long been in a death struggle with cultural nationalism, he has also long been a passionate evangelist on behalf of Canadian literature. He has a rare gift for analyzing and explaining literary technique, which when he brings it to bear on the work of Munro and other writers becomes infectious. One puts down a book by Metcalf impatient to read the many Canadian authors who excite him, excitement he instils like few other critics.

Metcalf's abiding preoccupation with Canadian authors distinguishes him from Connolly and other critics who were supremely concerned with the elucidation of style. It is often overlooked how this preoccupation complicates Metcalf's anti-nationalism. McGill professor Robert Lecker is a rare critic who has picked up on it. As Lecker mischievously remarks, "Metcalf is a nationalist who refuses to acknowledge that fact." Metcalf clearly rejects the critical tenets of cultural nationalism, but one way he has always been a kind of nationalist himself is on an institutional level. He is a great believer in the value of anthologies, presses, and journals specifically devoted to Canadian literature. Although Metcalf and Robin Mathews would come to blows if they had to edit a Canadian literary organ together, they share the view that a specifically Canadian literary infrastructure is necessary (even if, for Metcalf, that infrastructure should be private rather than public).

On all of the subjects—immigrant fiction, duty reads, institutional rather than cultural nationalism—Metcalf's writing foreshadows views that are now quite conventional. We take it for granted today that immigrant literature is a central part of Canadian literature, while the notion of the Canadian duty read has gone into a long decline. (How many millennials are even familiar with it?). We can debate the role of the Canada Council, but the idea that specifically Canadian media and other institutions are worth preserving remains popular. The once-common nationalist pastime of reading authors of the Confederation era with an eye to unpacking their "garrison mentality" does not.

To say that Metcalf was ahead of his time is not to say that he caused the decline of cultural nationalism. Enduring multicultural demographic trends surely made the marginalization of immigrant fiction unsustainable. The generations that have come after the boomers may also have been more comfortable with post-nationalism in part because the boomers succeeded at many of their goals. Robin Mathews, for example, achieved fame not as a literary critic but as a campaigner for the "Canadianization" of Canadian universities. When he took up the issue in the late 1960s, it was the norm for Americans to outnumber Canadians in many departments and for Canadian subjects, literary and otherwise to be neglected. After Mathews' efforts resulted in a 1981 law giving hiring priority to Canadian academics, the issue subsided. If post-boomer Canadians are less anxious about Canadian culture it may be partly because its value is more widely recognized and protected than when the boomers came of age.

Even if *Kicking Against the Pricks* did not single-handedly usher in the post-nationalist age, it remains a historically important work. Only four years separate Metcalf's book from Mathews' *Canadian Literature*, yet Mathews' work today feels badly dated in a way that Metcalf's does not. More than any other book, Metcalf's essay collection marks the end of the long 1970s in Canadian literary criticism. In this area if no other, the early 1980s were not so hideous after all.

After *Freedom From Culture*, Metcalf published two volumes of memoirs: *An Aesthetic Underground* (2003) and *Shut Up He Explained* (2007). These later works have fine passages, including a moving account of the extraordinary steps Metcalf and his wife took to help John Newlove, who won the Governor General's Award for Poetry in 1972, after Newlove succumbed to life-threatening alcoholism. But on the whole, the memoirs do not rise to the same level as the trilogy. Metcalf often recycles sections and chapters from book to book. He has also long made a practice of including many lengthy block quotes, both from works by other writers that he wishes to praise or disparage, and from his own fiction. Both of these traits, more or less under control in the trilogy, swell to problematic proportions in the memoirs, to the point that Metcalf sometimes seems inspired by Walter Benjamin's dream of a book composed entirely of quotations.

The main problem with Metcalf's memoirs however is their tone of complaint. Metcalf has often drawn attention to the fact that his short stories have been excluded from almost every national trade anthology published in Canada since 1980. (The second edition of *The Oxford Book of Canadian Short Stories in English*, coedited by Margaret Atwood and Robert Weaver, is the only exception I know of.) As he wrote in *Freedom From Culture*, "this would suggest either that my work is by common agreement very bad indeed or that the anthologists in question are possibly allowing extraliterary concerns to colour their judgement." Reviewers of Metcalf's fiction have concurred, rightly, in my view, that his work is unfairly neglected. But Metcalf's memoirs are marred by bitterness about the vagaries of literary life.

I wince at his cold treatment of a literary journalist I once worked with. She kept no blacklist and always spoke well of Metcalf. But when she had the temerity to mention in passing the low sales of an author published by Metcalf, he snarled, "What a squalid little mind she has!" Kafka wrote that literature must be the axe for the frozen sea within us. Too many of Metcalf's later passages extend the ice rather than attack it.

After *Shut Up He Explained*, ten years passed without Metcalf publishing another work of non-fiction. One picked up a new work by him with a certain amount of trepidation. The optimistic hope was for a late-career work written entirely in his generous mode. The realistic hope was to brace for something else.

***

Metcalf's book *The Canadian Short Story* outlines a history of the short story. In the nineteenth century, stories had the structure of a tale. The emphasis was on plot contrivance, which readers would follow for the pleasure of discovering what happens next. The tale structure lent itself naturally to stories of adventure set in exotic locales, as in the work of Robert Louis Stevenson or Rudyard Kipling. Their stories, like the realist novels of Dickens and Hardy, gently pulled the reader along and so could be enjoyed by a wide audience.

The arrival of modernism changed everything. By the 1920s, story-writers such as Katherine Mansfield and James Joyce had come to view the tale structure as imposing a false order and tidiness on the chaos and flow of experience. Their work is deliberately fragmented, allusive, and more demanding of the reader. The modernist story therefore "banishes the urbane, charming master of ceremonies who explains, provides a commentary, suggests where laughter or tears are required." As a result, the short story genre splits away from mass-market entertainment.

Early modernist story-writers were influenced by film, from which they learned the jump-cut technique, and by poetry. In 1913, Ezra Pound codified the tenets of Imagism, according to which poets were advised to strip away all superfluous words, and to not use a phrase such as "dim lands of peace." According to Pound, "it dulls the image. It mixes an abstraction with the concrete. It comes from the writer's not realizing that the natural object is always the adequate symbol." During the same decade, Gertrude Stein published experimental works that broke radically free of nineteenth-century diction. Pound and Stein influenced modernist writers such as Ernest Hemmingway and Sherwood Anderson, who strove to cut away all "familiarity, conventional diction [and] routine deadness of observation" from their writing.

Canadian story-writers lagged behind. Some, such as Raymond Knister (1899–1932), aspired to modernism in prose but failed. Others continued to write tales well into the twentieth century. Then in the 1950s, Munro, Gallant, Blaise, and Levine (whose postgraduate study was on Pound) began to produce bodies of work deeply stamped by modernism. In 1962, Hugh Hood published *Flying a Red Kite*, the first Canadian book of modernist short stories. An effervescence of great Canadian story writing begins, one that continues into the twenty-first century.

Part of what causes Canadian story-writers to excel is their recognition of a problem faced by modernist story-writers of all nationalities after the mid-twentieth century. By this time, the modernist story has developed a familiar and predictable structure organized around an epiphany. A character would experience a sudden rush of insight, a revelation that would "neatly deliver little packages of emotional 'growth' and 'fulfillment,'" as Metcalf puts it.

Contemporary writers shared with earlier modernists a dubious attitude toward tales. At the same time, however, the modernist story structure had for them become an obstacle, one that stood in the way of formal innovation. Different writers respond to this challenge with different forms. Munro, the supreme master, revolutionizes the story structure with frequent jumps backward and forward in time and subtle shifts in perspective. But Canadian story writing as a whole is now too diverse to generalize about, beyond a commitment to innovation itself and an ongoing willingness to make demands on the reader that separate stories from light entertainment.

Metcalf devotes approximately a hundred pages to this history, interspersed with detailed examinations of particular stories, including "Miss Brill," by Mansfield, which is reprinted in its entirety. There are also many asides on stylistic matters, including a thought-provoking criticism of similes. ("Similes usually clog up the works and do nothing a well-chosen verb can't do better, and besides, tempt writers into 'Look Ma! No hands!' showing off.") But the majority of the book is devoted to discussing the Century List. It is Metcalf's estimate of the fifty best short-story collections published in Canada. Metcalf originally conceived the list as starting in 1900 and ending in 2000, hence the name. But both the beginning and end dates soon proved nominal. The list does not include any stories published before 1950, the dividing line Metcalf appears to have settled on, while it does include twenty-first-century collections Metcalf found too essential to ignore. The name notwithstanding, the Century List is a guide to the best short fiction published in Canada between 1950 and 2015.

The fifty collections on Metcalf's list include authors whom Metcalf has edited (Steven Heighton, Annabel Lyon, and

Russell Smith) alongside well-known names who achieved international prominence independently of Metcalf (Margaret Atwood, Alistair MacLeod, and Carol Shields). There are collections by writers whose names are familiar from recent prize lists (Zsuzsi Gartner, Lisa Moore, and Kathleen Winter) and by members of an older generation whose names were, at least to me, obscure (Ann Copeland, Shirley Faessler, and Isabel Huggan). In entries on each collection Metcalf makes the case for its inclusion, often accompanied by notes on literary form solicited from the author in question. The list as a whole Metcalf describes as "the starting point for a literary discussion which has not yet taken place but that is essential for our literary sanity."

Metcalf is again in recycle mode. Of the fifty story collections named, forty appeared in a previous version of the Century List published in *Shut Up He Explained*. There is again a battery of block quotations, and the narrative is sometimes disorganized. The first five pages denounce *Quill and Quire* magazine, Josef Skvorecky, Al Purdy, Margaret Atwood, Robertson Davies, the editors of the New Canadian Library reprint series, *Ottawa Citizen* journalist Bruce Ward, as well as "big house publishers, bleating media savants, agents and low-wattage academics, hacks, hucksters, and flacks." Yet despite its flaws, *The Canadian Short Story* is a rich and rewarding book, at times even a great one.

After the opening pages, Metcalf chops off few hands and instead offers a sustained affirmation of Canadian writing. More than once he engages in a prolonged examination of an individual story, each time offering a tour-de-force example of craft-based criticism. I cannot recommend highly enough his brilliant analysis of Munro's piece, "Walker Brothers Cowboy." Metcalf lifts up the watch face of the story to illuminate how its rhetorical mechanics achieve emotional effects. Also superb are Metcalf's analyses of stories by Gallant and Mansfield. The essays on Munro and Gallant have appeared in print before, but having all three in one volume helps make this Metcalf's most generous and admiring book to date.

The Canadian Short Story ultimately highlights a theme running through all of Metcalf's work since *Kicking Against the Pricks*. It is Metcalf's fraught relationship with academia. As he wrote in his memoirs, "not for me logic-chopping in a littered classroom with orange plastic chairs but, rather, intense concentration in the presence of the thing." Metcalf's oppositional stance toward academia is reinforced by the fact that the nationalist critics his trilogy went after were often professors. A noteworthy feature of *The Canadian Short Story* is that it updates Metcalf's status as an academic outsider in a way that is relevant for the twenty-first century. As with his previous works of criticism, Metcalf's latest is a helpful corrective to the current ticks and quirks of literary academe.

Metcalf was not the only critic dissatisfied with literary nationalism in the 1980s. New approaches to studying literature, often highly theoretical, were sweeping through literature departments. Today, academic critics are interested in a wide variety of frameworks—queer theory, comparative literature, Asian-Canadian writing, eco-criticism—that eschew cultural nationalism. Like Canadian short stories, these frameworks are hard to generalize about, and certainly many offer valuable and important insights. Yet prominent within them is an approach that does not so much criticize works of literature as debunk them.

This strain was analyzed by University of Chicago English professor Lisa Ruddick in a widely read article, "When Nothing Is Cool." After interviewing over seventy graduate students in English, Ruddick noted the demoralizing effect their field of study sometimes had on them. Students were trained in critical approaches that were "all about the thrill of destruction. In the name of critique, anything except critique can be invaded or denatured." More than one young academic Ruddick interviewed described being left with a feeling of numbness. "After a few years in the profession, they can hardly locate the part of themselves that can be moved by a poem or novel."

Metcalf has one affinity with academic practitioners of critique. If they have often expressed skepticism about the idea of a canon, Metcalf has echoed them in going after one particular canon. Like his more theoretical counterparts, Metcalf draws attention to how questions of politics and power can make a purported canon seem more credible and authoritative than it really is. (Only in Metcalf's view, it is not because the very idea of a cannon is suspect, but because the works in question are pipsqueaks.) This affinity however is overshadowed by a crucial difference. Unlike wielders of critique, Metcalf is simultaneously a canon *builder*. The purpose of his Century List is to canonize those short story collections that in his estimation best succeed aesthetically. The passages he cites bring the reader directly in contact with that part of oneself that can be moved by literature. In this way, Metcalf's book serves as a refreshing antidote to the excesses of critique.

The Canadian Short Story makes explicit that the story as something to be experienced is a feature that Metcalf associates with modernist stories but not earlier forms such as tales. This suggests that his critical method may not be well suited to analyzing the work of historically distant authors—Sophocles, Dante, Shakespeare —who are surely worth reading alongside Gallant and Munro (although I concede that Dante could dial down the religion or at least change up the settings a bit). Many readers will also be reluctant to go the full Metcalf and say stories are better than novels.

But given his focus on contemporary stories, Metcalf is well served by his method of quoting individual passages at length and subjecting them to loving, painstaking scrutiny. Among other benefits, his approach nicely showcases the work of previously unfamiliar writers. I was not familiar with the stories of Ann Copeland, Libby Creelman, and Alexander MacLeod—to name just three—but put down the book haunted by their artistry.

Copeland, Creelman, and Macleod are edited by Metcalf or published by his presses. A cynic might say that such authors are overrepresented on Metcalf's list. This would be short-sighted. Roy MacSkimming, in his history of Canadian publishing, has called Metcalf's former press the Porcupine's Quill "Canada's pre-eminent literary press." Metcalf's legacy as an editor of short fiction is highly distinguished. One might dispute particular entries on Metcalf's list, but it is consistent with Metcalf's legacy and the size of Canada's literary community for it to contain many writers he has edited.

Rather than self-promotion, Metcalf's real motivation is his fealty to well-written sentences above all. There is a widespread view of story collections as a kind of apprenticeship before a writer turns to novels, which sell more. Similarly, when an author dies, interest in his or her work often falls off. Metcalf is indifferent to all such considerations of marketing. Many of the titles on the Century List are their authors' first collection, sometimes their first book. Others are by authors who died without reaching a large audience. In this way, Metcalf resembles those passionate music fans, often musicians themselves, whose collections range beyond popular acts to include obscure bands that never made it big. The casual collector is caught up in celebrity, awards, sales. The serious ones love the sound above all or, in Metcalf's case, the words on the page.

The beginning of cultural nationalism is often dated to 1967, Canada's centennial year. There is something fitting about Metcalf's book being sent out for review in 2017, Canada's 150th anniversary year. As an exercise in advocacy on behalf of Canadian literature, it is more convincing than any 1970s work. *The Canadian Short Story* should finally confirm Metcalf's status among critics of Canadian letters. Wayward and irascible his greatness may be, but it is greatness enough.

CHAPTER 4

THE LIBERALISM OF DIFFERENCE

What is Canada's leading intellectual export? Much evidence suggests it is the philosophy of Will Kymlicka. Over twenty years ago, *The Wall Street Journal* called Kymlicka a "global guru" due to his impact on lawmakers around the world, particularly in Europe. Since then, the influence of the Queen's University philosopher has only grown. When Nepal went through an acrimonious debate about a new constitution, for example, the country's largest English-language newspaper, *The Kathmandu Post*, editorialized in favor of incorporating Kymlicka's framework of minority rights. His influence has also been felt in Bolivia, where indigenous people make up a majority of the population yet are underrepresented in the military, and where Kymlicka was called in to address Bolivia's president and other dignitaries on how to make the army more inclusive. When the United Nations sponsored a workshop on African multiculturalism in Gaborone, the capital of Botswana, the organizers urged attendees to show up having read books written or edited by Kymlicka. Kymlicka has spoken to audiences at over one hundred universities, and his work has been translated into more than thirty languages (on a lower level of significance, he was also my supervisor when I was a master's student).

Kymlicka's unprecedented impact is due in part to the focus of his work. He has long been centrally concerned with so-called national minorities: groups such as the Quebecois or indigenous peoples, whose presence within a country's borders is not the result of immigration, but predates the country's official founding. Policies designed to protect minority cultures have long given rise to the concern that they can disregard the rights of other members of the political community. Rather than embrace one value at the expense of the other, Kymlicka takes the claims of cultural protection *and* individual freedom equally seriously. In this way, Kymlicka, along with other scholars who now build on his work, overcomes challenges to implementing minority rights in a liberal state that were long considered intractable.

In this and other ways, Kymlicka's theory has been deeply shaped by Canada's history as the home of three different national communities, English, French, and indigenous, living under a common set of laws. Canadian policy makers have had to improvise new solutions to the challenges presented by more than one nation sharing a government. When this improvising has resulted in workable measures, the principles on which those measures are based have not always been immediately clear. Canadian practices of accommodating national minorities rather have often come into being before anyone had formulated a well-worked out theory justifying such practices and outlining what precise form they should take. Kymlicka and other thinkers he has inspired spell out the principles of justice that have informed Canadian practice with clarity and rigor. In this way, Kymlicka's work puts an optimistic spin on Hegel's image of the owl of Minerva extending its wings slowly, at the falling of the dusk. Kymlicka has captured Canadian political experience in thought and distilled it into a philosophy of global relevance.

Kymlicka came of age intellectually during the 1980s, when Anglo-American political philosophy was dominated by John Rawls and Ronald Dworkin. The two Americans defended traditional liberal values such as individual rights and procedural justice alongside a more modern commitment to a radically expanded welfare state (or, on some readings, democratic socialism). Rawls and Dworkin achieved prominence in the 1970s, when they dethroned utilitarianism as the leading view among political philosophers in the English-speaking world. By the 1980s, their influence had become hegemonic. This spawned a critical reaction on the part of a diverse group of thinkers who, despite their inevitable differences, emphasized community as key value. Such a value, the critics charged, was one that philosophical liberals such as Rawls and Dworkin had woefully neglected.

A familiar way of locating thinkers on the political spectrum does so according to how much they support the government redistributing resources. When politics is understood this way, communitarians, as liberalism's 1980s critics came to be called, are difficult to classify. Prominent representatives include leftists such as Michael Walzer, a secular Jewish socialist who was active in the 1960s anti-war movement, but also Alasdair MacIntyre, whose otherwise hard-to-classify work would become an inspiration for Conservative Christians, who have historically favored less extensive redistribution. But when the economy is swapped out for culture as the site of government intervention, communitarianism gels into a recognizable view.

That view will be familiar to students of Canadian politics during the same period, the 1980s, when communitarians were challenging liberals for philosophical supremacy. This was the era of the Meech Lake Accord, which was negotiated by the government of Brian Mulroney to ensure Quebec would finally recognize the Charter of Rights and Freedoms and other constitutional instruments brought in under Pierre Trudeau in 1982. In return, Quebec would be recognized as a "distinct society" with new powers, unique among provinces, related to immigration, the Supreme Court, and other traditionally federal domains.

In 1990, Andy Stark, a former advisor to Mulroney, offered an explanation of the accord that goes some way toward making sense of communitarianism. Stark noted how the Accord represented a break from Trudeau's philosophy. Trudeau was fond of quoting a remark by the nineteenth-century French writer Ernest Renan: "Man is bound, neither to his language nor to his race; he is bound only to himself because he is a free agent." On a political level, Trudeau held, there is nothing special about language: The government should treat it the way governments of Trudeau's time hoped to treat race, sex, religion, or other aspects of our identity. Rather than something to be favored or disfavored, it should be left up to individuals to decide which language to speak and how much importance to attach to any given one. Hence Trudeau's mockery of unilingual Anglo business figures, "when these insular people insist, with much gravity, that their jaws and ears aren't made for [French] and can't adapt themselves to [it]."

The problem with this view, Stark observed, is that language is not like other attributes. Unlike religion, and more like race and sex, the barriers to changing one's language are "cognitive or physiological." Our mother tongues are not so easy to cast off in favor of new ones. But unlike race and sex, and more like religion, language, Stark pointed out, "needs community to survive. One can more readily remain black in a workplace of whites or female in a workplace of males than Francophone in a community of Anglophones."

The contrast between Trudeau and Mulroney on distinct society status is not a bad approximation of the liberal-communitarian divide. Notwithstanding Trudeau's many divergences from the liberalism of Rawls and Dworkin, his belief that there was no reason to treat language any differently from religion and the rest was a view he shared with the two American philosophers. As for the different philosophy underlying Mulroney's accord, Stark made explicit that it "embodies an awareness of this communitarian nature of language."

To say that language is communitarian is to say that it is an aspect of our identity that is shaped in a deep way by the community we inhabit. Communitarians, however, go farther than the drafters of the Meech Lake Accord and hold the same is true of many other aspects of the self. As MacIntyre put it in a famous passage, "I am someone's son or daughter, someone else's cousin or uncle; I am a citizen of this or that city, a member of this or that guild or profession, I belong to this clan, that tribe, this nation. What is good for me has to be the good for one who inhabits these roles." Communitarianism could attract adherents from across the economic spectrum because the left and right have historically ascribed importance to different collective identities, such as class, nation, or religious community, all of which can be made to fit a communitarian analysis as collective categories that have a formative influence on us.

As a student, Kymlicka was "hugely impressed," with the work of Rawls and Dworkin, which he viewed as combining "the best of the liberal commitment to individual autonomy with the social-democratic commitment to ending involuntary disadvantage." But if Trudeau represented a fair approximation of their liberal approach to language and culture, that approach faced a major challenge when it was applied to Canada.

In 1969, Trudeau's government announced a plan to abolish "Indian" as a legal category. The Indian Act would be repealed, reserves would be converted to private property and sold to bands or their members, and indigenous people would have no special rights, whether to self-determination, land, or anything else. The government said its new policy would "enable the Indian people to be free—free to develop Indian cultures in an environment of legal, social and economic equality with other Canadians."

Trudeau's proposal was inspired by the push for civil rights in the United States. To the government's surprise, however, it was met with intense resistance on the part of the policy's supposed beneficiaries. Indigenous people viewed undifferentiated citizenship not as the culmination of their struggle for equality, but as an excuse for the government to ignore their unresolved land claims and treaty rights. It was, in the words of Cree lawyer Harold Cardinal, "a thinly disguised program of extermination through assimilation." Idealistic Canadian liberals thus seemed to face a dilemma. They could embrace liberalism or collective rights for Quebec and indigenous people, but not both at once.

This dilemma became acute for Kymlicka when he was a graduate student at Oxford University and the philosopher Charles Taylor showed up at one of his seminars. Although not quite a communitarian, Taylor endorsed many of that school's criticisms of mainstream liberalism, including that its commitment to individual rights was too rigid and dogmatic. During his visit Taylor argued, in Kymlicka's summary, that "Canadians could never endorse this theory of Rawls and Dworkin, this liberal egalitarian theory, because Canadians needed to provide collective rights for the Québécois, for Aboriginal peoples." Taylor rattled off all the collective rights—to language and self-government, land and treaty obligations—that were plainly incompatible with the American philosophers' culturally neutral vision of justice. As Kymlicka listened, he grew anguished by the force of Taylor's argument. "I was even more disturbed," Kymlicka later wrote, "when Ronald Dworkin, who was at the seminar arguing with Taylor, agreed with him that liberal egalitarians could not endorse these collective rights."

Kymlicka's anguish resulted in *Liberalism, Community and Culture* (1989). Its central argument, a liberal defense of the value of community and culture, may sound unremarkable, but it was a landmark work in political philosophy. It showed that liberal support for collective rights was far more plausible than Rawls and Dworkin ever acknowledged.

Kymlicka began with a core aspect of the traditional liberal rationale for individual rights: Each of us should be free to decide for ourselves what kind of life is best for us. This necessarily includes the freedom to re-examine our deeply held beliefs and adopt new ones. For liberals, such freedom is a precondition of a minimally adequate life.

Without the freedom to live in accordance with our own plans, we will be deprived of a crucial prerequisite of self-respect.

So far, so familiar. Kymlicka took the argument a step further. He discussed how we actually decide among different conceptions of the good life. "This decision is always a matter of selecting what we believe to be most valuable from the various options available, selecting from a context of choice which provides us with different ways of life." And that context of choice, Kymlicka argued, is provided by our culture.

"Our language and history," Kymlicka wrote, "are the media through which we come to an awareness of the options available to us, and their significance; and this is a precondition of making intelligent judgements about how to lead our lives." If that is the case, there can be a liberal rationale for protecting culture after all, whenever doing so is necessary to enable human beings to make sense of and choose among different life-plans.

Kymlicka's account of culture emphasized the centrality of language. If, as Andy Stark suggested, the language of public life is collectively determined, thereby distinguishing language from race and other aspects of our identity, this means that smaller languages and their corresponding cultures can be at risk of disappearing into larger ones. This can occur even when members of a minority culture remain attached to their culture and take steps to preserve it.

Because minority cultures have to worry about this outcome in a way that members of the majority do not, Kymlicka argued, considerations of fairness can justify the state stepping in to support smaller cultures. So in the case of indigenous people, for example, it was appropriate for the law to restrict the ability of non-natives to live on reserves or seek to serve on band councils. Similarly, it was appropriate for Quebec's

Law 101 to actively promote French as the language of public life, as a bulwark against the long-term erosion of French.

But not just any steps to protect a minority culture are permissible. A natural question to ask—and which many critics of minority rights have asked—concerns what happens once we allow the government to regulate who can own property on native reserves or what the language of storefronts will be. Where will the government's cultural powers stop? One reason Kymlicka's theory has been so influential is that it indicated clear limits on what kind of measures governments could impose in the name of protecting minority cultures.

The measures that Kymlicka endorsed restricted the options available to non-indigenous people or non-French speakers. Such limits are only justified to the degree that they can plausibly be said to make the situation of minority cultures more equal to that of the majority. Residency restrictions on reserves mean native people will be the majority there, making it easier for them to preserve their language and culture. Similarly, measures to ensure French is the language of public life in Quebec seek a role for French broadly similar to that which English plays elsewhere in Canada.

Such policies extend a form of cultural security to native communities and Francophones that members of the majority culture often take for granted. Such restrictions can thus more plausibly be thought of as legitimate forms of cultural protection than, say, a government program that subsidized native people taking vacations to Italy or one that banned Anglo-Montrealers from working in banks. Measures with no obvious connection to ensuring the stability of a minority culture, understood as possessing its own language, are non-starters on Kymlicka's account.

This rationale also meant that Kymlicka's theory would rule out some measures that minority communities have adopted over the years in the name of protecting their culture. The Pueblo Tribal Council of the Southwest United States, for example, has sought to restrict the ability of individual Pueblo people to practice Protestantism, which has displaced traditional indigenous spirituality in some Pueblo communities. This is an internal restriction on what members of the minority community themselves can do. It cannot be defended on Kymlicka's account, which seeks to preserve the freedoms of minority cultures and endorses only so-called external restrictions, which impose carefully defined limits on what non-members can do.

Of course, it is not just minority communities such as the Pueblo who have been guilty of overreach in seeking to justify arbitrary measures. In *The Enforcement of Morals* (1965), Patrick Devlin, a British Lord, infamously argued that British law could enforce the cultural preferences of the majority when it came to sexuality and other private matters, just so long as the majority's strength of feeling amounted to "intolerance, indignation and disgust." This rationale for regulating any aspect of culture is also ruled out on Kymlicka's account. Kymlicka's difference with Devlin is rooted in a distinction he drew between a culture's character and its structure. Character includes all the customs and habits that give a culture its specificity at a particular time: its attitudes toward religion and sexuality; its fashion, slang, cuisine, and the rest. These aspects of a culture can change considerably over the years, such that it would likely be impossible for any government to freeze them in time.

Kymlicka's concern is with something deeper: the enduring existence of a cultural community and language over generations. And an enduring cultural structure often exists over top of a changing cultural character. During the Quiet Revolution, for example, the *character* of Quebec changed dramatically overnight. In a few short years, attitude toward religion, sexuality, and the status of women became more secular and modern. The *structure* of a distinct Quebec culture, however, as exhibited by the continued existence of Quebec's national assembly and other institutions of self-determination, and by French remaining the language of public life, stayed in place. Lord Devlin, Islamic fundamentalists, segregationists, and other defenders of illiberal measures have often sought to preserve a specific cultural character. In this way, they all share an approach to cultural protection that Kymlicka rules out.

Nationalism was never the force in Canadian philosophy that it was in Canadian literature. Kymlicka's concerns are far removed from that of Margaret Atwood and other literary nationalists, and not only because Kymlicka is of a different generation. Kymlicka has commented favorably on the outsized influence that American philosophers have had in Canada since the 1960s. During this time, the expanding university system scrambled to accommodate a surge in enrolments, caused by the arrival of the baby boomers on campus, by hiring many American PhDs. "The Americanization of political philosophy in Canada," Kymlicka has written, "far from displacing a vibrant local intellectual tradition, in fact revived the field, and provided the tools for Canadian philosophers to make their own contributions." Needless to say, it is hard to imagine a cultural nationalist sharing Kymlicka's sunny view of American influence.

Yet despite this and other differences, Kymlicka's first book shares something with the literary criticism of Atwood and other nationalists. Like theirs, his stakes out and defends what we might think of as an underdog nationalism. Whereas Atwood and other cultural nationalists were concerned that Canadian identity not be made subservient to the power of the much larger country, the United States, with which it shares a continent, Kymlicka is sympathetic to the desire of the Quebecois and indigenous people not to be subservient to the much larger cultural community, Anglophone Canada, with which they share a state. In both cases, nationalism is seen as a vehicle for protecting an identity that is at potential risk of disappearing into a larger other. If all forms of nationalism are perennially at risk of tribalism and myth making, underdog versions are at least less able to engage in triumphalist imperialism than are their more powerful counterparts.

Kymlicka's first book propelled him to intellectual prominence when not just Canada but many countries were debating how to accommodate minority nationalisms. Events such as the fall of the Berlin Wall saw previously suppressed national groups assert themselves in a wave of what commentators called a new world of "ethnic pandemonium." Years later, a slightly baffled Kymlicka looked back on the fateful coincidence of publishing a liberal defense of minority rights just when the entire world was suddenly consumed by the idea:

> Confronted by this pandemonium, both policy-makers and academics desperately looked around to see what had been written about the relationship between liberal democracy and ethnic diversity, and my just-published doctoral dissertation —*Liberalism, Community and Culture*—was one of the few academic publications that addressed the topic. As a result, I quickly went from being a typical philosophy graduate student

to being an "expert" on ethnic diversity, initiating a string of invitations to write and advise on the governing of ethnic diversity that has continued unbroken for almost thirty years now.

Even this account however may undersell the influence of *Liberalism, Community and Culture*, which also effectively ended the liberal-communitarian debate. They say the best refutations of a philosophy are made by critics who feel its force: who intuitively understand why someone might be drawn to the philosophy in the first place. Kymlicka, perhaps because he shared their central concern with the shaping role of culture, presented searching criticisms of MacIntyre and other communitarians. One of his most powerful arguments called into question the degree to which communitarianism really was a rival philosophy to liberalism, as opposed to just another variant of it.

Grounds to doubt that communitarianism was a freestanding view were suggested by its proponents' habit of being vague and circumspect about what political measures followed from their arguments. One could finish a book by a philosophical communitarian without any concrete measures being put forward at all. In other instances, they seemed to wind up endorsing individual rights and other elements of liberalism that their surface arguments ostensibly found wanting.

MacIntyre, for example, admitted that even if we find our good in the social roles we inhabit, this "does not entail that the self has to accept the moral limitations of the particularity of this form of community." If that is the case, Kymlicka replied in *Liberalism, Community and Culture*, then it means that individuals can step back from their communities and social traditions to choose among them after all. If so, then the resulting political arrangements will not be very different from the current one, which allows individuals wide discretion in choosing which community roles and practices to identify with. And if these freedom-preserving arrangements are liberalism's central concern, then communitarians are a party not of opposition but of agreement.

Kymlicka further undermined communitarianism by removing its central appeal. It was thought to provide support for collective rights that liberalism supposedly could not. If liberalism was, as Kymlicka demonstrated, capable of generating not only a worked-out system of minority rights, but one that was relevant to national debates in a wide range of countries, there was no need to cast about for an alternative framework, as communitarianism was initially taken to be.

Yet if Kymlicka vanquished communitarianism, criticism of his own view was not slow in arriving from a different corner. An influential tradition of thinking holds that rather than strive to preserve the culture of our ancestors, we should embrace new ones. In the literary realm, the novelist Salman Rushdie has long been a proponent of this view. Rushdie has said his own work "celebrates hybridity, impurity, intermingling... It rejoices in mongrelisation." Such staunch cosmopolitanism also finds adherents among philosophers. One such proponent, Jeremy Waldron, wrote an influential critique of Kymlicka that faulted him precisely for paying inadequate attention to the cultural mixing that, according to Waldron, was a defining feature of modern life.

There is an obvious sense in which someone can become cosmopolitan by living in different countries. Waldron, however, argued that a person can be genuinely cosmopolitan even if they spend their entire life in the same city. This occurs when such an individual "refuses to think of himself as *defined* by his location or his ancestry or his citizenship or his language." Waldron elaborated his point with a vivid image of an American cosmopolitan:

> Though he may live in San Francisco and be of Irish ancestry, he does not take his identity to be compromised when he learns Spanish, eats Chinese, wears clothes made in Korea, listens to arias by Verdi sung by a Maori princess on Japanese equipment, follows Ukrainian politics, and practices Buddhist meditation techniques.

Like Waldron's San Franciscan, most of us have been influenced by more than one culture. Waldron, himself a New Zealander who has long been based in the United States, argued that this swirl of diffuse influences is not only inevitable but also desirable. Kymlicka's theory was essentially conservative, he charged, in seeming to resist this defining fact of modern life.

Waldron also suggested that Kymlicka had a deeper problem: He misunderstood the nature of culture itself. Even if Kymlicka is right that the plans and projects we choose from all have particular cultural meanings, Waldron wrote, it does not follow that those meanings must all be part of the *same* cultural framework. "Meaningful options may come to us as items or fragments from a variety of cultural sources. Kymlicka is moving too quickly when he says that each item is given its significance by some entity called our culture." Waldron reeled off a list of examples: The Bible, Roman Mythology, *Grimm's Fairy Tales*. We are exposed to a wide diversity of cultural fragments that, rather than cohere into a unified whole, are bits and pieces of many different narratives. Kymlicka may have shown that human beings need access to a wide range of social roles to choose from and cultural signposts to make sense of them, but he had not shown that they need membership in one particular culture.

Waldron's argument is a powerful rebuke to fundamentalists and arch-traditionalists regarding culture. But does it lay a fist on Kymlicka? Waldron does not take heed of Kymlicka's distinction between cultural character and cultural structure. Many of the items he mentions as influencing the modern cosmopolitan—cuisine, fashion, technology, media—would count as character in Kymlicka's terms, which Kymlicka does not seek to preserve. Kymlicka's argument does not prevent anyone from enjoying the churn of cultures that Waldron defends. In a Kymlickian world, a Francophone Quebecer, for example, is free to enjoy all the cultural delights that Waldron associates with San Francisco. If we change the example to involve someone in Montreal being forced to speak English at work against their will, that would more closely match the form of cultural "openness" that Kymlicka is concerned to prevent. And insofar as it is a forced and unwanted form of openness, in this instance, Waldron's preferred outcome, simply letting the swirl of modern culture take its course, does not seem so attractive.

Kymlicka acknowledged that the options available to us come from a wide range of cultural and historical sources. But Waldron's examples, he replied, actually support Kymlicka's original view. Consider what it means for a cultural item or idea to be available to us. If *Grimm's Fairy Tales* has had an impact on our culture, this is surely because it has been translated into English. Otherwise, it would have had as little influence as the folklore of other cultures that never penetrates our awareness. Kymlicka's notion of cultural structure was meant to capture this aspect of culture, which language typifies and which separates it from cuisine, religion, and other items on Waldron's list. "So the unavoidable, and indeed desirable, fact of cultural interchange," Kymlicka wrote, "does not necessarily undermine the claim that there are distinct cultural structures, once we recognize that they are based on a common language." He might also have mentioned that human beings tend to be more open to the delights of cosmopolitanism when they do not have to worry about their own culture disappearing.

Kymlicka's reply to Waldron appears in *Multicultural Citizenship: A Liberal Theory of Minority Rights* (1995). It tries to answer questions that *Liberalism, Community and Culture* left unaddressed. If human beings need access to a stable cultural structure, for instance, why must it be the culture of one's ancestors? Why not simply assimilate everyone into the majority culture, as the Pierre Trudeau government hoped to do with indigenous people? Without an answer to this question, Kymlicka's project was in doubt. A less sweeping but still serious issue concerned which particular groups are entitled to cultural protection. Would Kymlicka's argument oblige the Canadian and American governments to subsidize the continued use of Mandarin or Cantonese across North America's many Chinatowns? Such an outcome would reduce the theory's appeal, given that strong state support for immigrant cultures has less intuitive appeal than maintaining those of national minorities. Was there a principled way to avoid this conclusion?

Kymlicka's exchange with Waldron showed that culture can be an elusive concept, with proponents of different understandings talking past one another. Kymlicka sought greater clarity by now speaking of "societal culture" as his abiding concern. As the name implies, it refers to the culture that pervades an entire society, encompassing both the private and public realms, and which is "territorially concentrated, and based on a shared language." Whereas different uses of "culture" can refer to populations as small as subcultures or as vast as global civilizations, Kymlicka was explicitly referring to nations. And members of minority nations, he now argued, warrant state support for their cultures as a matter of self-respect.

This is because human beings commonly find a strong sense of identity in their societal cultures. The cultures in which we grow up play this role, Kymlicka argued, because we connect to them at the level of belonging rather than accomplishment. Of course we define ourselves in significant part through our individual achievements and losses. But there is a sense of security that comes with an identity that, rather than something we can earn or forfeit through our actions, is simply part of us. As Kymlicka put it in a passage that quoted two previous philosophers, national cultures matter to huge numbers of people because they provide an "anchor for [their] self-identification and the safety of effortless secure belonging." To deny Francophone Quebecers or indigenous people a stable societal culture was therefore a form of disrespect.

And immigrants? Kymlicka argued that they were entitled to distinct legal rights such as strong anti-discrimination laws, official government multiculturalism, and exemptions from laws that disadvantage them, such as motorcycle helmet laws in the case of male Sikhs. But these measures stopped short of the even stronger rights, to cultural protection and self-determination, which Kymlicka advocated for national minorities. Kymlicka argued that the two different kinds of cultural communities deserved different sets of rights because immigrants were unlike national minorities in a crucial respect.

"They have uprooted themselves, and they know when they come that their success, and that of their children, depends on integrating into the institutions of English-speaking society," Kymlicka wrote. Insofar as immigrants freely chose to migrate, they are unlike national minorities, who historically have most often become minorities due to conquest or other unchosen factors. Because immigrants voluntarily leave their countries of origin, it is reasonable for their new societies to make their admission conditional on waiving their right to live within their societal culture.

In addition to fending off objections, *Multicultural Citizenship* also presented a big new idea. Whereas Kymlicka's original argument for minority rights cited facts about minority cultures, he now cited a separate set of facts about governments. Prior to Kymlicka, generations of liberals had argued that when it came to culture, the state should adopt a stance of "benign neglect." Rather than favor or disfavor any particular one, the government should remove itself from the realm of culture altogether, leaving it up to individuals to decide what cultural activities or options to embrace. The liberal view thus had long been that culture should be treated much like religion. Kymlicka made a decisive break from liberal tradition by arguing that this stance was not only unattractive but also incoherent.

Government institutions cannot avoid embracing culture. This is most obvious when it comes to language, which all governments must use to function. A crucial political question therefore turns on which language or languages will become the language of government, which, as Kymlicka pointed out, encompasses "the language of public schooling, courts, legislatures, welfare agencies, health services" and many other institutions. A language of state enjoys a high level of security and is practically guaranteed to be passed down to the next generation. Conversely, when a language is not employed by public schools or other government institutions, this usually consigns it to marginalization.

Kymlicka further pressed his case against benign-neglect liberalism by noting other areas in which governments routinely favor one culture over another. Consider the fact that Christmas is a state holiday in Canada and the United States, whereas Hanukkah and Diwali are not. Such arrangements are far from neutral on a cultural level (or a religious one, for that matter). This is but one of several ways in which liberal-democratic governments foster identification with a particular societal culture. When immigrants apply for citizenship, for example, they are often tested on their knowledge of their new country. Such tests, rather than being culturally neutral, encourage newcomers to identify with the history and traditions of the country in question, which usually entails some degree of identification with the cultural majority. A similar sense of identification is fostered by the flags and anthems states employ, the statues and landmarks they commemorate, and the histories they promulgate, which frequently give prominence to the dominant societal culture.

While it would be possible to reduce the degree to which governments favor particular cultures in this way, eliminating it entirely would likely be very difficult. And in the case of language, there does not seem to be any realistic possibility of governments treating them all neutrally, which would require every language to be a language of state. Given that neutrality in the cultural sphere is a non-starter, Kymlicka argued, a reasonable alternative approach is to view protections for national minority cultures as a kind of equalization. As states are likely to favor the majority in matters like holidays and history, and must inevitably do so with language, enshrining legal protections for national minority cultures can be justified as a way of evening the cultural playing field by actively seeking to prevent the erosion of national minority cultures.

Multicultural Citizenship was Kymlicka's second pass at minority rights. Like his first book, it acknowledged clear and well-defined limits on how far state supports for minority cultures could go. Although Kymlicka argued that states inevitably played cultural favorites, the correct response to this was not to endorse unlimited state intervention in matters of culture (let alone religion). But part of *Multicultural Citizenship*'s power comes from its unique effectiveness in highlighting the many ways in which cultural majorities enjoy advantages that had long been overlooked.

To take but one example, shortly before the book appeared, Canada had undergone a debate about whether Sikh members of the Royal Canadian Mounted Police should be permitted to wear turbans instead of Stetsons. Arguments against doing so were often framed in terms of holding everyone to a uniform standard. But as Kymlicka pointed out, Mounties, like police in many Western countries, have historically been permitted to wear wedding rings. In some branches of Christianity and Judaism wedding rings are religious symbols, as is evident in the role they play in these denominations' wedding ceremonies. When police wear wedding rings for religious reasons, no one objects. Surely this is because the religious cultures in question include that of the cultural majority. *Multicultural Citizenship*, like few books before it, made cultural favoritism like this visible. In theory, we could potentially eliminate it by denying police the right to wear wedding rings, but that seems petty.

Kymlicka made a persuasive case that it was better to admit some flexibility in uniform requirements, especially if the result will be greater integration and inclusion of a visible minority. (In this way, his theory is at odds with Quebec's Laicity Act, which since 2019 has banned many civil servants from wearing religious symbols.)

Where Kymlicka's first book was often concerned with pointing out the problems of communitarianism and other rival approaches, *Multicultural Citizenship* is a sustained presentation of his positive case for minority rights. As such, it is his definitive statement of liberal multiculturalism and the work that may have most contributed to Kymlicka's global policy impact. If his previous book made Kymlicka a star, *Multicultural Citizenship* saw him explode into an academic supernova. It is among the most influential books—possibly *the* most influential—to come out of Canada in the last fifty years.

But if the book has been uniquely influential among global policy makers, its reception among philosophers has been more guarded. A recurring criticism, made by critics across the political spectrum, is that Kymlicka's distinction between national minorities and immigrants is overdrawn.

How can people immigrate at all, given what Kymlicka says about societal cultures? If a person's culture of origin is as important as he says, how is it possible that anyone could leave one culture for another? In *Multicultural Citizenship*, Kymlicka tried to pre-empt this concern by pointing out that the vast majority of human beings never leave the culture of their birth. When the book was published, for example, only 2.8 percent of the global population was made up of immigrants (and even that figure included those who move to countries where they already speak the language). "Some people seem most at home leading a truly cosmopolitan life, moving freely between different societal cultures," Kymlicka wrote. "But most people, most of the time, have a deep bond to their own culture."

In describing this bond, Kymlicka drew an analogy to taking a vow of poverty. Although some people can take such a vow and still lead fulfilling lives, this does not call into question that human beings have a right to a basic economic minimum. Similarly, the fact that some people can live outside their culture of origin does not undermine the fact that most people have a deep attachment to their own societal culture, to which they deserve secure access.

This aspect of Kymlicka's theory rested not on abstract political principles, but on empirical claims about human nature. Given this, it bears noting that the number of immigrants as a percentage of the global population has grown since *Multicultural Citizenship* appeared: In 2020, it was 3.5 percent. Not a lot, admittedly. But the fact that it has been growing, even if slowly, makes one wonder whether the number of people who can successfully embrace a new language and culture is larger than Kymlicka admits.

Even if Kymlicka is right that most people cannot leave their culture, migration poses a problem for his theory. Many people pull up stakes and migrate to a new culture not because they want to, but because they have to, in order to escape poverty or other deprivations. Even if the poorest of the global poor do not have the resources to migrate, refugees and other people do feel compelled to immigrate to escape economic or political problems. Many commentators have therefore asked just how accurate it is to characterize *all* immigrants as doing so voluntarily.

This worry about Kymlicka's theory becomes especially acute when we consider immigrant children. They often have no say in whether they will move to a new country. Indeed, they often find themselves in strange new classrooms where they do not speak the language. According to Kymlicka's mature theory, were a member of a national minority such as a twelve-year-old Cree child to suddenly be forced to operate in a new societal culture, it would have devastating implications, calling into question her self-respect and her ability to make sense of her life options. But when we imagine a Punjabi-speaking child being forced to operate in a new societal culture after his parents immigrate from Lahore to Toronto, this is no cause for concern. How can these different responses be reconciled?

In the case of adults, Kymlicka's answer is that they immigrated voluntarily. But their children usually do not make their own decision to immigrate. Moreover, Kymlicka's argument about the need for one's societal culture to provide a context of choice emphasized how damaging it is when human beings are forced to live inside new cultures. So if Kymlicka's account of societal cultures is correct, how can children not only enter new societies but also thrive in them, as immigrant children do with some frequency? And if immigrant children can turn out fine, why can't we expect the same when national minority children assimilate into the culture of the majority?

A final, less noted problem with Kymlicka's account concerns not immigrants but indigenous people. His case for special rights for them is based on protecting their societal cultures, Kymlicka's outline of which emphasizes their distinct languages. But according to the 2016 Canadian census, only 12.5 percent of indigenous people in Canada had an indigenous language as their mother tongue. On Kymlicka's account, the majority would be members of a societal culture centered around English or French. If the rationale of minority rights is to protect cultures that are understood to have a distinct language at their core, then that rationale will not apply to seven out of eight indigenous people.

After noting these limitations, one possibility would be to abandon the idea of minority rights. But there is another option. It is to distinguish between the particular arguments Kymlicka has made, and his broader project of seeking to reconcile liberalism and minority rights. Kymlicka's work has inspired other thinkers to offer their own theories of this kind, theories which break from Kymlicka on many points while preserving the spirit of his approach.

Kymlicka's most prominent intellectual descendant may be Princeton University theorist Alan Patten, whose book *Equal Recognition: The Moral Foundations of Minority Rights* (2014) offers a reformulated theory of liberal multiculturalism, one that consciously seeks to overcome the challenges that have bedeviled Kymlicka's theory. Like Kymlicka's, Patten's theory has been shaped by Canada's attempts to do justice to the cultures of its national minorities. ("To many of my American friends and acquaintances," Patten, who is from Montreal, writes in the preface, "my topic will seem, if not exotic, then at least awfully Canadian.")

Patten follows Kymlicka in arguing that the state can prioritize protecting national minority languages and cultures over those of immigrant communities (even if, like Kymlicka, he argues that governments have different responsibilities for immigrant communities). Patten, however, makes no appeal to the importance of culture as a context of choice for decisions about how to live. His argument is in this way closer to the one Kymlicka offered in *Multicultural Citizenship* concerning the obligation of states to protect minority cultures in the name of equality.

In Patten's formulation, those obligations include extending special accommodations to national minorities in a spirit of avoiding favoritism toward the majority. As in Kymlicka's theory, these accommodations seek to counteract the in-built tendency of government institutions to reinforce the culture and language of the majority. But also as with Kymlicka's account, this raises the question of why immigrants should not also have their cultures recognized and accommodated. Patten again follows Kymlicka by arguing that immigrants waive this right when they move to a country with a different culture. Patten, however, makes an original move by arguing that immigrants can meaningfully consent to such an arrangement, even though they do sometimes migrate out of necessity.

He defends this stance with a nuanced discussion of what makes a choice voluntary. Consider someone who is so sick that she will die unless she undergoes surgery. Patten thought-provokingly suggests that such a person can still give consent to the surgery, just so long as her condition has not impaired her faculties. Indeed, he plausibly argues that it would be wrong for a surgeon to operate on her without her consent. But if that is the case, it means that human beings can still make meaningful choices even in dire circumstances. By extension, even if the decision to migrate is not itself purely voluntary, immigrants can still consent to waiving their right to live in their culture of origin.

A natural question to ask about this argument is whether it might go too far in characterizing coercive scenarios as ones in which we can still exercise consent. When a mugger tells a couple leaving a bar that he will kill them unless they hand over their wallets, surely there is nothing voluntary about that kind of choice. But Patten maintains that we can recognize the possibility of consent in the surgery case (and, by extension, that of immigrants) without denying that mugging is coercion, full stop. The difference is that in the surgery case, the terms are reasonable. The surgery will benefit the patient, and the surgeon is not doing anything outlandish by asking her whether she wants to go through with it. Although the mugger's victims also benefit from having their lives spared, the robber is the one who puts them in danger in the first place, which is far less reasonable. People cannot meaningfully give or withhold consent in grim circumstances when the terms of the agreement are unreasonable. But when the terms are fair, Patten argues, consent remains possible. And it is reasonable for states to oblige immigrants to operate inside a new culture, as making every immigrant language and culture official would eventually make government dysfunctional.

If that is the case, then immigrants can reasonably be said to have voluntarily waived their entitlement to state support for their culture. This does not mean that a state can impose *any* conditions on immigrants. It would be ludicrous for example to ask immigrants to give up their right to a fair trial as a condition of arrival. But even so, governments can adopt a different policy stance toward immigrants than they do toward national minorities. As Patten points out, when a state deprioritizes the claims of immigrants it is "not denying them rights that are essential to freedom or a worthwhile life but is instead imposing on them a disadvantage that, in any case, will have to be imposed on some people given the impossibility of extending a full set of cultural and linguistic rights to all groups."

If Patten has a plausible answer to why immigrant cultures should not be treated exactly the same as those of national minorities, other problems facing Kymlicka's account simply never arise for his view. Because Patten's theory does not emphasize a need to have access to one's original cultural structure as a condition of choice or self-respect, it does not face the same problem Kymlicka's does in justifying why immigrant children can be made to grow up in a new culture. And because Patten presents his own subtle theory of culture, one that views it more as a matter of shared socialization than a shared language, his account does not face the problem Kymlicka's does in justifying legal rights for entire indigenous communities whose pre-contact languages have become dormant.

Patten may need to say more about how his theory applies to refugees and other migrants whose reasons for migrating are so extremely coercive that it does not make sense to view them to consenting to anything about their circumstances. But fruitful political philosophies sometimes arrive less than fully fleshed out. Just as Patten improved on Kymlicka, there may well be a bright graduate student out there who, as we speak, is grinding out a dissertation that improves on Patten. If so, they will be continuing a tradition that Kymlicka started, and which Kymlicka himself recognizes as having now progressed beyond his original arguments. As Kymlicka has written of Patten, "in most cases I'm happy to endorse his reformulations of the relevant culture-related interests and principles of distributive justice, which are often more careful and precise than my earlier works."

Kymlicka's status as the founder of an intellectual tradition that is still developing is further suggested by the work of Dale Turner, a University of Toronto political theorist who is also a member of the Temagami First Nation, an Anishinaabe community located in Northern Ontario. Turner's work is representative of how many indigenous people now approach the debate over indigenous rights. "Since most aboriginal communities claim that their special rights flow from their legitimate political sovereignty," Turner writes, "I take issue with liberal claims that Aboriginal rights imply a type of 'minority right.'"

According to Turner, most existing theories of minority rights are unsatisfying because they view the Canadian state, but not indigenous nations, as possessing sovereignty. This is not how indigenous people themselves conceive of political authority. If when Kymlicka first wrote incorporating minority rights into liberalism was a progressive step, Turner suggests that today it is necessary to recognize some form of indigenous sovereignty, even if he also emphasizes that the precise form is still being worked out, both philosophically and legally.

Turner argues that although we don't yet know what a final framework of indigenous rights will look like, it is likely to combine Western and indigenous elements. Given this, an important aspect of Kymlicka's theory is that it implicitly recognizes indigenous sovereignty. This is due to Kymlicka's account of what it is to be a national minority, which presumes some form of self-government. Although Turner is critical of some aspects of Kymlicka's approach, when it is judged by indigenous standards, it is clearly superior to previous theories of indigenous rights and policy proposals going back to Trudeau's White Paper. "Kymlicka's theory of minority rights," Turner concludes, "can be reformulated in a way that allows Aboriginal voices into the dominant non-Aboriginal discourse on Aboriginal rights." If or when such a reformulation occurs, it will be a fitting culmination to Kymlicka's project of outlining a new theory of justice. One that takes our difference seriously, while recognizing that we are equals all the same.

CHAPTER 5

THE ORENDA: A DEFENSE

Joseph Boyden is not native. The truth came out in 2016, a few days before Christmas, when Robert Jago, a political blogger, asked in a series of tweets, "Is Joseph Boyden actually native?"

Even as Jago was tweeting, the Aboriginal People's Television Network (APTN) was working on a story about Boyden. It soon appeared under the headline "Author Joseph Boyden's shape-shifting indigenous identity." Reporter Jorge Barrera wrote that Boyden had for years "variously claimed his family's roots extended to the Metis, Mi'kmaq, Ojibway and Nipmuc peoples." Barrera drew attention to Jago's tweets and cited genealogical research to show that Boyden's changing claims of indigenous ancestry, in addition to being inconsistent, were all false. By January, critics on Twitter were using the hashtag #CancelBoyden to call for Boyden's speaking invitations and other opportunities to be withdrawn. Successfully, it would turn out.

Boyden's change in fortune was stark. In 2016, he was the respected author of *Three Day Road* and other acclaimed novels on indigenous themes that had won the Giller Prize and other major literary awards, and that had transformed Boyden into an enthusiastic spokesperson for indigenous concerns. By 2017, Boyden's name had become, as a report in *The Globe and Mail* put it, "a byword for ethnic fraud and cultural appropriation." In 2017, Boyden gave a few interviews and wrote a *Maclean's* article in which he tried, without success, to defend himself from accusations of identity fraud. Since APTN's exposé, Boyden has been little heard from. As of this writing, no further books have appeared under his name.

Some observers have suggested that this is no great loss, as Boyden's writing now has little worth. This view was expressed at a 2017 panel at the University of Alberta. Janice Williamson, a professor of English and film studies, said, "I am not going to teach Joseph Boyden [as an indigenous author]. He takes up the space of indigenous writers." Fellow panelist Norma Dunning, then a PhD student in education, went further: "If I were you, I wouldn't teach Boyden. Period." Since the panel occurred, views similar to Dunning's have regularly appeared on social media. As David Gaertner, a professor in the First Nations and Indigenous Studies Program at the University of British Columbia, tweeted in 2020, "Joseph Boyden should not be on your syllabus unless you are teaching a course on fraudulence."

Williamson was making the fair point that in classes on indigenous writers, Boyden's work no longer has a place. But the thought that Boyden should no longer be taught, period, or only as an example of fraudulence, suggests that the revelation of Boyden's identity snuffs out whatever value his fiction possessed. In this way the backlash against Boyden has gone too far. If the case that Boyden misrepresented his identity is overwhelming, the case that we should no longer read *The Orenda* (2013) rests on a confused and complacent understanding of what it is for a writer to "appropriate" material from a culture not their own. Particularly in the age of reconciliation, we should be reluctant to cast aside a richly imagined novel such as Boyden's, which pulses with anti-colonial energy.

The case against reading Boyden hinges on accusations of cultural appropriation. The term is becoming amorphous through its application to everything from outsiders writing songs about minority cultures to indigenous land being seized at gunpoint. Are all of the activities condemned as appropriation really wrong? Or could there be value in a non-native writer depicting native experiences, so long as it is done in a careful and informed way?

Thoughtful answers to these questions are found in *Cultural Appropriation and the Arts* (2008), by James Young, a philosopher at the University of Victoria. When cultural appropriation is wrong, Young suggests, it often involves the wrongful taking of artifacts or other tangible goods, such as land. Young points to events during the 1890s when the Benin people of what is now Nigeria were fighting to maintain their independence after the arrival of British colonial expeditions. British soldiers plundered bronzes that had been made specifically for the Benin's traditional leader, the Oba. These culturally significant artifacts ended up in the British Museum and other foreign institutions. By taking the bronzes without permission, Young suggests, British soldiers engaged in wrongful object appropriation, which is a form of theft with added sting, given the cultural import of the items involved.

Young distinguishes object appropriation from the appropriation of artistic content that originated in a culture other than the artists' own, such as a song, story, or motif. The Japanese director Akira Kirosawa engages in this kind of appropriation when he uses Shakespearean plots in his films. A third category, subject appropriation, occurs when artists depict characters or institutions from another culture. Tony Hillerman, a mystery writer who has written frequently about Navajo characters but is not Navajo himself, engages in this kind of appropriation.

In Young's framework, "appropriation" is not always a bad thing. Hillerman's books, for example, for years were used in Navajo Nation schools. In 1987, the Navajo Tribal Council honored him with the Special Friend of the Dineh (Navajo) Award, which recognized him for "authentically portraying the strength and dignity of traditional Navajo culture."

Similarly, Kirosawa has received critical praise for his creative use of Shakespearean plots. Unlike the theft of objects, being artistically influenced by a different culture need not come at the expense of the autonomy of that culture's members. They can continue to tell their own stories and describe their own experiences. As Young sums up his view, "cultural appropriation is often defensible on both esthetic and moral grounds. In the context of the arts, at least, even appropriation from indigenous cultures is often unobjectionable." Young cites countless artists, from Picasso to Herbie Hancock, whose borrowings from other cultures resulted in works that resonated with audiences of many different cultures.

Young's book, with its careful distinctions between different forms of appropriation, as well as the overall view it expresses (one section is called "In praise of Cultural Appropriation"), offers a better approach than the one featured in heated literary debates over cultural appropriation. His account allows us to condemn the

The Canadian Mind

wrongful appropriation of objects and land, and a few stray cases of subject appropriation (such as that of the nineteenth-century missionary H. R. Voth, who violated the privacy rights of the Hopi people by taking pictures of sacred religious rituals). But when "cultural appropriation" is applied to literature, it is usually meant to condemn what Young terms "subject appropriation," regardless of the details of the depiction. Young, by contrast, sees subject appropriation as not only permissible but a potentially positive aspect of an artwork as well.

Young is white, but prominent writers of diverse backgrounds share his view that a presumption against subject appropriation is a bad idea. Many years ago, I attended a reading by Tomson Highway, then and now one of Canada's most prominent indigenous writers. During the Q&A, I asked Highway what he thought of the idea that non-indigenous writers should avoid writing about indigenous people. His answer consisted of six words: "I don't have time for it." The case for writing across cultural borders has also been well defended by the Palestinian literary critic Edward Said. Said, whose work is a monument to anti-colonialism, rejected the idea that "only women can understand feminine experience, only Jews can understand Jewish suffering, only formerly colonial subjects can understand colonial experience." Said argued that such a view relied on a dubious cultural essentialism, as it failed to "acknowledge the massively knotted and complex histories of special but nevertheless overlapping and interconnected experiences—of women, of Westerners, of Blacks, of national states and cultures—there is no particular intellectual reason for granting each and all of them an ideal and essentially separate status." As we will see in Chapter Nine, the notion that the meaning of a work of literature is fixed by the

82

cultural origin of its creator is satirized by Quebec writer Dany Laferrière, who is black.

Opposition to subject appropriation suggests a vision of the future in which indigenous, black, or other minority stories can only be told when an indigenous, black, or minority storyteller is available. It is hard not to see this resulting in a position of ongoing cultural privilege for narratives about Europeans and their descendants. Yes, we need more indigenous, black, and other creators telling their stories. But we should hope to see indigenous and other creators also become sources of inspiration in cultures beyond their own.

Many people other than Kirosawa have found Shakespeare to be a source of cross-cultural inspiration. Such borrowings are now the subject of an academic industry documenting Shakespeare's influence in countries as diverse as Indonesia, Kenya, and China. Although his material is overwhelmingly European, his reach is universal. Like other great artists, Shakespeare traveled well thanks to colonialism, but he has also achieved his status in part because his content and subjects are thought to belong to everyone. Opposition to subject appropriation stands in the way of non-white artists achieving the same level of universal authority and acclaim that is bestowed on Shakespeare and other celebrated European creators.

The double standard that sometimes informs the reception of writers of color has been pithily described by Indian novelist Amit Chaudhuri. "The important European novelist makes innovations in the form; the important Indian novelist writes about India." As Chaudhuri elaborates, "this is a generalization, and not one that I believe. But it represents an unexpressed attitude that governs some of the ways we think of literature today.... The American writer has succeeded the European writer. The rest of us write of where we come from." Chaudhuri refers to Indian writers, but what he says is true of how indigenous ones are often thought about as well. Talk of "cultural appropriation" only reinforces the view Chaudhuri criticizes, which, despite its progressive veneer, subtly marginalizes the work of indigenous, Indian, and other writers whose ancestry does not trace back to Europe.

Applied to Boyden, this suggests that we should distinguish the charge of identity appropriation from that of subject appropriation. The former is a wrong concerning how he represented himself. The latter is put forward as a wrong regarding his work that, upon examination, turns out to be dubious. There is nothing unethical in principle about a white author telling indigenous stories or writing about indigenous characters. No facts about an author, even an author guilty of something as serious as indigenous identity fraud, are sufficient to determine the quality of the work they produce. The debate over subject appropriation endlessly directs our attention to authors, when we ultimately must return to the work itself.

The Orenda takes place during the seventeenth century in what would later become Ontario. Among the indigenous peoples who lived there, the Wendat, whose historic homeland was between Georgian Bay and Lake Simcoe, were pre-eminent. They dominated regional trade to the point that other native peoples, from the Ottawa Valley in the east and perhaps as far away as Wisconsin in the West, had to learn their language as a condition of doing business. Their historic rivals, the Haudenosaunee, lived south of Lake Ontario but hunted north of it. Rather than trade, their interactions with the Wendat took the form of ambushes and raids, to which the Wendat replied in kind, sustaining ongoing cycles of small-scale violence.

The Orenda opens with a Wendat headman and his warriors kidnapping a Haudenosaunee girl, a response to the murder of the headman's family. On the same journey in which he kidnaps the girl, the headman also captures a Jesuit who had been sent from the new outpost at Quebec to convert the Wendat to Catholicism. The Jesuit, who takes turns narrating with the Wendat elder and the Haudenosaunee child, refers to the Wendat and Haudenosaunee by their respective French names, Huron and Iroquois, one of many ways in which each narrator reflects their particular culture. Much of the drama of the story concerns the interactions between the Wendat and French, who insist that the Wendat tolerate a growing number of missionaries as a condition of being players in the fur trade, and between the Wendat and Haudenosaunee. Wendat expeditions to Quebec require traveling upriver through Haudenosaunee territory, the danger of which, high to begin with, is exacerbated by the kidnapping and the Haudenosaunee desire for revenge.

According to the political economist Harold Innis, "the Indian and his culture were fundamental to the growth of Canadian institutions." Without being didactic, *The Orenda* illustrates what Innes was getting at. "The Anishnaabe came down from the north in strong numbers," the Wendat narrator observes, "their hunters loaded with deer meat and pelts to trade for Wendat corn." A so-called cultigen, corn is the result of human alteration and selection, and was likely first grown in ancient Mexico. By 500 AD, indigenous trade networks had brought it to Ontario, where an ancestor culture of the Wendat discovered how to grow it in a colder climate. This had a positive effect on the Wendat diet, and allowed them to settle in villages surrounded by palisades and cornfields.

It also gave them something of value to trade with neighboring nations such as the Algonquin-speaking peoples to their north, who lacked arable land and were nomadic by necessity.

The fact that the Wendat were already experienced traders when Europeans arrived enabled them to assume a prominent role in the early fur trade. That they occupied settled villages also made them a convenient missionary target, further entwining their fate with that of the colony at Quebec, three-weeks away by canoe. If today Ontario and Quebec are part of the same country, this is in part because of trade and missionary arrangements made possible by the Wendat's facility at agriculture. And if Canada does not include upstate New York, much closer than Quebec City is to Wendat territory, this is in part because New York belonged to the Haudenosaunee, who also mastered agriculture, occupied villages, and fought with the Wendat over hunting and fishing grounds.

Early in *The Orenda* the Wendat headman takes a dislike to the Jesuit, whom he correctly recognizes as a threat to his way of life. When the headman finds the priest praying over the Haudenosaunee girl while she is asleep, he mistakenly assumes the Jesuit is about to sexually assault her, one of many moments in the story of cross-cultural misunderstanding. The Wendat narrator then has an opportunity to kill the priest, but the girl talks him out of it. The headman later remarks that he should have killed the Frenchman when he had the chance, to which another character replies, "You know you can't... the elders won't condone it." The Wendat leadership will not tolerate the open murder of the Jesuit because accepting his presence is a condition of trading with the French. The headman decides instead to take the Jesuit, derisively referred to as the "Crow" due to his long black robe, on a journey to Quebec in the hopes that he will die in a Haudenosaunee attack.

A long-standing tradition of thought viewed the indigenous peoples of the Americas as savages. A prominent representative of that tradition, the seventeenth-century philosopher Thomas Hobbes, sought to illustrate the proper function of government by imagining what it would be like to live in a state of nature. Hobbes had in mind not life out-of-doors but life without the artifice of law or government, which regulates our interactions and checks our anti-social impulses, and which Hobbes considered a pre-condition of justice itself. Hobbes famously argued that such a state of existence would be so violent that people who lived in it would have "no knowledge of the face of the Earth; no account of time; no arts; no letters; no society; and which is worst of all, continual fear, and danger of violent death; and the life of man, solitary, poor, nasty, brutish, and short." Hobbes pointed to the New World as a place where people could be found living in such conditions. "For the savage people in many places of *America*, except the government of small Families, the concord whereof dependeth on natural lust, have no government at all, and live in this day in that brutish manner."

In depicting indigenous people as lacking culture and law, Hobbes was lending intellectual respectability to a prejudice already in circulation among European writers that would justify potlatch laws, which forbade the expression of indigenous culture, and other instruments for the "improvement" of native peoples. *The Orenda*, by offering a historically accurate picture of Wendat life, shows how ill-informed Europeans such as Hobbes were in their understanding of indigenous people.

One way the novel does this is in its depiction of sex and family life. Early on the Jesuit character decries local sexual mores as "shameless in their lack of modesty." The Wendat did not require women to always cover their breasts, thought it was fine for both women and men to initiate sex, including outside of marriage, and did not consider monogamy especially important until after a couple had children. In these and other ways, their approach to relationships differed from (some would say improved on) that of their European counterparts.

One familiar attitude that indigenous people held, however, was that they considered incest taboo. This meant that a person could only form a family by finding a partner who was not a relative. (In the Wendat case, this ruled out not only marriages between immediate relatives but also between cousins and other extended kin.) Contrary to Hobbes's image of endless war between nuclear families, starting a family required cooperation with other family units, particularly those who would become one's in-laws. The ties of extended kinship that resulted meant that it was possible to enforce cultural and moral norms, as indigenous characters do throughout *The Orenda*, even in the absence of presidents and prime ministers.

And if the Wendat did not have Western political institutions, they still had governments of their own. Wendat society took the form of a confederacy. It was composed of at least four autonomous nations, whose names are sometimes translated as the people of the Bear, Rock, Cord, and Deer (and may have contained a fifth, the people of the Marsh). Each nation had its own governing council that would deliberate over trade, war, and other matters of national interest. Representatives of all the nations would come together at least once a year to address issues of concern to the confederacy as a whole. A primary function of the confederate council was to suppress blood feuds and other violent disputes between members of different nations. The confederacy succeeded in bringing this peace, in part because different Wendat nations, estimated to have consisted of thirty thousand people at their height, shared a common language and culture.

The Orenda depicts meetings of the council of the people of the Bear, at which members gather around the fire and try to come to consensus on issues of national import, particularly as they concern interactions with the French and Haudenosaunee. It is because the council exists and wields political authority that the Wendat protagonist cannot simply murder the Jesuit. Although the inner workings of Wendat government are not a major focus of the novel, the depiction of Wendat government is significant as it illustrates the core falsehood in the myth of indigenous people living in a state of nature (which is further undermined by the fact that the Haudenosaunee, among other peoples, also maintained confederacies).

After the Haudenosaunee girl is captured, she accompanies the Wendat leader and his men to Quebec (a detail that may strain plausibility, given how rare it was for women to go on such journeys). While at Quebec, a French fur trader attempts to rape her, only for the Jesuit to intervene. The girl's assailant is then strapped to a stockade and publicly flogged with a cat-o'-nine-tails until he falls unconscious, after which the Jesuit again steps in to stop the violence. Although the Wendat who are at Quebec want the trader punished, they disapprove of the French authorities' brutal methods. "What is the point of this torture," one of them asks, "if he isn't [mentally] present to understand its point?"

The frank depiction of a Haudenosaunee girl being assaulted by a French character is a break from previous narratives of early Canadian life, which were known to romanticize sex between European men and indigenous women. Take *Company of Adventurers*, Peter Newman's acclaimed history of the Hudson's Bay Company, published in three volumes beginning in 1985. The first sentence of Chapter One, "The Bay Men," states: "For a time they were trustees of the largest sweep of pale red on Mercator's map, lording it over a new subcontinent, building their toy forts and seducing the Indian maidens they playfully called their 'bits of brown.'" Newman told history from the fur traders' point of view, taking at face value their accounts of sex with native women as playful and fun, all part of the big adventure. Boyden's narrative, perhaps because it is told mostly from indigenous perspectives, is far less romantic, foreshadowing as it does the sexual abuse of native children that would be institutionalized in residential schools and other organs of colonialism.

One way a modern author might react to colonial narratives would be to reverse them: Morally exquisite indigenous heroes triumph over depraved European villains. *The Orenda* rejects this strategy, which replaces one stereotype with another, in favor of a more complex approach. When the Wendat express bafflement at the cruelty the French inflict in the name of justice, it is one of many instances in which Europeans are found wanting by indigenous moral standards. (A similar moment occurs when some Jesuits are shocked to realize that the Wendat, unlike Europeans, never inflict corporeal punishment on children.) It is a testament to Boyden's skill as a writer that these moments are always believable. The indigenous characters have morally nuanced inner lives, resignation to practices such as kidnapping coexisting alongside gentle parenting and other habits of mind that reflect a well-honed moral sense.

Although the Jesuit character is less sympathetic, moral complexity also informs his make-up. His interventions to stop torture and rape draw on recognizably ethical impulses. Yet at the same time, his presence ultimately is a disaster for the Wendat. Both aspects come together in his religious fanaticism, which motivates him to commit acts of bravery and mercy as he seeks the destruction of Wendat culture. As a Catholic, he would never agree with Hobbes that morality is a product of human artifice rather than God's natural creation. Yet he shares the view that indigenous people are savage children and so in urgent need of his improvement. What he stands for is ultimately on display in a scene in which he uses his developing indigenous language skills to proselytize at a Wendat village. "Great voice, he loves you. Great voice is son child deer Christ. Christ kill for you to become him. Christ kill me. Die. Death for you. Christ."

The Orenda makes vivid many injustices to first nations that were a deliberate part of the founding of Canada. For readers aware of subsequent Canadian history and the unfinished project of achieving a just relationship with indigenous peoples, the effect of the book is to raise an old question with new force. That question was posed by anthropologist Michael Asch in *On Being Here to Stay* (2014), which takes its title from a famous passage, written by Chief Justice Antonio Lamar, in the supreme court's 1997 *Delgamuukw* decision: "Let us face it, we are all here to stay." Asch asks of people whose presence in Canada is a result of European settlement, "What, beyond the fact that we have the numbers and the power to insist on it, authorizes our being here to stay?" As befits a work of fiction, *The Orenda* allows the reader to imaginatively experience the history that gives this question force. As is also fitting, the novel calls this question to mind without answering it.

The Orenda is a respectable work of historical fiction, one that manages to inflame the reader's sympathies without being programmatic. Someone might accept this verdict on the book, yet still find fault with the fact that Joseph Boyden is its author. This view, or something like it, was suggested by the criticism that Boyden should not merely be removed from the reading lists of classes on indigenous authors, but no longer taught at all. This criticism is often expressed in a manner that assumes that Boyden "takes up the space" of indigenous authors, not only in classes on indigenous writing, but everywhere. Because it concerns the relationship of authors to other authors, rather than to texts, this objection is not rebutted by a defense of subject appropriation. But is this zero-sum view of reading really true?

Consider the history of Western films. When would have been the best decade to release one? Was it in the 1950s or 1960s, when the genre was at its height and other Westerns were in every movie theater? Or was it after 1970, when the genre went into a long decline? If engaging the work of one creator inevitably comes at the expense of engaging similar work by others, then it stands to reason that the best time to release a Western would have been after the genre became less popular, as there would have been fewer Westerns competing for viewers.

But the history of when creators of Western films had their best chance of success suggests that this is not true. It was during the period when the genre was popular that Westerns were most likely to find a wide audience. Rather than steal viewers from other Westerns, audiences who saw *The Searchers* (1956) were primed to also go and see *The Magnificent Seven* (1960). Of course, in the case of the Western, it is hard not to feel a sense of relief at the genre's decline, due to its perpetuation of the myth of the open frontier and other anti-indigenous tropes. But the same pattern holds true for opera, jazz, and other genres whose popularity has waned. The best time to produce them was often when many more similar works, not fewer, were widely available. This is because successful works of art can generate an interest in their subjects or themes that benefits other creators—hence all the bestsellers that now come with guides on what to read next and all those Hollywood sequels. Rather than ask which works *The Orenda* has stolen attention away from, we should ask for which works it has created new audiences.

One answer to this question is provided by historian Kathryn Magee Labelle. Labelle, who specializes in Wendat history, has described the positive effect *The Orenda* had on interest in her area. "It is fair to say that Boyden's book has brought the people and events of *Wendake ehen* (old Wendat country) back to the centre stage of popular culture," she wrote in 2015. "Indeed, in my conversations at history conferences, workshops, and book launches, *The Orenda* is ever present, and the question is often asked: 'As a Wendat historian, what do you think about the book?'" Labelle praises the novel as "a fair representation of the history that inspired it." In addition, she credits the novel with inspiring readers she has met "to research further and find out the details behind the characters and events."

Boyden may have made things easy for such readers by listing in his acknowledgments the works of nonfiction that inspired him. They include *The Children of Aataentsic: A History of the Huron People to 1660* (1976), by Bruce Trigger, and *Huron Wendat: The Heritage of the Circle* (1999), by Georges Sioui. These and other works that informed Boyden's research share a sensibility, one that is summed up in the subtitle of another book by Trigger (not cited by Boyden): *Natives and Newcomers: Canada's "Heroic Age" Reconsidered* (1985). Trigger and Sioui belong to a generation of historians who did much to overturn the longstanding view that the early contact period was a time when jaunty European explorers encountered indigenous peoples who had no cultural and political achievements to speak of.

Trigger's book is particularly effective in this regard (and has informed my earlier discussion). Although he may have referred to the Wendat as Huron, as was common at the time, Trigger's achievement was not lost on the Wendat themselves, who made him an honorary member. His description of the Wendat confederacy, to take but one example, remains thought-provoking decades after it was written. Beginning in the twelfth century, the confederacy afforded its subjects a degree of input into political affairs that was unknown in pre-Revolutionary France. It granted member nations significant local autonomy and sought to govern by consensus as much as possible. Ironically, after centuries of condescension toward indigenous peoples on the part of French traders and missionaries, France today is part of the European Union, a political body that also employs a norm of seeking consensus among autonomous nations. In this way modern Europeans follow political procedures similar to those the Wendat and Haudenosaunee pioneered centuries ago.

Georges Sioui is Wendat (and the first indigenous person in Canada to obtain a Ph.D. in history). He builds on Trigger's account, which he often cites with approval, by drawing on Wendat oral tradition. The Wendat and Haudenosaunee, he notes, never went to war to gain territory or in the name of religion. Rather than seek the total destruction of their enemy, the immediate purpose of many raids was to capture members of the rival community, who would be assimilated into the captors' culture to replace family members lost to disease or war (hence the expectation in *The Orenda*, which the Haudenosaunee girl struggles with, that she become Wendat.) Wendat and Haudenosaunee combatants also followed a strict honor code, in keeping with what was arguably the ultimate function of their conflicts, providing an opportunity for male warriors to gain status through acts of bravery. "It's a game we play with one another," the Wendat narrator reflects in a passage from *The Orenda* that recalls both Trigger and Sioui, "a chance for the young men to prove themselves and collect a little bounty." Sioui, who is thanked in Boyden's acknowledgments for reading the manuscript, provided a blurb praising *The Orenda* for allowing readers "to see through Native eyes the immense human tragedies that attended the birth of North American nation-states."

In addition to generating interest in non-fiction about the Wendat, *The Orenda* may also generate interest in fictional stories of colonial contact. In my own case, reading Boyden awakened an interest in contact novels set in Canada, such as *The Beothuk Saga* (2000), by Bernard Assiniwi, and far beyond, such as *Things Fall Apart* (1958), by Chinua Achebe. Like Boyden, these authors imaginatively reconstruct indigenous life, among the Beothuk of what is now Newfoundland and the Ibo in what would become Nigeria, in the lead-up to contact with Europeans. If they inevitably do so with different degrees of literary success, they nonetheless make vivid how indigenous people in different places and times thought about family and government, and how they contended with colonization. Assiniwi is a Cree author and Achebe is Ibo (now often rendered as Igbo). That *The Orenda* could generate interest in their work makes Boyden not their enemy but their servant.

The Orenda contains scenes of gruesome violence. After the Wendat capture some Haudenosaunee warriors, they slash the captives' torsos with knives and clamshells and jab burning sticks into their legs and buttocks. The prisoners are then brought inside a longhouse, where they are subject to ritualized torture. The purpose of the ritual, which lasts until dawn, is to make the victims cry out for mercy. For this reason, they are not allowed to pass out. When the prisoners appear on the verge of going unconscious, the Wendat villagers stop the torture to dress their wounds, and start the process again. The victims can die as heroes if, rather than break down, they go to their grave while singing their death songs, which they have memorized in anticipation of falling into enemy hands. The Wendat work hard to prevent this with beatings, bone-breaking, and burning. At the end of the book the Jesuit experiences an even more horrifying fate. His last memory is of a Haudenosaunee warrior cutting open his chest and pulling out his heart.

The excruciating detail with which these scenes are narrated has divided critics, including indigenous ones. This was evident when *The Orenda* was chosen for the 2014 edition of Canada Reads, during which the novel was championed by Wab Kinew, now leader of the Manitoba New Democratic Party. After another panelist said that the book depicted torture as pornography, Kinew, who is a member of the Onigaming First Nation, replied that "the violence is key to understanding the message":

If we look at the violence, the torture scenes in the book, from a Western perspective, then of course we're going to arrive at the same conclusions that people did 400 years ago, that these people are savage.... These people are engaged in a relationship with each other. And if you read historic texts from 400 years ago, the warriors from one nation would be upset if the warriors from another nation did not scalp, did not torture, their brethren. And the reason for that was that was your chance to prove your honor, and your dignity, one last time before you passed on to the spirit world.

Kinew's positive view of the book is in noticeable contrast to that of Hayden King, the Anishinaabe director of the Yellowhead Institute. King wrote a scathing review of *The Orenda* that condemned its depiction of violence. According to King, the book is "a comforting narrative for Canadians about the emergence of Canada: Indian savages, do-good Jesuits and the inevitability (even desirability) of colonization."

In addition to the violence, King draws attention to a genuinely puzzling feature of the novel. *The Orenda* is divided into sections, each of which is introduced by a short, enigmatic speech that appears to be spoken by beings from Wendat mythology. Part of one such mythic narrative states, "It's unfair to blame only the crows, yes? It's our obligation to accept our responsibility in the whole affair. And so we watched as the adventure unfolded, and we prayed to Aataentsic, Sky Woman, who sits by the fire right beside us, to intervene." King takes passages such as this to mean that part of the reason colonialism occurred was "because of the selfishness, arrogance and short-sightedness of the Huron." Boyden's book, in short, places part of the blame for colonialism on its victims.

King says that the novel portrays violence and torture as "the exclusive domain of the Indians." This overlooks the scenes of European violence that show it to involve its own special forms of cruelty, which the indigenous characters condemn. The narrative repeatedly juxtaposes indigenous and European violence, including in the scenes involving the attempted rape and its punishment, in ways that undermine the idea that European violence was nonexistent or somehow better. Crucifixes also play a symbolic role throughout the story. At one point the headman refers to the Jesuit and the "splayed and tortured man he always wears on his neck," suggesting that seventeenth-century Catholicism fetishized torture in its own way. If the European acts of violence in the book have not generated outcry, this may only be because we are already so familiar with them.

Yet even if the depictions of torture are historically accurate, there is an aspect of Boyden's rendering that remains disturbing. After 9/11, Western governments were revealed to employ or condone torture as an interrogation tool. One of the points that is often made in the torture debate concerns the falsehood of the popular image, found in countless movies and TV shows, of the masculine hero who is able to withstand torture without breaking down. Human beings who can resist torture, if they exist at all, are rare. The main function of the myth of the recalcitrant hero is to add to the burden of torture's victims by making them feel guilty for "confessing" whatever is necessary to make the torture stop. The fact that not just some but all of the book's torture victims, indigenous and

European alike, last hours or even days without breaking is a form of propaganda infecting Boyden's account.

This shortcoming is not noted by King, whose critique instead takes a strange yet revealing turn by endorsing Margaret Atwood's notion of survival as the concept that explains Canadian literature. King draws attention to the fact that, in outlining her theory, Atwood cited literature about the early Jesuit missionary Jean de Brébeuf, whom Boyden's Jesuit resembles. As Atwood wrote of her survival trope, "for early explorers and settlers, it meant bare survival in the face of 'hostile' elements and/or natives." For King, this is the key that unlocks *The Orenda*.

"Atwood even cites literature about Brébeuf as an example or Canadian survivance," King writes. "So *The Orenda* reinforces who and what Canadians believe they are. [The Jesuit] tells a story they know and can identify with . . . He becomes the protagonist, the doomed hero that reinforces colonial myths of savagery on the one hand, and salvation, on the other—'survival in the face of hostile Natives.'"

I argued in Chapter One that the idea of survival never shed light on Canadian literature. By the time King's article appeared, in 2013, few readers familiar with Canadian writing still considered Atwood's theory a helpful starting place. But even if we take Atwood's framework in its own terms, *The Orenda* does not fit her pattern. Atwood does discuss "literature about Brébeuf," but aside from a brief mention of his appearance in a Leonard Cohen novel, her discussion consists of an analysis of one E. J. Pratt poem about the famous Jesuit. Atwood quotes with approval Northrop Frye's remark, written four centuries after Hobbes, that in Pratt's poem, "Indians represent humanity in the state of Nature and are agents of its unconscious barbarity." As we have seen, *The Orenda* is a literary repudiation of this undying falsehood. It is as if, for King, the possibility that Boyden wrote an anti-colonial novel simply cannot be true.

This still leaves the sky people's strange remarks on who was responsible for colonialism. After King's article appeared, Boyden told an interviewer that the sky people should in fact be read as saying that indigenous people deserve some blame for their own colonization ("not *nearly* as much blame as the colonizers, of course," he was quick to add). Boyden here joins the long list of authors who make wayward interpreters of their own work. A more attractive possibility is suggested by one of Boyden's sources, Bruce Trigger, who calls into question the idea that Wendat mythical figures embody the characteristics of Wendat (or any other) people.

"Among the Huron, men committed most of the real and symbolic acts of violence," Trigger writes, referring to practices such as hunting and war. "Women were associated with life-giving pursuits: bearing children, growing crops and caring for the home." Despite this familiar division, Aataentsic is a violent and malevolent female figure, while her grandson Iouskeha is a male nurturer. "It is possible that by conferring certain human characteristics on mythical figures of the opposite sex, these myths aimed at compensating both sexes for the psychological limitations of the roles assigned to them in real life," Trigger suggests.

Trigger's observation about the sky people's gender roles should make us pause before assuming that any of their attributes, whether related to gender or anything else, are neatly transferrable onto the Wendat. What if, by taking on responsibility for colonialism, they actually contradict the idea that their Wendat subjects are somehow to blame? Such a reading is more in keeping with the compensation through reversal that Trigger highlights in the case of gender. It is *much* more consistent with the novel's grim depiction of the violence and plagues caused by colonialism. Indeed, by including sections narrated by Wendat religious figures and none by Christian ones, the novel subtly suggests that traditional Wendat beliefs were truer to reality than European religion.

The disagreement between Kinew and King over *The Orenda* may reflect a deeper disagreement among indigenous intellectuals over Canada's goal of making amends for the atrocities it inflicted on indigenous people. In introducing *The Orenda* on Canada Reads, Kinew said the book "gives voice to the indigenous so we can have a new conversation. Without that, no truth, no reconciliation." Kinew is one of the most prominent indigenous voices in favor of the project of reconciliation that the Truth and Reconciliation Commission of Canada called for in its 2015 final report. With the possible exception of Jody Wilson-Raybould, the former federal justice minister, Kinew may also be Canada's most prominent indigenous politician of recent years. His willingness to seek office and lead a political party is only consistent with his support for reconciliation. Accepting that Canada can make amends with indigenous people after all presupposes that Canada's political institutions are at least decent enough to deliver some measure of restorative justice.

King, for his part, may be the most prominent indigenous *skeptic* of reconciliation. His journalism in national newspapers and magazines often questions whether reconciliation, at least as normally understood, can ever succeed. This attitude was on display in his response to a 2018 speech Wilson-Raybould gave to indigenous leaders in British Columbia, in which she criticized indigenous thinkers who, "in the name of upholding Indigenous rights, critically oppose almost any effort to change [within the Canadian constitutional framework]." King retorted that "the heretics have ample evidence of corrupt institutions on their side."

It is unsurprising that King would have sympathy for reconciliation "heretics." Three years prior to Wilson-Raybould's speech, King coauthored a thought-provoking essay with criminologist Shiri Pasternak that is something of a manifesto for the pro-indigenous, anti-reconciliation stance. King and his coauthor were cool toward the political and legal changes that reconciliation is often associated with. They characterized "voting in or out unsupportive and delinquent governments, and using the courts to achieve justice as all reinforcing an unthreatening politics of charity: sophisticated and pragmatic, but also relatively benign." Against this they favor a different approach, one that takes seriously calls by indigenous thinkers for "disengagement from and alternatives to state forms of recognition and reconciliation."

King and Pasternak call their preferred approach indigenous resurgence. They do not go so far as to say that the attempts at electoral and legal victories that are normally thought to be crucial to reconciliation are pointless. Both outcomes, they concede, "can potentially lead to some gains." But the larger Canadian state that contains parliament and the courts is not a just entity, and is not likely to become one any time soon. As they candidly put it, "we do not believe in the legitimacy of the structures of the state." Insofar as reconciliation presupposes that Canada has attained some minimal level of justice, reconciliation will inevitably fail.

Much like Kinew's, King's view of reconciliation is of a piece with his view of Canada's political institutions. During the 2021 federal election, King commented on Twitter using the hashtag "#elxn44," only to then delete the tweet. As he explained in a follow-up tweet, "I had to delete a tweet because if you use election hashtag an icon pops up telling people to vote." Elections not only decide governments, they bestow legitimacy on democratic states. If that legitimacy is an illusion, then King's view entails that publicly endorsing elections, or ascribing much importance to their outcomes, is a form of naiveté.

The central problem with King's view was well captured by Wilson-Raybould in her speech criticizing indigenous reconciliation skeptics. "These voices, paradoxically, sometimes end up reinforcing the same outcome–inaction–that those who oppose rights recognition for Indigenous peoples and reconciliation pursue." And if Boyden's identity matters, then by the same logic, when it comes to elections, there will be an important difference between electing candidates such as Kinew or Wilson-Raybould as opposed to, say, Maxime Bernier of the populist People's Party of Canada.

The Orenda takes the reader back to indigenous peoples' first encounters with what would eventually become Canada. For someone open to the possibility of reconciliation, it can thus be read as an origin story. *We've got to do something to make up for this legacy* is a natural reaction to what the book describes. But because the novel, as a historical work, does not suggest any view pro or con on contemporary efforts at reconciliation, it does not provide any succor to readers who have already decided that reconciliation will be a failure. Indeed, if one takes the main lesson of Canadian history to be that Canada will always be too infested with colonialism to make reconciliation possible, then the novel may seem too gentle on Canada, despite all the violence and plagues it depicts.

By falsely characterizing *The Orenda* as a colonialist work, King does Boyden an injustice. He also sends an unhelpful message regarding literary progress. Novels of colonial contact have been around for a long time. Older versions of the genre really were colonialist. (*Heart of Darkness*, for example, gives African characters practically no speaking time.) If we are not going to distinguish an author such as Boyden from these predecessors, then novelists who write contact stories might as well produce colonialist propaganda, as there is no longer any point in trying to do otherwise.

Cross-cultural misunderstanding and prejudice is a central preoccupation of *The Orenda*, which describes it occurring in the minds of indigenous and non-indigenous characters alike. Given this theme, the passages in King's review that rely on pre-judgment, certainly of Boyden's text, and perhaps also of reconciliation (of which time will tell), issue an ironic lesson. Prejudice can cloud the mind of anyone, but achieving justice requires us to approach one another with open minds rather than cynicism and suspicion. King's criticism is a further reminder that the world is not divided between people entirely driven by prejudice and those purely committed to justice. His article, like the characters in *The Orenda*, is motivated by both impulses. In setting out to debunk *The Orenda*, King ends up illustrating the timeless nature of its theme.

In exposing Boyden, neither Jorge Barrero nor Robert Jago suggested that Boyden's novels should no longer be read. Barrero's news story offered no comment on Boyden's fiction. Jago, for his part, emphasized that his concern was not with the very idea of a non-native writer telling native stories. He cited the example of a white journalist who spent time on the reserve where Jago grew up before writing about members of Jago's family who had attended residential schools. "I don't mind him telling their story. He put in the time with the community, earned trust," Jago wrote, "and everyone knows it's an outsider's voice." Calls to no longer teach or read Boyden, whom everyone now knows is an outsider, only occurred later, after less careful critics began to pile on Boyden on Twitter and call for his cancellation.

What does it mean to cancel a person? Recent years have seen heightened sensitivity to language. Media and other organizations, for example, have stopped using the term "illegal immigrant" on the grounds, surely reasonable, that illegality should apply only to actions, not people. Online critics who denounced Boyden following his exposé showed no concern for such niceties. The hashtag #CancelBoyden suggested the problem was not Boyden's actions, but his being.

After his cancellation Boyden was divorced from his wife and moved from New Orleans to the Georgian Bay region of Ontario, where he lived with a new partner (who is indigenous) and their two children. In a 2019 article in *Georgian Bay Today* Boyden wrote, "I've faced some hard days the last years. Hard enough that for a frightening stretch in the grey world between Louisiana and Ontario I no longer believed I cared enough to live." This outcome should be recalled the next time social media calls on us to cancel a human being.

But this chapter is not called "Joseph Boyden: A Defense." No estimation of Boyden's fiction changes the fact that he was wrong to present himself as indigenous. The indigenous people in Boyden's historical novels are connected by lines of descent to people alive today. Efforts to determine how much Canada has changed from a colonialist society to one that shows equal respect to native people become impossible when we cannot identify who grew up in Canada as an indigenous person and to what degree society may still put obstacles in their way.

This consideration will apply when any white person falsely claims a different racial or cultural identity. There is however a further reason for concern in cases of indigenous identity fraud. This particular misrepresentation has long been all too common. In 1992, Bill Cross, a cofounder of the American Indian and Alaska Native Professors Association, was asked to estimate how many of the 1,500 American academics who presented themselves as indigenous were genuine. "We're looking realistically at one third of those being Indians," he replied.

Sociologists now use the term "self-indigenization" to describe this trend. The word was coined by Darryl Leroux, a sociologist at St. Mary's University in Halifax. His central example is the rise of so-called "Eastern Métis" groups: organizations composed of white Canadians and Americans who claim indigenous identities. Some Eastern Métis leaders have had histories of opposing indigenous rights or belonging to white supremacist organizations, but the practice is of concern even when practitioners do not have hate-group links. Self-indigenizers often seek to exercise hunting rights and other prerogatives reserved for indigenous people.

Dubious claims to indigenous identity are frequently justified through "a tenuous genealogical relation with a long-ago [indigenous] ancestor," Leroux notes. This relation is often presented as being especially important because of an oral tradition of indigenous identification in the self-indigenizer's family. Boyden's 2016 description of himself and other family members as "keepers of a number of oral histories passed down to us from previous generations that speak both to our European and to our Indigenous roots" fits the pattern Leroux and others have sought to counter.

The myth of the disappearing Indian is a recurring historical trope that characterizes indigenous people and their culture as long gone, a convenient belief in societies with unresolved land claims. Cases such as Boyden's suggest there is a second myth, that of the appearing Indian, which indigenous people must now also contend with. We should recognize the pernicious ways Boyden embodied this myth. But we should also recognize that the full story of Boyden's case cannot be summed up in a hashtag. We need to form separate judgments about his biographical narrative and his literary ones. Because in matters of truth, a critical mind is like a confederacy. It can recognize autonomous domains of veracity and falsehood, and allow both to coexist.

CHAPTER 6

MR. TAYLOR'S PLANET

In 1965, Canada's minority government collapsed, and an election was called for early November. In the country's largest city, two Université de Montréal faculty members would compete for the riding of Mount Royal. One, a forty-six-year-old law professor, had been successfully wooed to run for the Liberals. The lawyer's rival, a thirty-four-year-old philosopher, had been nominated for the third time by the New Democratic Party, which had never won a seat in Quebec.

When the philosopher ran in the previous election, in 1963, he set a riding record for NDP support. Indeed, one of his supporters had been the very Liberal he now found himself campaigning against. "I welcome the chance to challenge him to explain," said the philosopher of the former NDP lawyer, "what has changed in this Liberal party since then that has led him to give up the fight and change sides."

This time, the energetic philosopher would go on to perform the phenomenal feat of raising the level of NDP support upward still, winning 175 percent of the votes he had two years before, but still not enough. When the returns came in, no one was surprised that the lawyer had won.

Within three years the lawyer, known primarily for his contributions to the small intellectual journal *Cité Libre*, would be prime minister. Pierre Trudeau would hold power from 1968 to 1984, interrupted for only nine months in 1979–1980; long enough to shape the nation with his individualism, his liberalism, and his unyielding opposition to Francophone nationalism. He was the most influential Canadian politician of his generation, perhaps the most influential ever.

And the philosopher? By the time his old opponent left office, Charles Taylor had written an ambitious and internationally applauded book on Hegel; taught at Oxford as the prestigious Chichele Professor of Social and Political Theory; and distinguished himself as one of the most searching and most respected theorists and critic of modern liberalism.

In Canada, where Taylor returned from Oxford in order to work to preserve the federation, his extensive involvement in political debate would mark him as his generation's most prominent political intellectual and as a tireless critic of most of his old election rival's principles. In particular, he would become a champion of the view that Quebec could not be treated as a province just like all the others and that some constitutional recognition of its insurgent nationalism was ultimately what justice called for.

Looking back today, their 1965 election contest highlights interesting parallels between the careers of Trudeau and Taylor. Both played against type: The bilingual Francophone Trudeau was an early, sharp critic of Quebec nationalism; the bilingual Anglophone Taylor became an intelligent and sympathetic voice on its behalf. Both mixed academia with politics: Trudeau's undistinguished involvement in the former (entering Ph.D. programs at the London

School of Economics and Paris's École libre des sciences politiques, acquiring doctorates from neither) and mastery of the latter finds a mirror opposite in Taylor's failed bids for public office—forgotten disappointments now overshadowed by the achievements of his academic career.

Indeed, by the 1990s Taylor's ideas were everywhere ascendant. He was asked to speak before government commissions on the constitution and became a member of Quebec's Conseil de la Langue Francaise. But perhaps nowhere is Taylor's success and influence during this time more evident than in the reception of a short treatise he wrote crystallizing his political beliefs, a distillation of his views on liberalism, nationalism, and other issues Taylor had been thinking and writing about for almost forty years.

"The Politics of Recognition" was originally delivered as the inaugural lecture for the University Center for Human Values at Princeton University. In 1992, it was published by Princeton University Press as *Multiculturalism and The Politics of Recognition*. This first edition to Taylor's forty-eight-page essay included a fulsome twenty-one-page introduction by Amy Gutmann, the center's director, and three further replies to Taylor, including one by superstar political theorist Michael Walzer.

When the second edition appeared in paperback two years later, responses by German intellectual powerhouse Jurgen Habermas and Harvard philosopher K. Anthony Appiah were also included. There are scattered criticisms of Taylor throughout the work of these critics (particularly in Appiah's closing paragraphs), but when Michael Walzer declares, "I not only admire the historical and philosophical style of Charles Taylor's essay, I am entirely in agreement with the views that he presents," it is in keeping with the dominant tone.

The reaction has been similarly enthusiastic beyond the universities. In the months before the 1995 Quebec referendum, Stan Persky, then a prominent book critic, singled out the second edition of *Multiculturalism* for its "fresh thinking" on everything from Quebec to "collective identities [and] the question of what we ought to teach in our schools." The collection, Persky wrote, was "one of the liveliest, most readable and sanest debates on multiculturalism that I've seen to date." When "The Politics of Recognition" was published for a third time in Taylor's *Philosophical Arguments*, Oxford fellow David Miller reviewed in *The Times Literary Supplement*. Focusing almost exclusively on Taylor's political writings, Miller termed Taylor one of "the leading philosophers of our time."

That Taylor has played a positive, moderating role in Canada's interminable unity wars is obvious. And yet, if we separate "The Politics of Recognition" from the many areas where Taylor has earned our admiration, and instead approach it simply as an argument, it becomes clear that Taylor has been left, at the end of it all, with a political philosophy built on contradictions.

Taylor's essay is sometimes mistaken for a neutral presentation of ideas already in circulation, but it is in fact a work of advocacy, one that tries to convince us to think about politics in a certain way. In particular, Taylor wants to urge two ideas upon us. The first is that many political issues currently in the headlines "turn on the need, sometimes the demand, for recognition." The second is the impressive-sounding notion that our identities are "dialogical." These two ideas are critical to Taylor's overall account. Understanding the force of his argument requires understanding each of them in turn.

Taylor's concept of recognition is based on the premise that a person's identity is partially shaped by the view of him held by other people. Real harm can be inflicted on someone who lives among those who hold a demeaning conception of that person. As an example, Taylor cites feminist concerns about the negative self-understanding of women in male-dominated societies, self-understandings that can hinder women's emancipation even after some of the external barriers to their full citizenship are gone. Similar demands for recognition, he writes, are evident in black-white dynamics: White society projected on the black minority a demeaning image, one that some blacks adopted and now need to overcome.

Likewise, objections to Europeans' long-standing view of indigenous people as savages play out the same pattern. In each case, previously oppressed groups seek to replace the "grievous wound" of misrecognition with the "vital human need" of due recognition.

Much of Taylor's discussion of recognition is devoted to outlining how the idea came about historically, the call for recognition being largely a political phenomenon of the past two centuries. But only one part of Taylor's historical account needs to be grasped here: how the post-eighteenth-century view of people as being individuals contributed to the rise of struggles for recognition.

With a view of ourselves as individuals comes the ideal of being "true" to that individuality, true to that unique way of being a person. Borrowing a term from the literary critic Lionel Trilling, Taylor calls this the ideal of authenticity. It holds that we are being authentically ourselves when we do not allow social pressures to impose an external identity on us or lead us to copy someone else's. The ideal of authenticity demands that we acknowledge our own originality and look within to determine who we will be: We must cultivate a kind of self-contact in order to achieve genuine self-fulfillment.

Johann Gottfried von Herder, an eighteenth-century German philosopher, was an early exponent of this ideal. For Herder, authenticity worked on two levels: Not only should individuals be true to themselves, but societies should as well, in that they must each be true to their own culture. Italians should not try to be Germans, or vice versa, as that would be to adopt a derivative and therefore inauthentic cultural identity. Similarly, peoples colonized by European nations should be allowed to find their own measure. In this desire for cultural authenticity, Taylor sees the "seminal idea" of modern nationalism.

Taylor's account of recognition dictates that the individual can no longer seek after an entirely socially derived identity. But nor can she aspire to one that is purely individually derived either. And the reason for this is the "crucial feature of the human condition" which Taylor thinks modern philosophy overlooks. Just as luck would have it, this feature is also Taylor's second key idea: the dialogical nature of our identity.

According to Taylor, we acquire agency and the ability to understand who we are through the acquisition of languages of expression: Languages used here include not only words but also the languages "of art, of gesture, of love and the like." These languages are not something we learn in isolation but are rather picked up through interaction with the people in our lives. The languages this interaction imparts to us are crucial to our ability to understand ourselves, crucial to the genesis of mind itself. Taylor is at pains to say that this identity-composing dialogue goes on throughout life, and he expresses some dissatisfaction with the dominant view (what he terms "the monological ideal") that will at most concede dialogue a place in the early formation of our identity, in childhood alone. Not so, Taylor instructs. Our significant others, our parents especially, are always with us, and we conduct an inner dialogue with them long after speaking face to face. Similarly, some of our most cherished goods are possible only through sharing them with others (marriage, for example), and we are constantly interacting with other people in the political and social sphere. Here, too, dialogue is at work.

The upshot of all this dialogue? We don't forge an identity by ourselves, but rather "negotiate it through dialogue, partly overt, partly internal, with others." And this fact about us, when combined with the ideal of authenticity, grants a vital importance to recognition. Who I am crucially depends on what other people think of me, and so a demeaning view of my identity held by the people who shape me can be deeply damaging. Thus "the importance of recognition is now universally acknowledged." People understand its significance on an intimate plane, in the central role played by our significant others. On a public level, our democratic culture espouses a politics of equal recognition, evident in the many calls for recognition made by feminists, multiculturalists, and anti-racism activists.

Taylor's main concern is with recognition in the public sphere. Here, a politics of equal recognition has come to mean two things. The first is typified by the American civil rights movement, where equality takes the form of uniform rights for all, regardless of race, gender, and the rest. On this view, the point is to avoid different classes of citizenship—to prevent the political sphere from resembling a train with a first-class cabin reserved strictly for the majority. Taylor refers to this view as the politics of equal dignity.

But, he is quick to point out, another view of equality is also at large. And this one has given rise to demands for a different kind of equality. Taylor calls this second view the politics of difference. What it asks us to recognize is "the unique identity of this individual or group, their distinctness from everyone else." Why? "It is precisely this distinctness that has been ignored, glossed over, assimilated to a dominant or majority identity. And this assimilation is the cardinal sin against the ideal of authenticity." Here the move to equality is slightly more complicated, involving a two-step maneuver. The first step is to note that even though everyone has an equal right to their cultural identity, majorities often enjoy an unfair advantage in that the minorities who live in their shadow are forced into alien form by the pressures of assimilation and other unwanted forces. But if we incorporate a recognition of minority identities into our laws, those pressures can be relieved and minorities will finally achieve an equal footing with the majority. The point here is not to elevate one (minority) identity above all others, but rather to ensure that all identities are treated as first-class models of citizenship. The politics of difference therefore, through an acknowledgment of particularity, works towards this universal end.

Each in their own way, upholders of the politics of equal dignity and of recognition are both concerned with equality. They also have in common a tendency to take a dim view of the aims of the other. The equal-dignity crowd often feels betrayed by measures that take difference into account, particularly those measures that seek to make recognition of a minority identity a permanent fact of public life, not merely a temporary measure to be abolished once the playing field is levelled. And just such a belief in the importance of permanent recognition is what animates some of the measures taken in the name of the politics of recognition. "After all," Taylor writes, "if we're concerned with identity, then what is more legitimate than one's aspiration that it never be lost?"

To the "universalist" upholders of equal dignity, the outcome of all this "recognition" often appears to be discrimination, period. Equality in their view just is equal treatment. Advocates of difference, in turn, argue that the "blind" liberalism Universalists favor negates minority identities by assimilating them into a mold not their own. That mold is not neutral, but that of the society's dominant or majority culture: minorities alone are forced into an inauthentic cultural existence. The result is that, despite all the talk about equality for everyone on the part of the Universalists, "the supposedly fair and difference-blind society is not only inhumane (because suppressing identities) but also, in a subtle and unconscious way, itself highly discriminatory." And this, it turns out, is Taylor's criticism. He writes that the version of liberalism that is blind to the cultural identities of its citizens is "guilty as charged by the proponents of a politics of difference."

A concrete example is perhaps the best way to make sense of these two abstract notions of equality and the accusations and counter-accusations that fly back and forth. Taylor provides one in the form of a long discussion of Quebec's language laws. Briefly, the original language laws ("Bill 101") legislate three things: Francophone and immigrant parents cannot enroll their children in non-French schools; businesses with more than fifty employees must operate in French; English-only commercial signs are not allowed. The goal of the laws is, of course, to ensure that French remains the language of public life in the province, and their effect in this regard has been rightly described as spectacular. (Introduced in the late 1970s, by 1990 Bill 101 had resulted in 90.2 percent of Quebec students below the university level attending French schools. Among students whose first language was neither French nor English, the rate increased from 38.7 percent to 72.7 percent between 1980 and 1989.) But it is the philosophical underpinning of the language laws that Taylor is most concerned with. In his own words:

> It is axiomatic for Quebec governments that the survival and flourishing of French culture in Quebec is a good. Political society is not neutral between those who value remaining true to the culture of our ancestors and those who might want to cut loose in the name of some individual goal of self-development... It also involves making sure that there is a community of people here in the future that will want to avail itself of the opportunity to use the French language. Policies aimed at survival actively seek to create members of the community.

Measures such as Quebec's language laws, then, are not strictly neutral in their treatment of different cultural identities. In this case one particular identity, that of French Quebecers, and its corresponding aspiration for survival through future generations are recognized by the state and legally acted upon. Thus, Quebec politics is an example of the politics of difference and recognition in action.

Taylor describes what he sees going on in Quebec using the terminology of liberalism: "a society can be organized around a definition of the good life" when it is the nature of that good that it must be sought in common. Liberal theory has traditionally held that no version of the good life is to be favored by the state. But Taylor stresses that the model he endorses need not compromise liberalism's ultimate goals: The fundamental liberties it has fought to establish—habeas corpus, freedom of speech, religion and assembly, and so on—can be distinguished from less fundamental "privileges and immunities" that can be restricted when strong reasons are presented. A society animated by strong collective goals, therefore, can still be liberal if it protects the essential liberties of all. To Taylor's mind, this is the singular achievement that Quebec represents.

The ramifications of this are international in scope. An ever-increasing number of countries are becoming multicultural. In our age of immigration, more and more members of Western societies "live the life of diaspora, whose center is elsewhere." The immigrant, too, has her culture, and if her aspirations for its survival are to be respected, as Taylor feels they should, then "our philosophical boundaries" are called into question. Compared to traditional liberalism the Quebec model is a better guide to dealing with tomorrow's new multicultural world order; only it can meet the increasing demands for cultural recognition.

Taylor understandably does not outline in detail how this would work out in practice. Instead, he concludes "The Politics of Recognition" with some guiding principles to employ when interacting with cultures not our own. We must be open to what Taylor, borrowing a phrase from the German philosopher Hans-Georg Gadamer, calls a "fusion of horizons." Rather than using our own culturally specific standards and values to judge the other culture, we should cultivate an inner transformation by allowing that culture's standards to mingle with our own. In this way, we will forge a new, truly inter-cultural perspective, a deep openness that is, ultimately, edifying. Taylor points to Saul Bellow, author of *Herzog, Mr. Sammler's Planet,* and other well-known works, as an example of a prominent cultural voice who overlooks this crucial insight. Other cultures that have provided contexts of meaning for a substantial number of people through long periods of time, "that have, in other words, articulated their sense of the good, the holy, the admirable—are almost certain to have something that deserves our admiration and respect." In the end, cultivating openness to a fusion of horizons has the power to take us beyond "our own limited part in the whole human story."

One can't help but have sympathy for Taylor's concern that cultural minorities be treated fairly. But insofar as we value an argument in defense of multiculturalism that is consistent and well-informed, the more we are compelled to recognize that Taylor's isn't.

Recall Taylor's description of why he supports measures such as Quebec's language laws. It is because, as a member of the minority culture at hand might put it, they preserve and perpetuate "the culture of our ancestors." This strikes Taylor as a good idea, one that even heralds a new variant of liberalism. And yet, he is equally emphatic that we should be welcoming, in a deep sense, to the changes that can result from contact with a culture not our own. But how so? If a culture passes laws designed to preserve the culture of its ancestors, a "fusion of horizons" with other cultures is precisely what it is trying to prevent. A judgment has been made, and the ancestral culture is deemed to take priority.

Two problems stem from this. First, Taylor's endorsement of measures that seek to ensure cultural homogeneity across generations overlooks the possibility of misrecognition occurring through one generation imprisoning the next in a false vision of itself. Quebec, for example, was once a deeply Catholic society. Would it have been fair for the old Catholic establishment to have used public policy to ensure the church a permanent position of power?

A culture's self-understanding can change, and efforts to force a contemporary understanding on the future are hardly immune to the problems around imposed identities Taylor seeks to avoid.

Second, consider how things would play out if an individual Francophone Quebecer were to take one of Taylor's central conclusions to heart. In his discussion of intercultural penetration and fused horizons, Taylor writes that the "main locus of this debate is the world of education." And Taylor characterizes the fusion of horizons he is in favor of in linguistic terms: it operates "through our developing new vocabularies of comparison." Reading this, and acting on the common-sense belief that we can't really know a culture without learning its language, a French Quebecer could not be faulted for wanting to send her child to a school where the language of instruction was something other than French. But Taylor, as a supporter of Law 101, believes the government should forbid this. Similarly, an immigrant to Quebec who wanted to send her child to an English school to "fuse" with that culture would seem to get an equally mixed message from Taylor: by all means, open yourself to another culture—but do try and make sure that it happens to be French.

The inspiring vision of being inwardly transformed by other cultures that Taylor holds out at the end of his essay seems to exist in a room with no connecting corridor to the one where, moments before, he held forth on the need to legally prohibit certain forms of cultural horizon-fusing. As it stands, the students who would seem most able to enjoy the edifying experience of being transformed by another culture are the members of the cultural majority—in the Quebec case, English speakers most like Taylor himself. It's hard not to see in this a silent privileging of the majority culture.

The English can be pushed to arrive at a mind-expanding overcoming of their "own limited part in the whole human story." But the French? Ah, yes, well. The French. Best not to expect too much. Not everyone can meet standards of self-development as exacting as our own.

Taylor might try to get around this by making the reasonable argument (which does not appear in "The Politics of Recognition") that a person can profit most from other cultures if she is first relieved of the worry that her own culture is about to disappear. This, however, would only bring Taylor in contact with a still larger problem he sets for himself. It concerns the two irreconcilable views of cultural assimilation he wants to support. Most of the time, Taylor is opposed to minorities being homogenized into majorities, as this results in a "grievous wound" of misrecognition, a harm on the level of "inequality, exploitation and injustice," and one that occurs even when it is not explicitly sought by the majority culture. And yet, in his defense of Quebec's language laws, Taylor comes out emphatically for policies that "actively seek to create members of the community."

In other words, were Quebec's Francophones to be subsumed into Canada's English majority, the result would be a serious injustice. But the French goal of culturally assimilating other minorities is perfectly laudable. Strangely, Taylor's concern over unwanted assimilation leads him to endorse government measures, the explicit aim of which is unwanted assimilation. This would seem to make inevitable the very type of misrecognition Taylor is at pains to avoid, the only difference in the Quebec case being that the burden of having an external culture inflicted upon them is shifted to cultures with less power than the French: immigrant cultures.

Taylor could have avoided this problem had he allowed for some distinction between groups such as the Quebecois and immigrants. This distinction is usually made in common-sense discussions of Quebec politics, just as it as it is in Will Kymlicka's *Multicultural Citizenship* or Alan Patten's *Equal Recognition*. But Taylor, bizarrely, goes out of his way to deny it. He argues that Quebec's language laws hold the answer for countries that are becoming increasingly multicultural through immigration and so multicultural "in the sense of including more than one cultural community that wants to survive." That he is in effect here arguing that immigrant desires for cultural survival are best served by using the law to assimilate them into the majority—something Bill 101 does by his own account —seems an enormous difficulty, yet one to which Taylor is cheerfully oblivious.

One can argue that the law should push immigrants into the dominant culture in places like Quebec, or one can argue that the law should prevent them from ever being pushed because their cultures also deserve recognition; but one cannot simultaneously argue for both positions. This is quite a serious problem for Taylor's theory, so much so that it is hard to imagine things getting any worse. And yet, this is what happens when Taylor's view of immigrants is examined alongside his other foundational idea, his dialogical view of human identity.

The problem stems from Taylor's claim that immigrants "live the life of diaspora, whose center is elsewhere." To describe someone's cultural identity in this way means you don't really see it as being composed by much of a dialogue at all: The immigrant, rather, is shaped by the old country alone, and the dialogue that shapes her ends when she leaves it. Hence her center, her identity, is left behind.

If anything, this is a "monological" understanding, of just the sort Taylor criticized for not acknowledging that dialogue is a lifelong process. When it comes to immigrants, it turns out Taylor believes dialogue is present only in the genesis of their cultural identity after all.

Taylor is resolutely opposed to unwanted assimilation and very much in favor of it; Quebecers must fuse with other cultures and not fuse with them; immigrants' cultures must be recognized by the law and immigrants' cultures must be swept away by the law; our identities are formed in dialogues and our identities are formed in monologues. Over and over again, Taylor nimbly pulls together the most powerful ideas from a dazzling array of sources—Rousseau and Herder, Trilling and Gadamer—only to harness them in service of practical measures that do total violence to the very ideals he stands for.

The overall effect is like seeing someone displays great ingenuity and presence of mind in leading a bull through the door of his own china shop: utter bewilderment, yet tinged with a strange sort of admiration.

Why has Taylor's theory, despite its debilitating defects, proven to be so popular? Precisely because his essay treats a topic that so many of us—particularly we liberals—have a deep intuitive attachment to, our critical faculties are somewhat disarmed by "The Politics of Recognition." We want there to be a profound philosophical argument that lends support to our intuitions about how cultural minorities ought to be treated. And we want Charles Taylor, who has written brilliantly on many other topics, to be the one who delivers it. For many people, his gentle, decent approach sets the standard to be aspired to in scholarly and political debate. But the effect of this and Taylor's other winning qualities has been to obscure the fact that, philosophically speaking, his argument is a mess.

CHAPTER 7

THIS AMERICAN
GANGRENE

David Frum's journey to the White House began in Toronto. In 1975, Frum was a teenage volunteer on a provincial political campaign. The candidate belonged to the New Democratic Party, but Frum, whose political views had yet to solidify, was not supporting him out of solidarity. Frum had signed on because he wanted to see a political race up close and his family happened to know the nominee. "The campaign's headquarters was a forty-five minute bus and subway ride from my parents' house," Frum wrote in the Canadian edition of his book *What's Right* (1996). "I devoted the resulting reading time to a book that my mother had given me: the first volume of Aleksandr Solzhenitsyn's *The Gulag Archipelago*. The horror of Soviet communism burst upon me like a bomb. A kind of evangelical fervor gripped me: everybody had to know about this! (Remember, I was fourteen.)"

Frum's encounter with Solzhenitsyn as a precocious Canadian teenager set him on the path that eventually led to writing speeches for George W. Bush. In that capacity, Frum is perhaps best known for helping coin the term "axis of evil," a phrase intended to legitimize the invasion of Iraq by depicting it as part of a network of terror-supporting states as dangerous as the Axis nations of World War II. Frum's primary career, however, has been as a journalist, and in this role the *Wall Street Journal* has fairly called him "one of the leading political commentators of his generation." Since Donald Trump's rise, Frum has arguably been his most outspoken critic on the right. Less than a week before Americans went to the polls to choose between Trump and Hillary Clinton, Frum published a strongly worded article ridiculing the Republican talking point that Clinton was so vicious that any GOP candidate, even one as offensive as Trump, would be better. "To demonstrate my distaste for people whose bodies contain mean bones, it's proposed that I give my franchise to a man who boasts of his delight in sexual assault?" Frum wrote in the *Atlantic*. "Who mocks the disabled, who denounces immigrant parents whose son laid down his life for this country, who endorses religious bigotry."

Given this background, it is no surprise that *Trumpocracy: The Corruption of the American Republic* is an indictment of Trump. The book recounts the major moments of Trump's election campaign before cataloging and criticizing Trump's many scandals. Frum is clear-eyed about the disastrous consequences of Trump's presidency. But one of the questions Trump raises is historical. What is his relationship with organized conservativism? Frum depicts Trump as the corruption of a previously wayward but ultimately respectable political tradition. "He has ripped the conscience out of half of the political spectrum and left a moral void where American conservatism used to be." Such an account requires us to forget the moral void that was already present during the Bush years.

That void is powerfully illustrated by Mohamedou Ould Slahi. Slahi was a prisoner at Guantánamo Bay between 2002 and 2016.

In 2005, he managed to complete a 446-page hand-written manuscript in his cell. It was composed in English, a language Slahi achieved fluency in only while incarcerated. After Slahi tried to have the manuscript released, it was classified secret and deposited in a facility near Washington, D.C., where it languished for years while Slahi's lawyers fought to clear its publication. Eventually, a censored version, with 2,500 black-bar redactions, was published in 2015 as *Guantánamo Diary*. Now a second edition has been published without redactions. It documents the Bush administration's embrace of torture and related crimes straight out of Solzhenitsyn. Contrary to Frum's portrait of Trump as a break from a conscientious US conservatism, the real story is one of amoral continuity.

A distinctive feature of Frum's writing, aside from its nimble prose style, is that his brand of conservatism has long been a contrarian one. Well before Trump, Frum regularly criticized American conservatism in the name of making it stronger. He once wrote a magazine article that condemned Pat Buchanan, then on the verge of seeking the Republican presidential nomination, for his "sly Jew-baiting and his not-so-sly queer bashing." Frum's first book, *Dead Right* (1994), was published shortly afterwards. It again took aim at Buchanan-style paleo-conservatism, but also argued that more mainstream conservatives had compromised their commitment to small government in favor of "triviality and faddishness."

After the 2008 financial crisis, Frum's message changed. He argued that conservatives should accept a larger role for government. "There are things only government can do, and if we conservatives wish to be entrusted with the management of the government, we must prove that we care enough about government to manage it well," he wrote in *Comeback: Conservatism That Can Win Again*. Frum's post-2008 writings on issues such as social security, health care, and the environment have often staked out positions that a left-wing reader can agree with. The venerable left-wing magazine the *Nation* has gone so far as to call Frum "one of the media's most effective anti-conservative, or at least anti-Republican, commentators."

What makes Frum an anti-Republican rather than an anti-conservative—a critic of a party more than a set of first principles —is his stance on immigration, which he wants less of, and, especially, foreign affairs and national security. On Iraq, for example, Frum has subsequently criticized how the invasion was managed and sold, but not the decision to go to war itself. As Frum told his interviewer from the *Nation*, "I believe in an American-led world order. I believe in the strength and power of America." If Frum's views on many domestic issues have moderated, he remains recognizably conservative on international issues related to war and terrorism (hence the title of his *Atlantic* election article: "The conservative case for voting for Clinton").

Trumpocracy contains a chapter on Trump's stumbling and farcical efforts at diplomacy, the main outcomes of which have been to alienate the United States from its allies and to embolden Russia, whose military intelligence service is widely thought to have hacked the servers of the Democratic National Committee to aid Trump's election. Overall, however, the book focuses on Trump's domestic politics, an area in which Frum, apart from some qualified sympathy for Trump's view on immigration, finds little common ground. The book as a whole offers a sober warning against Trump's ongoing assaults on liberal democratic norms.

Much of Frum's material will be familiar to anyone who follows the news: Trump's pathological narcissism; a White House staffed by fiends and hobgoblins (communications director Anthony "the Mooch" Scaramucci, assistant to the president Omarosa Manigault-Newman); a Twitter account that re-circulates material from Nazis; the constant efforts to delegitimize the press and other organs of accountability; Trump's admiration for the most sadistic and repugnant figures in public life, as evinced by his pardoning of racist ex-sheriff Joe Arpaio and his dismissal of the sexual harassment accusations against former Fox News CEO Roger Ailes ("It's very sad. Because he's a very good person"). Frum catalogs Trump's depravity in unflinching detail.

Frum aptly identifies Trump's disregard for truth as a defining feature of his presidency. "No American president in history —no national political figure of any kind since at least senator Joe McCarthy—has trafficked more in untruths than Donald Trump," Frum writes. If this aspect of Trump has long been familiar, there is something to be said for Frum bringing many specimens of Trump's dishonesty all together in one place, so as to document the full scope of his mendacity.

Trump's enablers have included Republican media personalities, politicians, donors, and more than a few intellectuals. In some cases, Trump's enablers have been corrupted by him. In others, their function has been to reinforce Trump's own worst tendencies. Frum notes that Trump made unprecedented appointments of former or current military commanders to his cabinet and other positions. They included his chief of staff, secretary of defense, homeland security secretary, director of the federal bureau of prisons, and two national security advisors. Given the otherwise incompetent nature of Trump's administration, Frum suggests that this is a dangerous arrangement. "High among those dangers is impatience with law," he writes. A common outcome of military training is a willingness to do whatever it takes to win a battle. "That outlook, good in its place, must always be balanced in a republic of laws by the lawyer's insistence on the supremacy of legality." Trump's contempt for law is likely only to be exacerbated by his decision to surround himself with advisors with military instincts.

Frum argues that Trump ultimately represents an unprecedented assault on the norms that have constrained the American president since Watergate:

> Tax disclosure refused for the first time since Gerald Ford. Conflict-of-interest rules ignored for the first time since Richard Nixon. Running a business corporation while in office for the first time since Lyndon Johnson. The first appointment of a relative to a senior government position since John F. Kennedy named his brother Robert attorney general. The first appointment of a presidential son or daughter to a senior White House position since Franklin Roosevelt's son James. The first use of presidential patronage to enrich the president's family since Ulysses S. Grant.

The one positive trait Frum associates with Trump is a lack of hypocrisy. His flaws were plain during his presidential campaign, during which he did not present himself as a traditional politician but as an outsider who would cleanse Washington with fire. In this way, he spoke authentically to the concerns of his supporters within the GOP who felt shut out of the traditional two-party system.

"Just 13 percent described themselves as 'very conservative,' " Frum writes. "What set them apart from other Republicans was their economic insecurity and their cultural anxiety." Trump tapped into that insecurity and anxiety in a manner that allowed him to break free of the rules of partisan politics. "Donald Trump created in effect a three-party system in the United States, by building a new Trump party in-between the Democratic and Republican parties."

Trumpocracy contains scattered references to the presidency of George W. Bush, not all of which are positive. Their primary function, however, is to posit Bush and Trump as opposing figures. Trump expects servile deference and hysterical praise from his subordinates. The president whom Frum once served, by contrast, "distrusted flattery and flatterers. His eyes would narrow and a cynical smile would form, as if to say, 'Now I see what you are.' " Trump's rants about the European Union and the North Atlantic Treaty Organization are contrasted with Bush's wise European policy. "During his own tenure in the White House as speechwriter for George W. Bush," the jacket of *Trumpocracy* states, "Frum witnessed the ways the presidency was limited not by law but by tradition, propriety, and public outcry, all now weakened." The Bush years are portrayed as a time when, unlike now, morality and sanity prevailed. But how plausible is Frum's attempt to cabin off Trump from Bush?

"Modern political lies are so big," Hannah Arendt wrote, "that they require a complete rearrangement of the whole factual texture—the making of another reality, as it were, into which they will fit without seam, crack, or fissure, exactly as the facts fitted into their own original context." Arendt, somewhat eccentrically, used "lies" to include false statements a speaker believes but should not. Bush and Trump both created their own alternative realities in this sense.

The basis of Trump's fantasies is mostly egotistical: He has the biggest crowds; he cuts the best deals; he is amply endowed (financially and otherwise). Bush's delusions were geopolitical: Iraq had weapons of mass destruction, mission accomplished. But Trump and Bush both rival Richard Nixon in their propensity to create dream-palaces of the kind Arendt described. Each poisoned the public sphere with enormously destructive falsehoods. If there is a difference so far regarding their alternate realities, it is in Trump's favor: His fantasies did not claim hundreds of thousands of lives.

American conservatism has long exhibited an antagonistic attitude toward instruments of international justice. Conservative parties in Canada, Australia, and across Europe have reconciled themselves to the fact that their countries are states signatories to the International Criminal Court (ICC), a flawed but necessary institution. The United States has never ratified the ICC treaty. To be sure, support for the ICC on the part of the Clinton and Obama administrations was lukewarm at best. But conservative Republicans have long opposed any version of a global court due to their hostility to all attempts to hold the United States accountable for its actions abroad.

During the lead-up to the Iraq war, United Nations weapons inspector Hans Blix warned that Iraq had no weapons of mass destruction. Vice-president Dick Cheney and other Bush administration officials responded by attacking the credibility of Blix, his agency, and the United Nations as a whole. When Trump, during his campaign, referred to "the utter weakness and incompetence of the United Nations" he was only following the lead of Bush and many other Republicans.

Among the most important issues faced by both Bush and Trump has been human-caused climate change. Rising global temperatures now exacerbate everything from wildfires in California to rising sea levels at Trump's Mar-a-Lago resort in Florida. The Bush administration withdrew the United States from the Kyoto Protocol. Rather than replace the problematic treaty with an adequate response to climate change, Bush appointees suppressed the findings of government climate researchers and engaged in repeated "incidents of political interference [as] part of a larger pattern of attacks on scientific integrity by the Bush administration," as a scathing 2007 report by the Union of Concerned Scientists and the Government Accountability Project put it. Trump, who has called global warming a hoax, withdrew the United States from the Paris Agreement at the first available opportunity (under the withdrawal rules, the day after the 2020 presidential election; the United States soon re-joined under President Biden). Trump also appointed numerous climate change deniers to high-level positions in his administration, including —tragically, pathetically, inevitably—the head of the Environmental Protection Agency.

Trump may have campaigned as a populist, but he has clearly governed as a conservative. In the Senate, votes by conservative Republican Ted Cruz agree with Trump's views 92 percent of the time, those by left-wing Democrat Elizabeth Warren only 11 percent. In December 2017, after Frum submitted the manuscript of *Trumpocracy*, Trump tweeted on behalf of Alabama senate candidate Roy Moore, who at the time was beset by credible allegations that he had harassed or sexually assaulted teenage girls: "The people of Alabama will do the right thing. [Moore's opponent] Doug Jones is pro-abortion, weak on crime, military and illegal immigration, bad for gun owners and veterans and against the WALL." One hopes Bush would not have supported an alleged sex offender such as Moore.

But the issues cited in Trump's tweet all play to the concerns of conservative Republicans, who largely supported Bush. Frum, in short, exaggerates the differences between Bush and Trump.

There is a more significant difference between the two politicians. It can be seen by recalling a description of modern political debate that sees all minimally plausible political theories as occupying an egalitarian plateau. Each theory affirms in its own way that members of the political community are moral equals. This notion of equality is a moral idea, not to be confused with equality of resources or talents. Rather it amounts to the belief that all members of the political community have interests that matter equally. The government therefore must respond to them, not necessarily with equal treatment, but with equal consideration and respect. Where the left and right have historically disagreed, on this account, is on the necessary preconditions for treating people as equals. In the economic sphere, for example, the left has defended some form of resource equality while the right has emphasized equal rights to one's property and economic opportunity.

It is not hard to name right-wing thinkers whom this model doesn't fit (Ayn Rand, Leo Strauss), but these thinkers are often considered cranks in part because they do not occupy the egalitarian plateau. The diversity of right-wing thought has long included more respectable voices whose central arguments do endorse moral equality. They range from social conservatives such as Canada's own George Grant to Harvard philosopher Robert Nozick, arguably the twentieth century's most rigorous libertarian. This wide acceptance of moral equality is not surprising: In the modern world, it is far more philosophically plausible and politically palatable to argue over what equal respect entails than it is to reject moral equality outright.

This is why American presidents have long paid at least lip service to all men, and more recently all women, being created equal.

George W. Bush was no exception. In the same speech in which he referred to an axis of evil, Bush spoke of the "need to prepare our children to read and succeed in school," taking "our children" to include all American children. Today, it is normal to extend moral consideration beyond state borders and affirm the moral equality of all human beings, a perspective American presidents have been happy to adopt when convenient. Hence the passages in Bush's speech graphically describing human rights violations the Iraqi regime had committed against its own people.

Critics of American presidents have often charged that their affirmations of equality are lip service. Certainly in Bush's case it was a strange response to the Iraqi regime "leaving the bodies of mothers huddled over their dead children," as his speech put it, for him to do the same. Whether it comes to America's school programs or its foreign policy, critics of Bush and other presidents have often called for them to act in a manner that better lives up to their egalitarian rhetoric.

Trump is distinctive for not even paying lip service to equality. His rhetorical attacks on Mexican immigrants, African-American football players, and Muslims; his reluctance to condemn white supremacists; his sympathy for the racist conspiracy theory that denies that the United States' first black president is American—it is impossible to reconcile these nauseating aspects of Trump's record with even a minimal commitment to moral equality. This is what Frum is getting at when he says there is no hypocrisy in Trump. Particularly during the campaign, Trump did not employ noble rhetoric about equality (or anything else). He was instead open about his contempt: for communities of color; for his female opponent; for everything except himself and his cramped; and exclusionary vision of American society.

One of the most extreme things Trump said during the campaign concerned how he would prevent terrorism: "When you get these terrorists, you have to take out their families." Trump was indicating his willingness to disregard human rights in pursuit of national security. For Bush, this was not just rhetoric. It was policy.

Solzhenitsyn Aleksandr observed that people who fell into the hands of the secret police usually did not try to escape. "It isn't just that you don't put up any resistance; you even walk down the stairs on tiptoe, as you are ordered to do, so your neighbours won't hear," he wrote in *The Gulag Archipelago*. Because the victims of Stalinism were so often innocent, they were unprepared for the knock on the door. This sometimes left them with a nagging sense of complicity after the fact. After his own arrest, Solzhenitsyn was haunted by questions he found difficult to answer. "So why did I keep silent? Why, in my last minute out in the open, did I not attempt to enlighten the hoodwinked crowd?"

Mohamedou Ould Slahi had a similar reaction to his own arrest. It occurred in 2001 in his native Mauritania, when members of the West African country's security service showed up at his door. After a week in detention, he was informed he was being transferred to Jordan and was taken to the airport by agents, who left his legs unshackled, thereby providing an opportunity to break away. Rather than seize it, Slahi cooperated with his escorts. "I could easily have run away and reached the public terminal before anybody could catch me," he writes. "I could at least have forcibly passed the message to the public, and hence to my family, that I was kidnapped. But I didn't do it, and I have no explanation for why not."

Slahi did not know it at the time, but the Jordanian rendition team that brought him to Jordan was following a pattern, one that Human Rights Watch described in a 2008 report. It noted that "from 2001 until at least 2004, Jordan's General Intelligence Department served as a proxy jailer for the US Central Intelligence Agency (CIA), holding prisoners that the CIA apparently wanted kept out of circulation, and later handing some of them back to the CIA."

Slahi was originally told that he would be in Jordan only for a few days, but this soon proved false. During his first interrogation his captors asked him what he had done. When he said he had done nothing, they burst out in laughter. "Oh, very convenient! You have done nothing but you are here!" To be a detainee was to be deemed guilty, a rationalization Solzhenitsyn's captors had also employed. As a colonel in the Soviet ministry of state security put it: "We are not going to sweat to prove the prisoner's guilt to him. Let *him* prove to *us* that he did *not* have hostile intent."

Slahi was incarcerated in Jordan for eight months. Prison rules ostensibly allowed the International Committee of the Red Cross (ICRC) access to all prisoners. Whenever the ICRC visited the prison in which Slahi was housed, however, he was hidden in a cellar, one of several steps taken to deny him contact with the outside world. Throughout his detention, Slahi experienced acute stress and depression. His interrogations, which revolved around terror charges he knew nothing about, eventually turned violent. Slahi, however, suggests that the worst part was the psychological abuse. It involved having to listen to another detainee be beaten with an unidentified hard object outside the interrogation room. This lasted until the detainee was crying for his life and Slahi was shaking with fear.

In July 2002, Slahi was transferred to the Bagram Air Base in Afghanistan, where he was again interrogated about a terror operation he knew nothing about. Two weeks later, Slahi underwent rendition for the third time, to Guantánamo. During his previous transfer to Afghanistan, Slahi was already so broken that he had to be dragged on board the airplane; during that grueling flight he was shackled, blindfolded, earmuffed, and made to wear a diaper. The conditions of his longer flight from Afghanistan to Cuba were worse. He was again earmuffed, this time with a set that had such an excruciating grip that his ears bled for several days. Equally painful goggles blocked out his sight. Every so often, a guard would remove his earmuffs and speak into his ear, "You know, you didn't make any mistake: your mom and dad made the mistake when they produced you." After being strapped into the plane, Slahi had a mask placed over his face and a bag put on his head. The belt strapping him in was so tight it constricted his breathing. A terrified Slahi did not know how to say "tight" in English: "I kept saying, 'MP, Sir, I cannot breathe!... MP, SIR, please.' But it seemed like my pleas for help got lost in a vast desert."

At Guantánamo, Slahi was sexually humiliated by female interrogators. He was warned that, if he did not confess, he would spend the rest of his life at Guantánamo; he was told that his family was in danger if he did not cooperate; subjected to extreme noise and light; constantly shackled by his wrists to the floor so that he was unable to stand without stooping, triggering sciatic pain in his lower back; and made to experience extreme cold in a punishment cell known as the cold room. This last technique, Slahi notes, has long-term health consequences that are difficult to trace back to a torturer. "The torture squad was so well trained that they were performing almost perfect crimes, avoiding leaving any obvious evidence."

Slahi's renditions to Jordan and Afghanistan were at the hands of the CIA. After he arrived at Guantánamo, responsibility for his interrogation was divided between different agencies. The redacted edition of *Guantánamo Diary* left open the possibility that the CIA was among them. The restored edition makes clear that it was the work of the Federal Bureau of Investigation and various branches of military intelligence. Military interrogators had a much higher cruelty threshold than their FBI counterparts, to the point that a schism developed between the FBI and military intelligence, due to the latter's adoption of the extreme interrogation methods that the CIA had been employing at its rendition sites. The FBI viewed such tactics as so inhumane and counter-productive that it eventually withdrew from joint interrogations.

Military interrogators subjected Slahi to extreme sleeplessness. It occurred when he was placed in an isolation cell that admitted no light:

> The cell—better, the box—was cooled down to the point that I was shaking most of the time. I was forbidden from seeing the light of the day; every once in a while they gave me a rec-time at night to keep me from seeing or interacting with any detainees. I was living literally in terror. For the next seventy days I wouldn't know the sweetness of sleeping; interrogation 24 hours a day, three and sometimes four shifts a day. I rarely got a day off. I don't remember sleeping one night quietly.

The methods used on Slahi recall those used on Solzhenitsyn. The Russian writer's interrogation had lasted for ninety-six hours and was made up, Solzhenitsyn wrote, of sleeplessness, lies, and threats.

The sleeplessness in particular was "a great form of torture: it left no visible marks and could not provide grounds for complaint even [in] an inspection—something unheard of anyway." Forcing prisoners to go without sleep for days did more than make them experience extreme tiredness. Withholding the biological imperative of sleep "befogs the reason, undermines the will, and the human being ceases to be himself, to be his own 'I.' "

The CIA has long been aware of the lineage of the methods it employs. *Guantánamo Diary* cites a 1956 CIA report titled "Communist Control Techniques: An Analysis of the Methods Used by Communist State Police in the Arrest, Interrogation, and Indoctrination of Persons Regarded as 'Enemies of the State.'" Whereas in recent years apologists for torture have preferred to speak of "enhanced interrogation techniques," and "special interrogation plans," the CIA report is refreshing in its avoidance of euphemism. "These methods do, of course, constitute torture and physical coercion. All of them lead to serious disturbances of many bodily processes."

If Slahi was unable to provide information about terror operations he had no knowledge of, this was not an aspect of reality Guantánamo could easily accommodate. Slahi had to be withholding what he knew. For this reason, a year after Slahi arrived at Guantánamo, he became subject to a "special interrogation plan," approved by then-secretary of defense Donald Rumsfeld. After it went into effect Slahi's captors became less concerned not to leave traces of their work.

The plan saw Slahi removed from his cell by soldiers in riot gear who blindfolded him and placed a bag over his head before placing him on a boat that drove around for several hours. The purpose was to deceive Slahi into believing he was undergoing rendition for a fourth time, to Egypt, where he would experience torture beyond human limit. During the boat ride Slahi nearly suffocated and was beaten so badly he could not stand or speak. When he passed out he was woken with ammonia and beaten again.

Solzhenitsyn observed that greed played a central role in keeping the gulag running. Transportation to the gulag was a long, brutal process. It involved being packed into crowded train cars and unloaded at intermediate transit prisons where non-political prisoners served the role of trustees. Such an arrangement allowed officials to keep a portion of the money budgeted for salaries. Rather than having to pay the trustees, the gulag's managers gave them a free hand in their dealings with newly arrived political prisoners, whom they often robbed. And, as Solzhenitsyn put it, "they also take things from us *honestly*." Political prisoners could pay trustees for various favors, such as changing their departure time or not putting them in a cell with thieves, non-political criminals who were even more vicious than the jailers.

Guantánamo operationalized greed in a different way. This is documented by Murat Kurnaz, whose detention coincided with Slahi's. Kurnaz, a resident of Germany, was on a religious pilgrimage in Pakistan when police at a checkpoint ordered him off a bus and took him into custody before turning him over to the United States. Once at Guantánamo, Kurnaz was told that his arrest had been facilitated by a financial incentive directed at local agencies in Pakistan. "When I was apprehended, everyone knew that there was money to be made by turning in foreigners. Lots of Pakistanis were sold as well. Doctors, taxi drivers, fruit and vegetable sellers, many of whom I later met in Guantánamo." Kurnaz's discussion of his bounty, which he was told was US$3,000, appears in his own 2006 memoir, *Five Years of My Life: An Innocent Man in Guantanamo.*

Although Slahi was not brought in this way, Guantánamo as a whole was the product of large numbers of bounties paid in Pakistan and elsewhere.

A major difference between Guantánamo and the gulag is that Guantánamo has been within the reach of law. Human rights groups working on behalf of prisoners launched lawsuits that challenged their lack of basic procedural safeguards. One such challenge resulted in the 2008 US Supreme Court decision *Boumediene v. Bush*, which allowed Slahi to challenge his detention in 2009. Thus his case, unlike Solzhenitsyn's, did include a trial to determine whether his detention was justified, albeit one held eight years after his arrest.

Slahi was arrested because he was believed to be an active member of al-Qaeda. Multiple pieces of Slahi's background appeared to suggest as much. He received weapons training in Afghanistan at an al-Qaeda camp; he was in contact with Ramzi bin al-Shibh, who was accused of helping organize the 9/11 attacks; and his cousin was on al-Qaeda's shura council, the body just below Osama bin Laden in the terror organization's hierarchy. Finally, Slahi was thought to be part of the so-called millennium bomb plot. It involved Ahmed Ressam, who was arrested in 1999 after getting on a ferry in Victoria, BC, and trying to disembark in Port Angeles, Washington state. US Customs agents found the makings of a bomb in the trunk of Ressam's rental car, with which he had been planning to destroy the Los Angeles airport. Ressam lived in Montreal, where Slahi also briefly resided. Canadian and US intelligence agencies suspected Slahi, who attended the same mosque as Ressam, of having provided assistance to him.

These allegations were enough for Slahi to be presumed guilty by his torturers. When the case against him was finally subjected to courtroom scrutiny, however, it fell apart. The judge noted that the training Slahi received in Afghanistan had taken place in 1990, before al-Qaeda had taken up terrorism against the United States. Slahi's training had been for the purpose of fighting the Soviet-sponsored communist government, a cause the United States supported. As for Ahmed Ressam, his time in Montreal did not overlap with Slahi's. The two never met. Slahi did have contact with his cousin who was in al-Qaeda, but this relative had been opposed to the 9/11 attacks and had tried to persuade Osama bin Laden not to carry them out, an effort documented in *The 9/11 Commission Report*. Slahi occasionally performed favors for his relative, but they involved activities unrelated to violence, such as helping to electronically transfer money to a family member. As for al-Qaeda member bin al-Shibh, Slahi barely knew him. Both men were living in Germany in 1999 when bin al-Shibh and two friends met a stranger on a train with whom they discussed jihad and their hope to go to Chechnya to fight the Russians. The stranger suggested they contact Slahi. When the three did so, Slahi put them up for the night and suggested that they could train for fighting Russians as he had, in Afghanistan. But there was no discussion of violence beyond the Chechen-Russian conflict, and no discussion of Slahi harming anyone.

"The evidence does show that [Slahi] provided some support to al-Qaeda, or to people he knew to be al-Qaeda," Judge James Robertson concluded. "Such support was sporadic, however, and, at the time of his capture, non-existent." Slahi's interactions with al-Qaeda members, importantly, did not show he was a member himself, the ostensible grounds for his imprisonment. "Rather, they tend to support Slahi's submission that he was attempting to find the appropriate balance—avoiding close relationships with al-Qaeda members, but also trying to avoid making himself an enemy." Judge Robertson ordered Slahi freed in 2010, but an appeal by the Obama administration meant he was not let go until 2016, fourteen years after his initial arrest.

In addition to his civilian trial, Slahi was also subject to military commission hearings at Guantánamo. A primary purpose of his interrogations was to gather evidence that could be used against him in such hearings. A central lesson of his case concerns the profound procedural inadequacy of military terror courts relative to civilian ones. By favoring military tribunals over civilian trials, the Bush administration exhibited a cynical contempt for truth, both factual and moral.

This became clear to the prosecutor assigned to assemble the case against Slahi at his military tribunal, a Marine named Stuart Couch. Couch had joined the prosecution in the hope that, in his words, he would "get a crack at the guys who attacked the United States." In 2003, after reviewing Slahi's file, Couch saw that Slahi had falsely confessed to being a terrorist as a result of his torture. Couch was moved, in particular, by a fake letter that stated Slahi's mother had been detained and was in danger of being transferred to Guantánamo, as well as a sudden admission of guilt that Slahi offered after being subject to the US-approved torture plan. *Guantánamo Diary* quotes an interview in which Couch describes the effect these discoveries had on him:

> It was at the end of this, [after] hearing all of this information, reading all this information, months and months and months of wrangling with the issue, that I was in church this Sunday, and we had a baptism. We got to the part of the liturgy where

the congregation repeats—and I'm paraphrasing here, but the essence is that we respect the dignity of every human being and seek peace and justice on earth. And when we spoke those words that morning, there were a lot of people in that church, but I could have been the only one there. I just felt this incredible, all right, there it is. You can't come in here on a Sunday, and as a Christian, subscribe to this belief of dignity of every human being and say I will seek justice and peace on the earth, and continue to go with the prosecution using that kind of evidence. And at that point I knew what I had to do.

Couch's epiphany amounted to the realization that he had fallen off the egalitarian plateau. Like the FBI, he deemed the methods used against Slahi so objectionable that he removed himself from Slahi's case and refused to be part of his prosecution.

At its height under Stalin, the gulag is estimated to have incarcerated at least two million people. Guantánamo, at its peak, housed 779 prisoners. Even factoring in Guantánamo's network of feeder sites in the Middle East and Afghanistan, there is no comparison in scale. The Center for Constitutional Rights and other non-governmental organizations (NGOs) have also done important work exposing injustices at Guantánamo. The legal universe that generated the gulag permitted no equivalent NGO ferment.

But if Guantánamo does not match the gulag either in size or pure lawlessness, it is recognizably an island in the archipelago that Solzhenitsyn described. According to a Seton Hall University analysis of US government data, less than 10 percent of detainees were classified as al-Qaeda fighters. The same 2006 study, which examined 517 detainees, found that 86 percent were arrested after the payment of a bounty. In addition to Couch, six other military prosecutors requested reassignment or resigned due to concerns that hearings conducted at Guantánamo have failed to meet minimal standards of justice. Opposition to the twilight world described in Solzhenitsyn's prison saga should entail opposition to Guantánamo. Not because the two are identical, but because the affinities between them, which include the imprisonment and torture of innocent people, are terrible enough.

Frum has often retold his origin story tracing his politics back to his reading of Solzhenitsyn. Yet as an axis-of-evil speechwriter, he served the administration that created the Guantánamo Bay detention camp. That administration responded to terrorism in a manner not subject to strong legal oversight. It was, to borrow a phrase, impatient with law. Ironically, the case Slahi was accused of being mixed up with—Ahmed Ressam's bomb plot—ended in what has long been an example of a well-handled terror trial. It demonstrated that suspected terrorists are best tried by open civilian courts because their respect for the rights of the accused allows them to more accurately address questions of guilt and innocence. Insofar as the Bush administration's response to terrorism was analogous to a war, this entailed that it was conducted with fewer rights safeguards. By coming up with a pithy way of expressing the thought that opposing terrorism, and the regimes that allegedly sponsor it, is akin to waging war, Frum contributed to the climate of unreason in which the methods inflicted on Slahi became possible.

Of course, as a mere speechwriter, Frum did not write policy or weigh in on decisions regarding Guantánamo. Accountability, however, is something we face not only for our individual actions and the differences they make. We can also be judged for our actions as part of a group. Imagine a group of people who decide to hide a body. One of them is physically weak, so that when they all push the corpse into a river one night, her effort contributes nothing. On an individual level, she plays no causal role in making the body disappear. She is still complicit in the group's wrong. Frum is complicit in the moral disaster of Guantánamo in a similar way. Not because he caused it, but because he participated in the administration that made it possible. In particular, he participated actively in the project of justifying and selling a war on terror.

Frum has also been complicit as a journalist. Not long after Guantánamo began receiving prisoners, it attracted criticism in the international press. "As American forces advanced [in Afghanistan], Europe's left-wing press invented atrocity stories to keep them company," Frum wrote in *The Right Man*, his 2003 White House memoir. "The left-wing British tabloid the *Mirror* accused the United States of torture for the offence of handcuffing al-Qaeda terrorists in transit to Guantánamo Bay and issuing them plugs to protect their ears from engine noise en route." Accusations of human rights violations were the invention of unreliable critics; all Guantánamo detainees are terrorists; Slahi's bloody ears were for his own protection. The falsehood quotient in Frum's account was high.

Frum's writings have sought to delegitimize not only external critics of Guantánamo, such as the European press, but also internal ones, such as the FBI. The federal agency was deeply implicated in Slahi's ordeal, having twice questioned him in Africa before he was arrested and shipped to Jordan. Nevertheless, the FBI's institutional ethos did not tolerate torture, which made it unwilling to participate in the methods used on Slahi and other prisoners. Frum had this ethos in mind when he called for a transformation of American security institutions in his 2004 book *An End to Evil: How to Win the War on Terror*, coauthored with Richard Perle.

"The transformation must begin with the single worst performer among those institutions: the FBI," Frum and Perle wrote. "The FBI is essentially a police force, and like all good police forces, it goes to great lengths to respect the constitutional rights of the suspects it investigates." This concern with respecting rights renders the FBI "inherently disabled" in dealing with accused terrorists who are not citizens. "Noncitizen terrorist suspects are not members of the American national community, and they have no proper claim on the rights Americans accord one another."

The reference to "suspects" is chilling. This is not because the rejection of torture presupposes that every victim is innocent. Reasons not to torture even convicted terrorists include the fact that people will say anything to make torture stop, resulting in worthless intelligence (such as Slahi's confession). But Frum's reference to suspects takes in a wider class of individuals than those convicted at trial. This is consistent with the view of national security as a theater of war. According to that view, being unwilling to deprive someone of basic liberties until they have been found guilty is a pathetic feature of procedural liberalism. Slahi was not American and was a terror suspect. It follows that the methods employed on him were appropriate. Conservatism and Stalinism kiss.

In 2006, Frum took a tour of Guantánamo. One reason the US military may offer such tours is to generate favorable press coverage. If so, Frum's visit paid off. In a *National Post* article about his trip he cited transcripts of detainee testimony given at review tribunal hearings. The detainees' words suggested that they were, in Frum's sarcastic summary, "innocent goatherds and blameless wedding guests swept up by blind American injustice." According to Frum, the testimony was remarkable in each case only for its implausibility. There was no excuse for "those in the west who succumb so easily to the deceptions of terrorists who cannot invent even half-way plausible lies." Frum's account of his visit uncritically recycled the official administration view. Tours of the kind he went on do not permit visitors to speak with detainees such as Slahi, or to concerned military staff such as Couch. This renders them worthless as fact-finding exercises.

Finally, as recently as 2009, Frum defended the Bush administration from criticism of its interrogation practices. Frum was prompted to do so by Barack Obama's admission that the United States had used torture. Although Obama's admission was limited to the use of waterboarding, Frum argued that it went too far. "Maybe waterboarding was wrong even in 2002–2003. The Bush administration itself has acted on the understanding that it was unnecessary after 2003," he wrote in his *National Post* column. "But make no mistake: What is going on in this so-called 'torture' debate is an attempt to hijack humanitarian feeling to smuggle into international law new claims on behalf of the world's most conscienceless criminals." The use of scare quotes around torture and the robotic insistence that torture's only victims are terrorists are bad enough. But the most pernicious aspect of Frum's statement may be its insinuation that the use of torture at Guantánamo, which at the beginning of 2018 still housed forty-one prisoners, is old news no longer worth dwelling on.

A longstanding fantasy has been that torture can be institutionalized in a controlled way. But torture is like a fire that always escapes the fireplace. It is inevitably directed at the innocent.

And on a national level, it inevitably corrupts the institutions of any country willing to use it. During the Algerian war of independence, the colonial French government employed torture on a widespread scale. The phrase *"la gangrene"* was used to describe how torture, in the words of historian Neil MacMaster, "was seen as a form of cancer that inexorably led to the degeneration of the liberal democratic state, its institutions (particularly the army and the judiciary), its core values and fundamental respect for human rights and dignity."

The United States under Bush was infected by the gangrene seen in Algeria and other torture regimes. One of the institutions most affected was the Republican Party. When Trump during his campaign called for "a total and complete shutdown of Muslims entering the United States," he was singling out for abuse a group that had long been mistreated under Bush, the former president's rhetoric about recognizing Islam as a religion of peace notwithstanding. For years, Frum has participated in the gangrene's advance as a Bush speechwriter and a Guantánamo apologist. This prevents him from seeing how the annihilationist conservatism of the Bush years foreshadowed Donald Trump.

In addition to creating Guantánamo Bay's detention camp and invading Iraq, Bush signed the *Patriot Act*, which legalized warrantless wiretapping and indefinite detention. Although his administration took steps to eliminate racial profiling in federal law enforcement, it also instituted regulations that facilitated profiling on religious or national-origin grounds, with the result that "immigrants and visitors from Arab and Middle Eastern countries were subjected to increased scrutiny, including interviews, registration, and in some cases removal," as a 2004 US Commission on Civil Rights report put it. Bush opposed the *Employment Non-Discrimination Act*, which would have prevented discrimination based on sexual orientation, and announced his support for a constitutional amendment to deny legal recognition to same-sex unions. The common theme running through these and other initiatives of Bush's administration is a glaring disrespect for rights. A similar disrespect emanated from Trump in his utterances on Muslims, Mexican immigrants, transgender people, and countless other groups.

Unlike Bush, Trump was sometimes too incompetent to turn his utterances into law. His contributions to public discourse are bad enough in themselves. The president is a loud voice in the public sphere, and what he says has a huge influence on what counts as acceptable. Hence the renewed prominence of far-right groups since Trump's election. More importantly, equality is the philosophy of democracy. It is naive to think that a president who is openly contemptuous of equality can be a reliable manager of democratic institutions. For these reasons Trump's rhetoric has indeed been a step down from Bush's, which is no small loss.

The United States may someday have a president who respects moral equality in both words and action. To date, few presidents have fallen farther from the egalitarian plateau than Trump and Bush. Frum's view of Trump as a break from his predecessor relies upon a self-serving amnesia we have long been warned against. In Milan Kundera's words, the struggle of man against power is the struggle of memory against forgetting.

CHAPTER 8

THE LAST NATIONALIST

In November of 1988, Canadian literature began to disappear. Before then, writers who had come of age in the 1960s regularly produced novels and stories set in modern Canada. They also established presses and other institutions devoted to fostering Canadian culture. Then free trade arrived. Literary values gradually gave way to commercial ones, marking the end of the period when writers such as Mordecai Richler and Alice Munro could launch international careers with works set in a real Canadian neighborhood such as Mile End, Montreal, or a fictional Canadian town such as Jubilee, Ontario. Following the free trade election of 1988, literary fiction that achieved critical or commercial success was increasingly published by foreign-owned presses, and increasingly set in the distant past or outside Canada altogether. Both trends, which were intertwined, worsened after Canada's entry into the North American Free Trade Agreement in 1994. As a character in a Russell Smith novel published a few years later put it, "novels are like movies now. They can't be about things here."

So runs an argument by Stephen Henighan. Henighan has a well-earned reputation as a literary cosmopolitan. A novelist and short story writer who teaches Spanish and Hispanic Studies at the University of Guelph, Henighan's fiction is often set in Central America, Europe, and other foreign locales, while much of his non-fiction addresses Latin American subjects. For many years Henighan has also served as General Editor of the Biblioasis International Translation Series, whose catalog includes works that Henighan has personally translated from Portuguese and Romanian. These international interests notwithstanding, Henighan is a writer-critic in the tradition of Margaret Atwood and John Metcalf: a practitioner with a comprehensive vision of Canadian literature. And in this guise Henighan has kept cultural nationalism alive into the twenty-first century.

Henighan inherits some familiar problems from nationalists of Atwood's generation. Yet for all the areas where he continues their approach, there are others where he embraces views long advanced by cultural nationalism's critics. In this way, Henighan reveals cultural nationalism to be a fluid and historically changing idea. A question that his work raises is whether literary nationalism might evolve even further along the trajectory that Henighan has begun. His criticism should prompts us to ask whether we might retain cultural nationalism's concern with the fate of a specifically Canadian literature, without the fear of American influence that has long accompanied it.

The text in which Henighan's nationalism is most evident is *When Words Deny the World: The Reshaping of Canadian Writing*, which was nominated for the Governor General's Award for Non-Fiction in 2002, a rare achievement for a work of literary criticism. The book attracted attention in part because it was unusually abrasive.

In response to a literary critic who praised a Canadian novel for being set outside Canada, Henighan retorted that the critic had "a pathetically provincial attitude." Another critic who appeared on television and said something Henighan disagreed with was guilty of "TV-lobotomized, all-American simple-mindedness." Henighan assaults books by Timothy Findley, Margaret Atwood, Carol Shields, Jane Urquhart, and many other much-loved Canadian authors. His comments on writers or literary institutions based in Toronto are especially savage. In addition to venal agents and philistine publishers, he characterized the city as the home of phony writers who cheer on the replacement of literature by commercial fiction. "These are people who are writers in the way that other yuppies are software developers or management consultants: all questing, all uncompromising ferocity of inquiry into life and human experience, has been tamed."

Henighan's brutal takedowns of iconic Canadian authors, like the prominent internationalist strand in his work, may not make him sound like much of a nationalist. But Henighan's nationalism is evident everywhere in the book, particularly in its central message that Canadian literary history is a story of rise and fall.

Into the 1950s, Henighan writes, Canada barely had a literature. There were few publishers, and among the handful of literary writers the country produced, a disproportionate number—Mordecai Richler, Mavis Gallant, Margaret Laurence—left for Europe. In the 1960s everything changed. The combination of post-war prosperity, an expanding university system and an upsurge of nationalism contributed to a cultural boom and a new literary infrastructure, one made up of flourishing small presses, the Canada Council for the Arts and other institutions with a literary rather than commercial ethos.

In addition to these domestic factors, Henighan plausibly suggests that the carnage of the Vietnam War also caused Canadians to place more value on their differences from the United States. "It is one of the peculiarities of this vital period that virtually all of the best Canadian [works] of the time," Henighan writes, "were published between 1965, when the United States first committed combat troops to Vietnam, and 1975, when the North Vietnamese Army captured Saigon."

The boom years of 1965–1975 resulted in literary works that are now part of Canada's literary canon. Laurence and Richler came back to Canada and, along with Atwood, Munro, and other writers who had never left, wrote novels and linked story collections that reflected Canadian life. They also adopted more complex literary forms. As Henighan puts it in an essay published in 1990 that became a chapter in *When Words Deny the World*, Canadian literature as a whole seemed about to "leap to the sort of modernist or postmodernist epics of cultural identity to which other peripheral and postcolonial societies have given birth in the last thirty years."

Many of the epics of cultural identity that Henighan has in mind are Latin American: He points to novels by Mario Vargas Llosa, Gabriel Garcia Marquez, Carlos Fuentes, and other representatives of the Latin American Boom. Beginning in the 1950s and lasting into the 1980s or later, these writers produced an enduring body of work that combined narrative innovation with the felt documentation of Latin American life. Henighan argues that this is no accident: Writing about societies that were once colonies requires literary forms that go beyond those used by writers in the United States, Europe, and other cultural powers. "If your reality is marginalized," Henighan urges, "mythologize your marginalization! Innovation occurs in the moment when you discover that you cannot both remain true to your own experience and write like John Updike."

Henighan argues that Canadian writers occupied a marginalized cultural circumstance similar to that of Latin American writers, yet they squandered the opportunity to produce masterpieces on the scale of *One Hundred Years of Solitude*. As a result, where Latin America's boom was a multigenerational affair resulting in more than one masterpiece, Canada's lasted little more than a decade, after which we were left with many good novels but no great ones.

According to Henighan, after the mid-1970s, the literary infrastructure that Canada's nationalist generation created remained in place. But the books themselves became less ambitious. Atwood, Munro, and other prominent writers achieved international success, "at the price of being packaged as veritable brand names. Each new book must resemble its predecessors in order to satisfy the mass market." Even more disappointingly, the writers who followed them often opted for competence rather than innovation.

Crucially, the settings of successful Canadian novels also changed. "In response to the demands of the new international market, many Canadian writers are discarding their Canadian subject matter," Henighan's 1990 essay argues. "The mid-1980s has witnessed a rash of novels set in Boston and Iowa and London and Paris," Henighan writes, referring to bestsellers such as W.P. Kinsella's novel *Shoeless Joe* (1982), set in Iowa, and Atwood's *The Handmaid's Tale* (1985), which takes place in a dystopian Boston.

If Canada's literary decline began in the 1980s, it only grew worse as the conservative decade wore on. "The collective idea of Canada was demolished on November 21, 1988, when Canadians voted to subordinate our national project to the requirements of continental free trade," Henighan laments. On an institutional level, the literary ethos that once predominated was eroded by a garish commercialism. Henighan associates the 1990s with many negative developments. They include the rise of literary agents, an outsized concern with foreign rights, and the arrival of the Giller Prize, which Henighan accuses of favoring Toronto's larger (and eventually mostly foreign-owned) presses over regional literary ones. Small presses and Canada Council grants, although they did not disappear, were "superseded by a slick, image obsessed, Toronto-centric commercial publishing industry serving as a supply depot for the global book market."

Supporters of free trade and open borders often argue that such policies are no threat to cultural identity by pointing to the European Union. The freer flow of goods and people has allowed diverse European identities to thrive, to the point that smaller societies such as Scotland and Catalan have given rise to viable secession movements. Henighan thought-provokingly argues that this defense won't work in Canada, where "globalization means Americanization." Europe is home to many sustainable cultures, none of which is individually powerful enough to absorb the rest. Without the active state support for culture that has waned since Canada's literary boom, Henighan suggests, English-speaking Canada is in danger of becoming culturally subservient to the United States.

Henighan offers different kinds of evidence for his claim that Canadian literature became fatally commercialized in the 1990s. Some of that evidence is anecdotal, as when he recounts a conversation with a big-shot literary agent in Britain. During a meeting in a café to discuss a manuscript, the "irredeemably English" agent acknowledges that while Henighan's novel is well written, it is "too Canadian." As the unnamed Brit explains, "you can't sell a novel set in Canada internationally. The country's image is boring and the fiction plays up to the image." The meeting ends with Henighan receiving some unsolicited career advice. "You've moved outside Canada. Now it's time to move your fiction outside Canada." Henighan describes other agents in London, New York, and even Canada similarly rejecting books (not all written by Henighan) on the grounds that they are "too Canadian."

Further evidence Henighan offers to support his rise-and-fall narrative is textual. A widely discussed chapter of *When Words Deny the World* is called "Free Trade Fiction." It criticizes at length two bestsellers of the 1990s, Michael Ondaatje's *The English Patient* and Anne Michaels' *Fugitive Pieces.* Henighan's discussion of Ondaatje's book begins by announcing, "It is easy to make fun of *The English Patient,*" a remark that sets the tone for the critical onslaught that follows.

Henighan argues that *The English Patient* is evidence of Ondaatje's "flight from history into metaphor." In part this refers to Ondaatje's self-consciously beautiful writing style, which contains an excess of poetic imagery. Because the novel's characters are essentially opportunities to deploy images, they walk around the crumbling Italian villa in which the novel is set expressing important thoughts rather than believable dialogue. ("I thought I was going to die. I wanted to die. And I thought if I was going to die I would die with you. Someone like you, young as I am, I saw so many dying near me in the last year.")

The English Patient takes place in 1945, yet Ondaatje's characters refer to "North American troops," and to a "North American" identity. Henighan argues that Canadians of the 1940s would have been unlikely to use these phrases, given that they lived in a colonial society that considered itself closely tied to Britain rather than the United States, which only entered the war two years after Canada, and under different circumstances. In this way, Henighan argues, Ondaatje's characters lack historical believability.

Henighan is equally scathing about *Fugitive Pieces*. An overreliance on poetic language and imagery again comes at the expense of a felt engagement with history, Canadian or otherwise. This is the case even though *Fugitive Pieces* is concerned with the legacy of the Holocaust and has scenes set in Toronto. Henighan argues that Michaels' language is too often "shapeless showing off" that fails to illuminate her important material. Michaels' depiction of Toronto ("a city built in the bowl of a prehistoric lake") is also framed in geological rather than social terms, and so fails to engage with its large immigrant population and other political features.

Like Ondaatje, Michaels fails to write believable scenes with Canadian protagonists, Henighan charges. He quotes a passage in which an older male character with a European sensibility attends a party at which he meets a young Canadian woman. Michaels describes the older man taking an immediate interest in her, both intellectually and romantically:

> She moves through history with the fluency of a spirit, mourns the burning of the library of Alexandria as if it happened yesterday. She discusses the influence of trade routes on European architecture, while still noticing the pattern of light across a table...

> There's no one left in the kitchen. All around us are glasses and small towers of dirty dishes. The noise of the party in the

other room. Michaela's hips lean against the kitchen counter. Voluptuous scholar.

"To anyone who has spent time in European intellectual circles," Henighan tartly remarks, "this passage is beyond inanity. Persuading continental European intellectuals to take seriously the thoughts on Western culture of a Canadian—even a recognized authority of the weight of, say, the literary critic Northrop Frye or the philosopher Charles Taylor—is excruciatingly difficult." The male character was born in the 1930s and the meeting takes place fifty years later. For a European of his generation, Henighan objects, the possibility of being struck by a twenty something Canadian woman's intellect is zero ("her 'voluptuousness,'" he dryly adds, "is a different matter").

When Words Deny the World was followed by A Report on the Afterlife of Culture (2008), which continues the pessimistic argument of the first book, while supplementing and refining the thesis here and there. The title essay argues that the print culture that gave a central place to literature has been displaced by "the neon-lit glare of the mass world." A stranger speaking loudly into his phone on the bus; video games beckoning from countless screens; the rise of film and television as dominant modes of storytelling. A public sphere that once allowed the sustained concentration required to appreciate literary works has been displaced by technologies of distraction.

According to Henighan, the cultural content that mass technology makes available often has a recurring sameness. As a result, the more we allow ourselves to be distracted, the more our culture becomes homogenized. "This 'mass' element pervades all contemporary cultural activity," Henighan writes, "from the cherry-picking of downloaded tunes on a teenager's iPod that expresses her 'individuality' to the book club reading lists that try to fill the void left by the disintegration of literature by establishing a common ground for literary discussion." In addition to Itunes and book clubs, other aspects of modern culture of which *Afterlife* disapproves include blogs ("sloppy, fractured . . . intellectually malnourished"), contemporary "ethnic fiction" (a product of "the intensification of globalization since 1990"), and the Canadian Broadcasting Corporation's book show Canada Reads ("hugely reprehensible").

Henighan's criticism attracts attention in part because of how provocative it is. If his account of Canada's literary history is true, then our culture is doomed. Yet although Henighan differs from previous nationalists in many ways, he continues the traditional project of analyzing literature in national terms, albeit in a way that avoids many of that project's traditional problems. To appreciate the innovative aspects of Henighan's work, however, requires first separating them from his less plausible claims.

Henighan is surely right to be worried about Canadian writers setting their work in the United States for the wrong reasons. The comedian Martin Short once said that when Americans watch television they watch television, but when Canadians watch television they watch American television. Short's remark captures the inwardness, even at times provincialism, of the American cultural sphere, as well as the familiarity with American culture that Canadians first learn as children. The desire to break into the US market can provide Canadian writers with a crass and commercial, rather than literary incentive to set their work there.

But Henighan suggests something stronger. His anecdotes about literary agents turning down well-written books because they are too Canadian are naturally read as suggesting a deep bias against novels with any kind of Canadian setting. At times, however, Henighan suggests that not all Canadian settings are equally damned. Canadian novels can achieve international bestseller status, Henighan allows, if they are set "in other countries, in the Canadian past, or in parts of Atlantic Canada where the present can be made to feel like the past." In other words, the bias is not against novels with a Canadian setting per se, but against those set in contemporary urban Canada.

A prejudice against urban Canadian fiction would be bad enough. But Henighan often gives the impression that the more sweeping bias, against Canadian settings outright, is his real concern. Regardless of which version of the argument we have in mind, an odd feature of Henighan's extensive writing on this subject is how little evidence he provides to document either version of the problem.

The main evidence for Henighan's broader claim comes via his anecdotes about frustrating conversations with literary agents. Henighan mentions showing them a manuscript, one that bears similarities to *The Streets of Winter*, a novel Henighan published with Thistledown Press in 2004. A social novel set in Montreal during and after the free trade election of 1988, the book chronicles the urban experiences of a wide range of characters: French and English, immigrant and native-born, gay and straight, brown and white-skinned. Although the novel contains good writing and builds to a dramatic climax, many details of Montreal life seem less imagined than recorded. Characters contemplate the economic make-up of particular neighborhoods, the fate of Quebec separatism, and the diversity of Montreal itself. ("Montreal is like the ocean.

The whole world swims these streets," remarks a Portuguese immigrant at one point, articulating a theme of the book.) This material too often feels informational, and the novel works better on an intellectual than an emotional level. One wonders if some agents, by telling Henighan that his writing was "too Canadian," may have been gently trying to tell him something else.

Henighan offers stronger evidence for his narrower claim of a bias against urban Canadian locales. In a chapter of his book *Afterlife* called "Writing the City" he lists fifteen novels, in addition to *The English Patient* and *Fugitive Pieces*, which received major "critical and commercial attention" between 1989 and 2004. The list includes well-known novels such as *A Fine Balance*, *Alias Grace*, *No Great Mischief* and *The Colony of Unrequired Dreams*. Henighan notes that none of them has a contemporary urban Canadian setting.

This is true. But many novels set in contemporary Toronto, Montreal, and Vancouver were published between 1989 and 2004. If seventeen English-Canadian novels are enough to suggest a trend, it is possible to compile a list of equal length of urban Canadian novels that, after being published in Canada during the same period, were also brought out by American publishers. They include *Murther and Walking Spirits* and *The Cunning Man* (both by Robertson Davies), *Kicking Tomorrow* (Daniel Richler), *The Stone Diaries* and *Unless* (both by Carol Shields), *Minus Time* (Catherine Bush), *Headhunter* (Timothy Findley), *Childhood* (André Alexis), *Girlfriend in a Coma* (Douglas Coupland), *Mister Sandman* (Barbara Gowdy), *Flyboy Action Figure Comes with Gasmask* (Jim Munroe), *Baroque-A-Nova* (Kevin Chong), *Moody Food* (Ray Robertson), *Disappearing Moon Café* (Sky Lee), *Stanley Park* (Timothy Taylor), *The Robber Bride* (Margaret Atwood), and *Barney's Version* (Mordecai Richler).

These books attracted less acclaim than the books on Henighan's list. But in spite of their merit or popularity, it is hard to see how international gatekeepers were deeply biased against urban Canadian fiction if the American publication of novels set in Toronto, Vancouver, and Montreal during the 1990s was a common occurrence.

Henighan sometimes acknowledges that urban novels continued to appear in Canada and then quickly changes the subject to argue that the novel in question is not very good. So *The Stone Diaries* is "mediocre fiction," while *The Robber Bride* "seems to be amassing inventories of fresh fads." At other times he invokes generational or genre considerations. If Atwood, Davies, and Richler all continued to sell books with urban settings internationally, this was only because they became established before the age of agents. Similarly, if Andrew Pyper, a talented mystery writer, received a large international advance for his 1999 novel *Lost Girls*, this was because "the proven international salability of the mystery or thriller formula grants a large margin of freedom to adopt Canadian settings." Henighan's oddest take on a writer of contemporary urban fiction may appear in his discussion of Vincent Lam, whose 2006 story collection *Bloodletting and Miraculous Cures*, which is set in Toronto, was published in the United States after it won the Giller Prize. Henighan ignores the book and argues that it only won the Giller because of a conspiracy led by Margaret Atwood.

To sum up Henighan's case, there is an anti-Canadian bias across the English-speaking world that dampens interest in novels with a Canadian setting. Except when they are set in the past or in Atlantic Canada, when the author is a bad writer, when the author is long established, when the author writes mysteries, and when the author knows Margaret Atwood. On an individual level, Henighan's explanations as to why this or that book is an exception to anti-Canadian bias can strain credulity. But the fact that Henighan acknowledges so many exceptions to his rule suggests that it may not be much of a rule at all.

If Henighan's claim of a bias against Canadian settings is unconvincing in either of its main forms, the evidence for his depiction of the 1990s as an especially philistine decade also seems thin. He cites two novels, *The English Patient* and *Fugitive Pieces*, to argue that Canadian writing during the 1990s became "a literature dominated by poet's novels." But poet's novels existed in Canada before the 1990s. Well-known examples include *The Favourite Game*, by Leonard Cohen (1963), *Coming Through Slaughter*, by Ondaatje (1976), *A Short Sad Book*, by George Bowering (1977), and *Ana Historica*, by Daphne Marlatt (1988). Henighan never shows that the overly poetic writing he associates with the 1990s became especially common during that decade. His claim about free trade's impact on Canadian literature, which only examines books published after 1988, remains unproven.

In fact, if the 1990s are distinctive, it is actually because they marked a breakthrough in the reception of Canadian literature. Grounds for this view, ironically, are touched on by Henighan himself. In his discussion of Anne Michaels' depiction of an older European man becoming romantically interested in a younger Canadian woman, Henighan makes the fair point that someone born outside Canada before World War II would not associate Canada with cultural or intellectual achievement. But it is in just this regard that the 1990s marked a turning point.

Henighan mentions Charles Taylor as an example of a Canadian thinker whom European intellectuals were unlikely to take seriously.

This overlooks the breakout in international acceptance Canadian political philosophy experienced in the 1990s. Taylor's 1991 Massey Lectures, *The Malaise of Modernity*, had been translated into fourteen languages, most of them European, by the time W*hen Words Deny the World* appeared. In Chapter Six I criticized Taylor's essay, "The Politics of Recognition," but on the question of the essay's sheer influence, there is no question that its international impact has been enormous. This is reflected in the fact that the book containing Taylor's essay and replies by distinguished American and European intellectuals was translated into nine languages during the 1990s. Will Kymlicka, again, became globally influential during the same period.

It was not just Canadian philosophers who enjoyed a new level of international interest during the 1990s. The same was true of Canadian fiction writers, particularly novelists. The 1990s were the first decade in which Canadian novels swept major international awards such as the Booker Prize (*The English Patient*, in 1992), the Pulitzer Prize (*The Stone Diaries*, in 1995), the Orange Prize (*Fugitive Pieces*, in 1997; *Larry's Party* in 1998), and the International IMPAC Dublin Literary Award (*No Great Mischief*, published in 1999, won in 2001). These and other works were also translated into many languages—twenty in the case of *Fugitive Pieces* alone.

Of course, it is possible to exaggerate the cultural importance of foreign awards. But it is also a mistake to think they have no significance. The sheer frequency with which major prizes were bestowed on Canadian novels in the 1990s showed that Canada's international status has changed. This is significant given the prior history, to which Henighan rightfully draws attention, of European and other intellectuals considering Canada a cultural wasteland.

The 1990s was when it became unremarkable for international juries to deem Canadian books the best of those put before them.

This is why the fact that Ondaatje won the Booker Prize is important. Not because it shows *The English Patient* is well written. Henighan is surely right that the novel contains icky gobs of poetic imagery. Rather it is because the book's win marks a turning point in the international reception of Canadian literature. Canadian novels won international prizes before the 1990s, particularly during the 1980s. But winning the very most prestigious such prizes on a regular basis happened for the first time during the 1990s, the same decade in which Henighan claims everything went to hell.

If we can debate the merits of any particular prize-winner, this does not gainsay the fact that the overall trend was one of the wider world recognizing that Canada regularly produced good literature. There is an alternate universe in which no Canadians have ever won international prizes, and nationalist critics cite *that* as proof of anti-Canadian bias. We should be grateful that that universe is not the one we live in.

If Henighan offers an implausibly negative vision of Canadian literature, it may be because he shares with traditional cultural nationalism a gloomy and pessimistic sensibility. In *Arrival: The Story of CanLit*, literary scholar Nick Mount notes that the nationalist literary boom of the 1960s and 1970s was not just a product of new levels of affluence and education. "It was also fuelled by the most productive force in art: loss." As Mount elaborates, the uneasy feeling that Canadian identity was on the verge of being absorbed into its American counterpart (or, in the case of Quebec identity, into English Canada) "didn't just produce a string of elegies for a Canada that once was or might have been. It also fuelled an entire literature of loss—poem after poem and novel after novel about lost people and lost places." *Beautiful Losers, Civil Elegies, The Last Good Year,* and *The Last Canadian Poet* are just some of the fiction and non-fiction titles expressing this somber cultural mood.

An irony of 1960s nationalism is that it was at its most mournful just when Canadian culture was newly fertile. This is evident in the publication of George Grant's famous *Lament for a Nation: The Defeat of Canadian Nationalism* in 1965, when Canadian literature was beginning its historic rise. Grant was a cultural conservative, albeit a heterodox one whose suspicion of American capitalism and militarism gained him many left-wing admirers. Henighan quotes with approval Grant's prediction that Ontario would be integrated into the Great Lakes region of the United States, and shares with Grant and other cultural conservatives a tragic view of modern life.

Grant is not the only cultural conservative whom Henighan resembles. Allan Bloom, in *The Closing of the American Mind,* famously wrote that the value of the Western canon was lost on students who had grown up listening to rock music. "As long as they have the Walkman on, they cannot hear what the great tradition has to say. And, after its prolonged use, when they take it off, they find they are deaf." At one point Henighan writes of some of his own students, "the idea of historical and cultural change almost lies beyond their mental scope. Disciplined by the two screens [of TVs and computers] they see—literally—what is as always having been. The mere use of dates befuddles them." As in his negative depiction of a teenager innocently listening to an iPod, Henighan's pessimism recalls dour cultural conservatives such as Bloom at their least convincing.

One sometimes senses that Henighan's declinism has a personal motivation. This is due to the predictability with which he singles out particular Canadian novels for praise or condemnation. Henighan is well read in more than one national literature, and his chapters on Latin American, European, and African writers praise successful and little-known writers alike. In the case of Canadian writers, Henighan can be a generous champion of those he considers unfairly neglected. To take just one example, Henighan argues that *The Afterlife of George Cartwright*, John Steffler's novel about an eighteenth-century explorer of Labrador, is one of the most underrated novels of the 1990s. Henighan's claim is partly based on the mistaken belief that Steffler, who later became Canada's Parliamentary Poet Laureate, was never able to sell foreign rights. (In reality, Steffler's novel was published in the United States by Henry Holt.) Even so, I had not even heard of Steffler before reading *When Words Deny the World*. Thanks to Henighan's advocacy, I did, and it will be a long time before I forget Steffler's superb historical fiction.

When it comes to novels by Canadian contemporaries who have achieved commercial or critical success, however, Henighan is not so generous. He has kind words only for *Alias Grace* and *The Colony of Unrequited Dreams*, and even then only briefly. One often senses that Henighan's miserabilism is driven less by political or aesthetic concerns than by bitterness. Many of the things he attacks (the Giller Prize, large Toronto presses, Canada Reads, international sales) are the trappings of successful writers. The domestic writers whose works he praises by contrast are often those whose fiction, like Henighan's, is quietly published by regional presses. Of course this is not a reason to deny Henighan's arguments a fair hearing. But it does explain how Henighan, even though he is a nationalist, can sometimes sound like a colonialist critic of decades past, who routinely dismissed Canada for offering no literary works worth reading, the main difference being that Henighan recognizes an interregnum of good writing from the mid-1960s to the mid-1970s.

A final problem with Henighan's stance is more political. It concerns his protectionist view of foreign literary influence. On one level, Henighan approaches the discussion of Canadian literature in a spirit of letting the world back in. This is evident in his call to take Latin American writers as exemplars. Yet Henighan's more cosmopolitan view of what literary influences are acceptable has its own hard limits. If the old nationalist boundary was between domestic and foreign writing, Henighan's new dividing line is between writing from marginalized countries (Canada, Latin America) and powerful ones (Britain, the United States). The foreign influence that old-fashioned nationalists feared most was of course American. Henighan's approach, even though it is more inclusive, still looks down on American inspiration.

An unattractive upshot of this view is that it inevitably condemns most Canadian writing. Few Canadian authors have not been influenced in some way by counterparts from the United States and Britain. Recall Alice Munro describing the inspiration she found in Sherwood Anderson. Margaret Atwood has similarly said that *The Handmaid's Tale* was influenced by John Wyndham, Ray Bradbury, and other science fiction authors she read as a 1950s teenager. If Henighan's narrow view of what literary models Canadian writers should work with is correct, it is hard to see how good writing could arise in Canada in the first place, given that Munro, Atwood, and other pioneers had few English-language models other than British and American ones when they started out. Henighan's understanding of influence is difficult to reconcile with his recognition that good writing became common in Canada in the 1960s.

Henighan argues that Canadian writers should aspire to formal innovation because their cultural situation and subject matter, like that of Latin American writers, makes this necessary. But it is doubtful that there is any link between literary innovation and nationality. Modernist writers of the twentieth century certainly included many Irish writers, who would qualify as marginalized in Henighan's terms, but also many Brits and Americans, who would not. Henighan himself acknowledges, in a discussion of Faulkner's evocation of the American South, that writers in a culturally dominant country can identify with a subordinate identity within it. But if that is so, it puts in question the idea that the experience of marginalization neatly distinguishes Canadian and Latin American writers from their British and American peers.

Yet Henighan's problems are not the whole story. His unorthodox cultural nationalism includes many positive elements that update that approach for the twenty-first century. Henighan make a major step forward from 1970s nationalists by not fetishizing artistically dead nineteenth- and early twentieth-century works, and arguing instead that Canadian literature effectively begins in the 1960s. Of course some good books were written before 1960. But Henighan takes for granted that literature is something we read with artistic and emotional goals in mind, not merely scholarly or historical ones, legitimate as these goals are in an academic context. He is also writing years later than 1970s nationalists, and so has greater historical perspective. These considerations allow him to recognize the dramatic shift that Canadian writing underwent in the 1960s, in both quantity and quality.

It is also refreshing to read a nationalist critic who is too critical rather than not critical enough, even if Henighan sometimes goes too far in the other direction. He consciously avoids "the boosterism inflating the literary culture of the 1970s," as he aptly puts it, and an important aspect of his work is that it separates a concern with literature's ability to capture Canadian life, including urban life, from the apologetic and protective approach to Canadian writing that historically went with that concern.

A third virtue of Henighan's is that he avoids the temptation to invent literary traditions. Some critics, for example, have argued that there is a chain of literary influence that begins in nineteenth century sketches of Canadian life, extends to the stories of Duncan Campbell Scott at the turn of the twentieth century, passes through the satires of Stephen Leacock, and reaches all the way up to contemporary story-writers such as Alice Munro. John Metcalf, in *What is a Canadian Literature?* examined the evidence for this purported tradition and found it lacking. Henighan cites Metcalf's analysis and deems it "irrefutable," adding the thoughtful observation that critics who "discovered" such traditions were mistakenly trying to "forge for Canada a literary tradition as chronologically coherent as those of Great Britain and the United States."

Metcalf commissioned *When Words Deny the World*, so it may be unsurprising that Henighan has kind words for his editor. But it is misleading to think that Henighan and Metcalf share a critical approach. As Henighan notes in the acknowledgements to *When Words Deny the World*, Metcalf's "commitment to literary debate extends to the encouragement of writers with whom he may not agree."

Henighan's departure from Metcalf's view is evident in a thought-provoking chapter of *When Words Deny the World* that discusses how Canadian writers have innovated in the genre of the linked short story collection. Henighan offers a judicious examination of collections by Steven Heighton, Michael Winter, Elyse Gasco, and other writers all born within five years of 1960. Henighan criticizes and praises the work of his literary peers with a level of candor that is rare among Canadian writers. His argument provokes the thought that Alice Munro's pioneering example may have contributed to the linked story cycle becoming popular among a later generation of Canadian writers, which is a more plausible account of domestic literary influence than 1970s nationalists offered.

Finally, there *are* books with Canadian settings that do seem to be missing. At one point in *When Words Deny World*, Henighan wonders about the prospects of a certain kind of urban novel. "The new Canada is being forged in our multi-racial, multi-ethnic, multi-linguistic cities. But where are these big, synthesizing cities' big, synthesizing fictions?" Henighan acknowledges the existence of urban novels set in specific urban milieus, such as that of upper-class WASPs (*The Robber Bride*), anglophone Montrealers (*Barney's Version*), or South Asian immigrants from Africa (*No New Land*). But where are the novels that take the measure of Toronto or Montreal as a whole, as Dickens took the measure of London? Henighan accurately points out the challenges that stand in the way of the great Canadian urban novelist. "Dickens would require fluency in sixty languages to understand all the conversations he might hear in downtown Montreal or Toronto."

This is in effect a third version of Henighan's thesis about Canada's missing literature. It is not that we lack novels with Canadian settings or modern urban settings. It is rather that we are missing a particular *kind* of urban novel: the big, panoramic, synthesizing, Dickensian kind. Henighan is surely on to something in suggesting that there is a cultural and linguistic diversity to urban life in Canada that has yet to be adequately rendered on the page. It is a signature feature of Henighan's criticism that it can draw this missing literature to our attention and make us feel the force of its absence.

In offering his own distinct version of cultural nationalism, Henighan shows sensitivity to criticisms that have long been pressed by Metcalf and other opponents of 1970s nationalism. This illustrates a point that may sound obvious when stated plainly, but which has not been so obvious during decades of literary debate. An approach such as cultural nationalism is not something that we have to entirely accept or reject. It can be stripped for parts, rebuilt. In bringing together nationalist and anti-nationalist elements, Henighan takes a liberating step. It is not just that he offers a more careful and plausible version of cultural nationalism, important as that is. His precedent raises the possibility that we might go even further than Henighan himself does, and devise a variant of literary nationalism that is even more stripped down than his.

What might such a minimalist nationalism look like? It would retain a concern with the fate of Canadian literature between the 1960s and now. But it would separate this concern from the doom-mongering that Henighan combines it with. Once we let go of his suspicious view of fiction written during this time, we can return to the post-1970s period Henighan examines, and note reasons to be much more positive about it.

The first reason concerns novels that are set outside Canada. Just because a Canadian author chooses a foreign setting, it does not follow that their work says little or nothing about Canadian identity. Even a book set in the United States, the country about which nationalists have historically been most concerned, can reflect Canadian experience. To see this, consider just one of the books that Henighan views as insufficiently Canadian because of its US setting, *The Handmaid's Tale*. This is a short-sighted view of Atwood's novel, which offers a sustained commentary on Canada.

Thanks to the novel's adaptation into a popular TV show, its dystopian universe is now familiar. The United States has been taken over by a dictatorship called the Republic of Gilead, which imposes theocratic law in response to a fertility crisis. The regime's regressive measures include forcing fertile women to serve as handmaids: sexual servants who are assigned to households of the ruling class in order to conceive a child. Handmaids wear ankle-length skirts and bonnets; the visual allusion to the Puritan period became iconic after the TV adaptation, which was followed by the appearance of women dressed as handmaids at demonstrations for abortion rights, first in Texas, then in countries such as Ireland and Argentina.

An aspect of the novel that has attracted less attention is its depiction of Canada as a refuge from the United States. An underground resistance organization runs the "Underground Frailroad," a network of safe houses and couriers who help handmaids escape to Canada. The name obviously evokes the Underground Railroad that helped escaped slaves reach Canada in the nineteenth-century. If migration from Canada to the United States has historically been economically motivated, Atwood draws attention to one of several times in history when politically motivated migration traveled in the opposite direction, something that triumphalist American rhetoric about being "the last, best hope for mankind" has historically obscured.

In addition to being freer than the United States, Canada in the novel is also more peaceful. Not only is Gilead at constant war, but when women in Gilead are able to conceive at all, their babies often have birth defects. A clue as to why is offered in a description of one of the few women who have remained fertile. She is "a strong girl, good muscles. No Agent Orange in her family." Agent Orange of course was the chemical compound that American troops used to engage in herbicidal warfare in Vietnam, which caused American and Vietnamese children to be born with birth defects, among other devastating outcomes. The implication is that Gilead's fertility crisis, and the resulting imposition of handmaid status on fertile women, is due to a history of military adventurism on the scale of the Vietnam War.

Henighan, in his history of Canadian literature's 1960s boom, noted the relevance of the Vietnam War in explaining Canadian experience. Atwood was making a similar point in her book. Vietnam, the Underground Railroad and many other episodes in American history were also episodes in Canadian history. By setting *The Handmaid's Tale* in the United States, Atwood was on one level telling a story that drew on the legacy of Puritanism and other strands of American history. But she was also deepening the portrait of Canada found in her previous fiction, by highlighting differences between it and the United States. Indeed, by depicting a dystopian United States permeated by militarism and Biblical fundamentalism, Atwood emphasizes the two strands of American culture that arguably most distinguish it from Anglophone Canada. The novel is not *just* about Canada, of course. But rather than discarding her Canadian subject matter, Atwood was approaching Canada from a new angle.

If we can be more positive about Canadian novels with American settings than Henighan is, we can also be open to a more inclusive conception of Canadian literature, one that does not view it as always requiring Canadian authorship. Consider C. S. Giscombe, whom the critic Henry Louis Gates Jr. has described as "a major figure in contemporary African American letters."

Giscombe's book-length poem *Giscome Road* (1998) is inspired by Giscome Portage and other places in British Columbia named after John Robert Giscome. Giscome, whose name is spelled without a "b," was born in Jamaica in 1831, and may or may not be a relative of the contemporary Giscombe. In 1851 Giscome was one of 600 black people who left San Francisco in response to an invitation from the governor of the colony of Vancouver Island, which was experiencing a gold rush. The fragmentary historical record of Giscome's time in BC suggests that he "mined the Cariboo and the Omineca country with considerable success," as a document unearthed by Giscombe puts it.

The poem is a meditation on place and its relationship to genealogy and identity, racial and otherwise. Giscombe the narrator repeatedly tries to establish what his relation is to Giscome and to the Canadian landscape, only to fail at both. In a sense the poem is about the desire to possess such understanding, only to have to go on without it. A section of the poem addressed "to M. Atwood" quotes from *Surfacing*, in which a female protagonist also journeys through the Canadian bush in a failed attempt to find an ancestor (her father). "I am a place," Atwood's character says at the end of the novel, when she appears to be losing her sanity, a remark that

Giscombe's narrator quotes before adding, "I'm wilderness... I was/ Africa and America on the same bicycle." It is a self-description suggesting that Giscombe, like the namesake he is searching for, is essentially out of place in the Canadian bush.

Giscombe returns to Canadian subjects in *Into and Out of Dislocation* (2000), a work of literary non-fiction in which he again tries without success to pin down his relationship to Giscome. The book describes at length Giscombe's preoccupation with Canada, to which he repeatedly travels, but which sometimes makes him feel more African-American, at other times simply American, than anything else. Atwood appears again when Giscombe describes approaching the Canadian border in 1990, shortly after he has read *The Handmaid's Tale*. "Ms. Atwood's book isn't really about black folks, so we're just mentioned once or twice," Giscombe writes, drawing attention to a controversial aspect of the novel. Because Atwood has Gilead subject black Americans to a racist relocation scheme, one that collectively moves them to Detroit, they are also removed from the story, which some critics have argued is a form of literary marginalization.

Giscombe suggests dissatisfaction with Atwood's novel for a second reason. "It was a teachable, as we say, literary book: unambitious, full of the right gestures, and oddly smug in its holier than thou Canadianness; the last time I was in Montreal the huge graffiti on Rue. St.-Denis reminded BANQUE DE MONTREAL $=APARTHEID/CANADA COMPLICE." For an instant, Giscombe the American sounds defensive in his response to Atwood's portrait of the United States. But his next sentence shows a receptiveness to Atwood's outsider criticism. "[The novel] had an almost nauseating resonance to real life," Giscombe writes, "since that summer was also the summer of the flag-burning amendment, the summer of the Hon. Jesse Helms's continuing attack on the National Endowment for the Arts," and other measures that for him evoke Gilead's intolerance.

It turns out that Atwood's depiction of Americans seeking to escape to Canada holds personal poignancy for Giscombe. He and his wife, "had been talking, I'll confess, for months before I read it—pillow talk, talk over nightcaps—about driving casually into Canada and just never coming back, as the handmaid and her husband and *their* baby daughter had tried, unsuccessfully, to do." Giscombe's wife is white, but the historic resonance of his own crossing into Canada is highlighted by a jacket blurb by another African-American writer, Ishmael Reed, who says that Giscombe's Canadian memoir, "reads like the modern slave narrative, only the writer, a university professor, is seeking heritage instead of freedom." Giscombe's chronicle of dislocation, which is perhaps best described as a search for both heritage and freedom, issues a fair challenge to Canadian self-righteousness even as it finds inspiration, personal and political, in Canadian history.

In his own complicated way then, Giscombe is a Canadian writer. Of course, this is not instead of, but in addition to, being an American and an African-American one. Once we widen our understanding to include writers who are Canadian not just by birth or residency but also by subject matter, it will not only complicate, but also deepen and enrich, our literature. If Atwood can hold a literary mirror up to the United States in a manner that benefits from the perspective of the outsider, surely American writers can do the same in reverse.

Widening our perspective in this way will not only give us a new appreciation of American authors such as Giscombe.

It should also cause us to revisit Henighan's charge that Canadian literature disproportionately features books set in the Maritimes or the past. This may not be an accurate description of Canadian literature written by Canadians, but it is a fair description of Canadian literature written by Americans, even if what it describes is less a rule than a tendency.

The two American literary novelists who have written the most about Canada are probably Howard Norman and William Vollmann. Norman has written three novels (his Canadian Trilogy) set mainly in Atlantic Canada while Vollmann's seven-book series about the history of North America includes three novels set in territories (tenth-century Newfoundland, seventeenth-century Ontario, and the nineteenth-century Arctic) that would eventually be Canada. It is common for American writers, like writers of any nationality when they set their work abroad, to favor exotic settings. When American writers tell Canadian stories they often employ locales dramatically unlike the urban milieus in which most Americans live. Hence *The Shipping News*, by Annie Proulx, takes place in a Newfoundland fishing village, while *Canada*, by Richard Ford, when it gets to the country of its title, recounts events in a desolate corner of Saskatchewan. Giscombe's poetry and travel writing about Northern BC have a more personal motivation, but they fit the same pattern.

The literary documentation of urban Canadian life will likely always be a task performed primarily by writers who are Canadian by upbringing or residence. So long as this is the case, some form of literary nationalism will have a role to play in Canada. Even if it is not the same nationalism that Stephen Henighan defends, his heterodox version should be remembered, as both ancestor and inspiration.

CHAPTER 9

IMMORTAL LAFERRIÈRE

In 1976 Dany Laferrière was a twenty-three-year-old journalist in Port-au-Prince, the capital of Haiti. The country was under the rule of Jean-Claude Duvalier, who had assumed power five years earlier upon the death of his father, Francois Duvalier. Jean-Claude emulated his father by ruthlessly suppressing political opposition. A desire to improve Haiti's international reputation, however, as well as pressure from the Jimmy Carter administration, caused him to slightly ease media censorship. Although newspapers could not challenge the government, some were able to avoid running pro-regime propaganda. A paper that Laferrière had helped found, *Le Petit Samedi Soir* (Small Saturday Night), had a young staff that was willing to test the limits of press freedom. Its writers included Laferrière's best friend, Gasner Raymond, who published an article criticizing the government's use of troops to break a cement-factory strike. Not long afterwards, Raymond's body was found by the side of the road leading out of Port-au-Prince. Laferrière's mother happened to know a colonel in the military, who informed her that Laferrière was at risk of being next. A month later Laferrière was on a plane to Quebec, a destination he chose because a woman he had met there while participating in a Canada World Youth program agreed to pay his airfare.

Laferrière settled in Montreal, which had a freeing effect on his imagination. He was shocked to see couples kissing in public, a practice banned under the Duvaliers. Laferrière arrived when Montreal was hosting the 1976 Olympics, and after Nadia Comaneci scored the first perfect ten in the history of gymnastics he was swept up in spontaneous street celebrations, eventually winding up in a club where Dizzy Gillespie and Nina Simone were performing.

"She had a glass of whisky in her right hand, a lipstick smeared cigarette between her long, sophisticated fingers," Laferrière would write of Simone's performance and the sense of possibility that overcame him while watching her. "She sang looking out of the window, as though she could see a world which we were forbidden to enter. I don't know why, but my vocation as a writer was born precisely at that moment." Laferrière would later say that the best thing that ever happened to him was having to leave in a hurry for Montreal, "[a] new and unprecedented situation that allowed me to become responsible for my life."

Within ten years of his arrival Laferrière became one of Quebec's best-known novelists. After a steady stream of well-received works, in 2013 he conquered the wider Francophone literary world by being elected to the Académie Français. The Academy is an international authority on French language and grammar. Almost 400 years old, it is comprised of forty members, known as immortals, drawn from a range of occupations. Previous literary representatives include Voltaire, Montesquieu, Victor Hugo, Alexander Dumas, and Léopold Swédar Senghor (who, in addition to being a poet, was also president of Senegal). Laferrière's election was unprecedented in multiple ways. Not only is he the first immortal to hold Canadian citizenship, he is also the first who at the time of his election was neither a citizen nor a resident of France, an outcome that the academy's principal secretary cited as evidence that the venerable institution was modernizing. So far as membership criteria were concerned, she said, Laferrière's induction showed that "language is the nationality."

Laferrière's reception in English Canada has been less triumphant. Despite the fact that a Toronto publisher, Coach House Press, was an early champion of his work in translation, and although he has never stopped being a prolific author in French, his last book to be published in English, *The World is Moving Around Me: A Memoir of the Haitian Earthquake*, came out a decade ago. Laferrière's failure to achieve the same success in English Canada may be partly because his early work suffered from poor translation. That Laferrière does not give interviews in English may also dampen Anglophone media interest in his work. He perhaps further suffers from neglect because he eschews a role that the Anglosphere often expects immigrant writers and writers of color to fulfil, that of being a spokesperson for a race or nationality. (As Laferrière has put it, "I don't just come from Haiti or Quebec; I also come from the books in my library.")

Whatever the exact cause, Laferrière's neglect in English Canada is unfortunate. He is a singular voice, one whose work recounts Quebec's experience of its own version of cultural nationalism in the 1960s and 1970s, similar (but of course not identical) to that which gripped English Canada during the same period. Laferrière was uniquely positioned to chronicle Quebec's version of cultural nationalism and sympathetically bring out its ironies and contradictions. He was well suited to this task because of his gift for dramatizing the way in which nationalism and other forces of the public sphere deeply penetrate the private and intimate realm, as they pertains to sex and, especially, race. An enduring legacy of Laferrière's work has been to make vivid how intertwined the political and the personal are, not just in Quebec, but everywhere.

Laferrière's first book is a work of literary fiction. Beyond that general description, however, it defies easy categorization. The artistic approach it recalls the most may not be any tradition of writing, but the punk rock that was re-energizing music in the decade leading up to the novel's publication (in French) in 1985. Although the narrative only mentions punk in passing, Laferrière's style bears affinities to it. In particular, it share's punk's gleeful presentation of inflammatory material. This begins with the novel's title: *How to Make Love to A Negro Without Getting Tired*, which foreshadows the in-your-face racial satire that is to come.

How to Make Love's punk association is reinforced by its depiction of urban grit (Stephen Henighan, one hopes, would approve). The protagonist lives in a cheap apartment on rue St-Denis in The Plateau, Montreal's bohemian district, during the 1980s, before the neighborhood gentrified. The walls are too thin to keep out noise from the street and the summer heat is suffocating. Visible from the window is the Cross of Mont Royal, one of many references to Montreal landmarks. The protagonist describes himself and his roommate as "two blacks in a filthy apartment... philosophizing their heads off about beauty in the wee hours."

The two roommates spend much of their time pursuing white women, who are all referred to by nicknames such as Miz Literature or Miz Snob. While the men live in squalor, the women who go to bed with them come from tony Westmount homes and pursue graduate degrees at McGill. As their names—the only ones they are given in the book—indicate, they are deliberate caricatures. If sexual desire brings them in contact with the two men, every aspect of their identity—white, female, affluent, native-born—simultaneously places them at a distance from the pair as well.

Like a good punk song, Laferrière's raw and sometimes raunchy narrative wins the reader over through sheer guts and energy. He is absolutely fearless in his willingness to write explicitly about sex, something many literary writes shy away from (one chapter is memorable titled "And Now Miz Literature is Giving Me Some Kind of Blow Job"). But as was also sometimes true of punk, it is not always clear at first glance whether a provocative line or image is being offered ironically. The lusty enthusiasm of the well-heeled women, for example, ("you could hold a gun to her head and she wouldn't do the tenth of what she does here for a white guy") prompts the protagonist at one point to reflect on the dynamics of sex between a white woman and a black man:

> In the scale of Western values, white woman is inferior to white man, but superior to black man. That's why she can't get off except with a Negro. It's obvious why: she can go as far as she wants with him. The only true sexual relation is among unequals. White women must give white men pleasure, as black men must for white women. Hence the myth of the Black stud. Great in bed, yes. But not with his own woman.

Taken at face value, the racial and sexual hierarchy this passage describes is retrograde and off-putting. Something similar seems true of a later scene in which the roommate entices two women ("both of them were dogs") into the apartment to drink beer, which prompts the protagonist to reflect, "I was laying in wait for the big one behind the eleventh beer." Is the image of a man hoping (plotting?) to have sex with a woman who has had eleven beers satirizing something? If so what, or whom, exactly?

Then there is the matter of the book's title, already discomfiting in its time, surely only more so now. Recent years have seen academics be disciplined for uttering the n-word in class. The n-word in question of course is not the one in the name of Laferrière's book, but the even worse six-letter slur. In 2019 a professor at Augsberg University in Minnesota was suspended for mentioning the n-word in a discussion of a passage from James Baldwin's anti-racist classic, *The Fire Next Time*, in which the slur appears as a means of giving shape to the precise form of racism that the book challenges. The same year another professor, at the New School for Social Research in New York, was investigated after she quoted an interview in which Baldwin used the n-word (the university soon dropped the investigation). In both cases the academics were not using the slur but mentioning it, a distinction often lost in subsequent media coverage.

Academics have been sanctioned for mentioning, not the n-word itself but a term or redaction that calls it to a listener's mind. In 2020 a business professor at the University of Southern California sought to make a point about filler speech terms such as "um" and "ah" by using an example from Mandarin. "Like in China the common word is 'that'—'that, that, that, that,'" he said. "So in China it might be 'nèi ge'—'nèi ge, nèi ge, nèi ge.'" The professor employed a common Mandarin pronunciation, *NAY-guh*. After students complained, the professor was suspended from teaching the class. In 2021 a law professor at the University of Illinois Chicago administered an exam that employed the redacted term "n_____." This time student complaints resulted in the professor being placed on administrative leave and required to take an eight-week diversity-training course. An assigned reading for the training course used the same redacted term (the professor is now suing the university).

In none of these cases was there any suggestion that the speaker was wielding the n-word or a sound or symbol that might recall it with the goal of humiliating or demeaning a black person. Rather there now seems to be a widespread view that the power of the n-word, which is undeniable, stems not from its use as a rhetorical weapon, but from its appearance, or even just the suggestion of its appearance, in any context. Ironically, such an approach may only invest the slur with power. Taken to its logically conclusion, a view of the n-word as beyond the realm of calm examination would put obstacles in the way of studying, analyzing, and counteracting racism. Not only anti-racist works by James Baldwin and readings for diversity-training courses, but texts by historians and journalists who seek to draw attention to racist language in forthright ways would be subject to bowdlerization and sanction.

Laferrière's chapter titles often reference previous literary depictions of black people, including several that are bluntly racist. Chapter One, for example, "The Nigger Narcissus," alludes to a novella by Joseph Conrad. A later chapter, "The Negro is of the Vegetable Kingdom," recalls a line from a 1951 poem by the white French writer René-Guy Cadou. Contemporary norms give black writers wider latitude than white ones in using the n-word, so one might think that this explains the book's frequent mentions of racist speech. But Laferrière's complicated relationship to the category of "black writer" sees him reject the view that his blackness places him a different class than writers of other races. Of course authors are not the final word on how they should be read. Yet Laferrière's rationale for rendering racist words and ideas as they are actually expressed, as a first step toward draining them of their power, has independent appeal. His work takes it for granted that we can encounter racist terms in more than one way, not merely as weapons, but also as specimens.

In this way, Laferrière's stance is similar to that described in a 2021 law review article, "The New Taboo: Quoting Epithets in the Classroom and Beyond." The authors, Randall Kennedy and Eugene Volkh, both distinguished law professors, document a wide range of cases in which instructors have been sanctioned or subject to controversy for mentioning racist speech or writing. "To us, enunciating slurs for pedagogical purposes is not simply defensible. We think that, used properly, such teaching helps convey and reinforce important academic and professional norms of accuracy and precision in use of sources." Like the two legal academics, Laferrière is an enemy of euphemism because he wants to depict racism plainly and accurately.

This is the case even though Laferrière, as a French-language author, is faced with a slightly different set of choices. *How to Make Love* most often uses the term *nègre*, which can, but need not always be, translated as "nigger." According to Laferrière's translator, David Homel, the word "black" is "too free of stereotype and too politically cool" to capture the prejudicial image of black men as sexually voracious that Laferrière's title evokes. "I finally decided on 'negro,'" Homel writes in the novel's introduction, "alternating when the occasion called for it. 'Negro' is outdated, it smells of pre-Black Power liberalism, and because of those echoes it is particularly well suited to Laferrière's satirical intent." Of course "negro," although not as bad as the n-word, has ample offensive potential of its own.

If the novel's English text is engaging, yet also puzzling and sometimes unsettling, this may in part be due to differences between it and the French edition, differences that have changed over time. When the book was first published in English, by Coach House, the title was shortened to *How to Make Love to a Negro*. This rendering was criticized by Lee Skallerup Bessette, a critic who considered it too serious to capture the ribaldry in Laferrière's original: "we no longer expect humor, and in fact we no longer know what to expect."

Bessette's remark about the English title appears in a 2005 article noting a series of omissions in the English translation. She recounts how Laferrière, upon meeting his future translator, Homel, joked, "Don't worry about the translation. The book's already in English. Just the words are in French." Homel later wrote an article that cited Laferrière's offhand remark, as well as the book's allusions to Anglophone writers and musicians, as evidence that the novel continues an Anglo-American tradition of writing:

> There is a manic, immigrant energy that is perfectly suited to the English language (some would say that the energy is the English language). Since it turned out that Laferrière was right—that the book was indeed already in English—I had the rare and delicious opportunity to do what all translators secretly want to do: outwrite the work, outdo it, *be better than the original*, the attempt at which is the duty of all translators.

Of course, all translators make creative decisions. But Bessette persuasively argues that Homel's view of the novel as essentially English caused him to translate many passages that refer to Quebec or French writers in a way that distorts or obscures their meaning. One such example (not mentioned by Bessette) may be the title of the final chapter. In French it is "On ne naît pas Negre, on le deviant." This recalls a famous sentence from Simone de Beauvoir's feminist masterpiece, *The Second Sex*: "On ne naît pas femme: on le deviant." In English the line, possibly the most widely quoted one de Beauvoir ever wrote, has become well-known in the form in which it was first translated: "One is not born, but rather becomes, a woman." De Beauvoir was drawing attention to the fact that gender roles are a matter of culture rather than nature. But Homel's translation of the title, "You're Not Born Black, You Get That Way," at least for this reader, made the allusion to de Beauvoir undetectable.

That allusion is important for making sense of the novel. As historian Sean Mills puts it, "just as the book appears to be articulating crass chauvinism, its very last section, entitled 'You're Not Born Black, You Get That Way,' evokes Simone de Beauvoir and reveals the central meaning of the work." The narrator is grappling with racial and sexual stereotypes that black people living in a majority white society have long had to contend with. (Laferrière once said that it was only after he moved to Montreal that he discovered that he was black. "A black person," he wryly noted, "only exists in the presence of a white person. Before, in Port-au-Prince, I was only a human being.") *How to Make Love* makes these stereotypes ruthlessly explicit in order to deflate them. As the narrator remarks, "I'd like to be one hundred percent sure whether the myth of the animalistic, primitive, barbarous black who thinks only of fucking is true of not. Evidence. Show me evidence... no one can." Similarly, an attribute of the narrator that defies pernicious stereotype (and which is, I concede, not at all punk) is how supremely well-read and cultured he is, conversant with a dazzling range of literary and musical works from France, the United States, Quebec, Japan, and elsewhere.

In 2010, Douglas & MacIntyre republished Homel's translation, this time with the full title. Yet as if in exchange for this restoration, something else was now missing. The French text has an epigraph: "'*Le nègre est un Meuble.*' *Code Noir, Art. 1, 1685.*" The Black Code was a decree by the French King Louis XIV regulating slavery in the French Empire. It was meant to ensure that French sugar plantations in the New World had an ample supply of slave labor. The reasons for the code's inclusion at the start of Laferrière's narrative are subtle yet clear. Not only is Quebec a former French colony, but *How to Make Love* is frequently concerned with racial scripts and expectations: codes that, although they are social rather than legal, have their own restrictive power. The epigraph's mention of article one of the Black Code reminds the reader of how long racial codes have been around and the circumstances in which they originated. Yet the epigraph, and the historical context it provides, does not appear in the 2010 edition, which is the one most North American readers now have access to.

Laferrière's concern with social scripts would partially explain why the women in *How to Make Love* are types rather than characters. Such depictions are meant to draw attention to how sexual stereotypes, like racial ones, limit our perception of the human beings to whom they attach. This explanation is, admittedly, not entirely satisfying. As many critics have noted, the female characters are little more than symbols, an aspect of the book that, even if it is deliberate, is still a weakness. But this flaw, real as it is, is not as bad as Laferrière unconsciously endorsing "crass chauvinism." It is rather his weak and ineffective way of challenging such chauvinism. (It also seems significant that as soon as the narrator allows himself to imagine sleeping with a woman after she's had eleven beers, his world literally comes crashing down on him, in the form of his apartment ceiling collapsing. The outcome suggests that his wolfish intentions were wrong enough for him to deserve being disabused of them in dramatic fashion.)

How to Make Love was a sensation in Quebec. To be sure, not everyone enjoyed the book. Feminist critics and established Quebec-Haitian writers found much to criticize (Laferrière's irreverence toward questions of race, as well as his plain prose style, both departed wildly from Haitian literary tradition). But the novel was a bestseller that came to be regarded as a turning point in Quebec literature as the first breakout work by a black author. In addition to the greater clarity of the original French edition, and the fact that controversy over the book's title helped increase sales, this was also due to the way that Laferrière rewrote narratives of Quebec nationalism.

The year Laferrière arrived in Quebec, 1976, was the year the Parti Quebecois came to power. Immigrant communities often have positive feelings toward the parties in office when they immigrate and many Haitians who arrived in the late 1970s expressed sympathy for the PQ. There was also a longstanding view in Quebec of Haitians as fellow Francophones. In general, this was not true, as most Haitians spoke Creole. But it meant that Quebec nationalists saw their movement as having a place for Haitians, whom they tended to characterize as "good immigrants" who could easily assimilate. Laferrière, as a child of the Haitian elite (his father had briefly been mayor of Port-au-Prince), had been educated in French, which allowed him to take a return interest in nationalist debates. And in the 1970s a well-established trope of those debates was that there was a special connection between Francophone Quebecers and black people.

The Quiet Revolution was famously driven by a sense that Quebecers were not "masters in our own house." In the 1960s Francophones were in the majority but controlled only 20 percent of the Quebec economy and had higher rates of unemployment than their Anglo counterparts. Nationalist intellectuals and artists frequently made sense of this situation by comparing it to that of black subjects of colonialism. As Quebec feminist Marjolaine Péloquin has written, during the 1960s, "the French language was dirty, was the color of the soot that covered our village. The white language, the langue of the *boss*, was English." A famous poem by Michele Lalonde, "Speak White," immortalized a familiar insult that also associated French with blackness. Perhaps the most well-known expression of the idea that Francophone Quebecers share a political status with black people was in the title of Pierre Vallières' nationalist manifesto *Nègres blancs d'Amérique* (1968), a bestseller known to English-speaking readers by its translated title, *White Niggers of America*.

Yet even as nationalist intellectuals associated Frenchness with blackness, Quebec society still exhibited racism toward actual black people. Examples that occurred after Laferrière arrived include a 1983 scandal in the Montreal taxi industry. After white passengers repeatedly asked not to have black drivers, a local taxi company responded by firing twenty Haitian cabbies, and Haitian drivers in general were effectively barred from servicing Dorval airport. (In a book published the same year as *How to Make Love*, Bharati Mukherjee argued that English Canada was little better. "In the years I spent in Canada—1966 to 1980—I discovered that the county is hostile to its citizens who had been born in hot, moist continents like Asia.") Mills, the historian, plausibly argues that by associating themselves with blackness, nationalist intellectuals were not so much transcending ethnocentrism as they were forgetting the history of racism in their province toward black, indigenous, and other non-white communities. Like their English-Canadian counterparts during the same period, Quebec nationalists of the 1960s and 1970s had their own narrow and simplistic conception of belonging.

How to Make Love often references people or places of significance to Quebec nationalists. The protagonist's apartment, for example, is near Carré Saint-Louis (Saint-Louis Square), a park that has long been associated with the sovereignty movement because it was the symbolic heart of the bohemian neighborhood in which many nationalist artists and intellectuals lived and protested during the Quiet Revolution. The protagonist is also writing a novel, which he imagines being reviewed in Montreal's major French newspaper: "Pierre Vallières took five columns in *La Press* to say: 'Finally, the true *Black Niggers of America*!'" That Laferrière's novel would be of interest to nationalist intellectuals was further reflected in the fact that the book's editor, Jacques Lanctôt, was a former member of the Front de liberation du Québec who had served two years in prison for his role in the kidnapping of British Trade Commissioner James Cross.

These aspects of the book have a connection to its sexual material. During the Quiet Revolution, the idea that "Quebecers are the irrefutable proof that one can have white skin and a Negro soul," as one nationalist (and white) writer put it, was sometimes said to be confirmed by the popularity of interracial relationships between Quebecers and Haitians. This view combined truth with wishful thinking: As historians have noted, relationships between Quebecois women and Haitian men were far more common than the reverse. Nevertheless, the fact that many Quebecers perceived interracial sex as having a salient political meaning created a local racial code that Laferrière's could transform into pungent literary material.

All of the women Laferrière's black characters sleep with are Anglophones. Their associations with McGill and other bastions of English Montreal present them in a manner that nationalist readers would have appreciated. The fact that Francophone women were not similarly depicted allowed Laferrière to satirize the interracial sex myth without offending Francophone sensitivities. This is because his depictions of interracial sex reinforced a view of Anglos as colonialists. In depicting Miz Literature and the rest through the eyes of a black protagonist, the novel adopted a point of view that resonated with Francophones and their sense of themselves as cultural underdogs. Although Laferrière may have been an outsider in the sense of being an immigrant, he was an insider in that he had familiarized himself with nationalist thinking after arriving in Quebec. His book also appeared after sovereigntists had experienced major disappointments, including the loss of the YES side in the 1980 referendum. That Laferrière gave voice to nationalism through irreverence and satire was likely welcomed by readers who had grown weary of militant struggle.

How to Make Love turned Laferrière into a celebrity. Soon after the book appeared Télévision Quatre-Saisons hired him to be its weatherman (his practice of using his airtime to offer barbed commentary on prominent Quebecers, as well as his decision to give one report in the nude, may explain why his meteorological career did not last). In 1989, a film adaptation of *How to Make Love* set a record in France by being shown in 120 theaters, more than any other previous film from Quebec. But when the film was shown in the United States, the controversy that had dogged the book was re-ignited. Many newspapers refused to print the entire title, often referring to it as "How *To Make Love . . . Without Getting Tired.*" (*The New York Times* used the full title in its review, but under a headline that called the film "*How to Make Love...*"). By 1990 Laferrière's increasing fame had become so distracting that he and his family moved to Miami, where he could write in peace, and where he would live for over a decade before returning to Montreal.

By the end of the 1990s Laferrière had written eight more books, none matching the success of *How to Make Love.* "I could go ahead and write the novel of the century, and people would still talk about the first book," he wrote ruefully in *Why Must a Black Writer Write About Sex?* (1994), a work of "autofiction" in which a writer named Dany Laferrière is the protagonist. In addition to recounting the controversy over the movie title, it describes Laferrière attending the film's premiere in New York, where an unidentified woman approaches him and asks, "Aren't you ashamed of using a title like that?" When he says no, she throws a glass of wine in his face.

Why Must a Black Writer often seems to be addressed to critics who took an equally negative view of Laferrière's first book. It depicts a young black woman approaching him in a park, for example, where she demands that he write about her because "you give too much press to white women." The long discussions with her that ensue seem to be Laferrière's way of addressing the criticism, made by more than one reviewer, that despite its concern to tear up all racial and sexual scripts, *How to Make Love* focused on interracial relationships between white women and black men to the exclusion of any others, such as those involving black women or same-sex relationships. In other places Laferrière seems to suggest that his first book was justified by the rewards it brought him. "I got what I wanted: to be famous and have all the girls I want," he writes, a thought that, although it may be offered ironically, echoes comments Laferrière has made in interviews. In places the narrator sounds like Sex Pistols manager Malcolm McLaren who, when asked what punk amounted to, used to cynically answer, "cash from chaos."

At the end of *Why Must a Black Writer* Laferrière declares, "I'm not a black writer anymore." This is one of many places in Laferrière's fiction that draw attention to how he wishes to be read. This tendency reaches its peak in *I am a Japanese Writer* (2010), which again has a protagonist reminiscent of Laferrière himself. After the protagonist tells his publisher he is writing a book called *I am a Japanese Writer,* they sign a contract on the spot, and the book becomes a critical sensation before it is even written, one of many touches that satirize the notion that a writer's work is defined by their identity. As the writer-protagonist later remarks, "When I became a writer and people asked me, 'Are you a Haitian writer, a Caribbean writer or a French-language writer?' I answered without hesitation: I take on my reader's nationality. Which means that when a Japanese person reads me, I immediately become a Japanese writer."

These passages again recall remarks Laferrière has made in interviews, stating that he prefers not to be identified as an "immigrant writer," "ethnic writer," or "black writer." "I want to be taken as a writer, and the only acceptable adjectives in this case are a 'good' writer ... or a 'bad" writer." Part of his rationale for doing so, he has said, is to escape "that paternalistic attitude that [critics] use when they're dealing with exotic writers." That attitude recalls Amit Chaudhuri's ironic observation that European novelists make artistic innovations while Indian novelists, and by extension immigrant ones, write about where they're from. Laferrière has sometimes called himself an American writer, but his usage of "America" refers not to the United States but the Americas as a whole, deliberately including Miami, Montreal, and Port-au-Prince. Laferrière may be comfortable with that label in part because there are no stereotypes about writers who are "American" in his cosmopolitan sense of the term.

It is hard not to sympathize with Laferrière's desire to be judged first and foremost as a writer. But while his interviews expressing this thought are often eloquent and insightful, his expression of the same idea in his fiction often has a didactic feel. Immediately before offering his remark about becoming a Japanese writer, for example, Laferrière draws attention to Basho and other Japanese writers who have influenced his work. He is surely right to suggest that classifications such as "Haitian writer" or "immigrant writer," like "Canadian writer," can too easily obscure cross-cultural influences of this kind. But it seems a problem that the only interesting thing about *I am a Japanese Writer* is its satirical take on the tendency to devote excessive attention to an author's identity. The story about a writer who comes up with the idea to write a novel called *I am a Japanese Writer* that he then struggles to complete is clever and self-referential, but not emotionally engaging. *Why Must a Black Writer,* similarly, often reads like an essay or a work of journalism. In more than one of Laferrière's books that followed *How to Make Love,* having something to say came at the expense of having something to feel.

In *Why Must a Black Writer Write About Sex?* Laferrière's narrator seemed worried about being the literary equivalent of a one-hit wonder who never matches the success of his first record. By the time of Laferrière's induction into the Académie Français, few observers were likely to have shared that concern. In 2009 Laferrière won France's prestigious Medicis Prize for a novel that would be published as *The Return* (2011) in English Canada, where it was longlisted for the Giller Prize. The novel, if that is the right word for a narrative that switches back and forth between prose and poetry, describes Laferrière's return to Haiti following the death of his father in New York, with the goal of reaching the village where his father was born. The prize turned the French version of *The Return* into a bestseller in France and Quebec and had a major impact on Laferrière's career. But the English version (which was also translated by Homel) again seems undone by Laferrière's didacticism, with the verse passages often reading like prose with line breaks ("In the international media / Haiti always appears deforested. / Yet I see trees everywhere").

A different work from Laferrière's later career, also set in Haiti, is more successful. The text in question has an even more unusual publishing history than Laferrière's first book. In 1997, Laferrière published *La Chair du Maître* (the Flesh of the Master), a collection of short stories. In 2005 one of the stories was adapted into the engaging French-language film *Vers le Sud,* which won some awards and was a hit on the art-house circuit. Shortly after the film came out, Laferrière's Parisian publisher released a new version of the collection, which drops several stories, adds new ones and revises others, under the same title as the film. Whereas *La Chair du Maitre* was never translated into English, the heavily revised edition appeared as *Heading South* (2009).

This editorial history caused one critic to ask whether *Heading South* "[should] be seen as a movie novelization? If so, it is by far and away the best cinematic tie-in ever penned." *Heading South* is certainly a good book. But novelizations are a familiar means of wringing more money out of material originally presented in another medium. *Heading South* is more a reflection of Laferrière's rule-breaking sensibility, which often sees him disregard established literary conventions, including that of taking a text's published form as its final one. *Heading South* is one of several works of both fiction and non-fiction that Laferrière has extensively revised after their initial appearance. (A similar indifference to established practice may inform *Heading South*'s jacket copy, which characterizes the book as the basis of the film rather than vice versa. The jacket also slyly presents it as a novel, when it is probably more accurately described as a collection of linked stories.)

Laferrière's changes to the text gave *Heading South* a unified concern with sexual tourism. Much of the sexual activity in question again involves white female characters with black male counterparts. But *Heading South* has a wider frame of reference than *How to Make Love to a Negro Without Getting Tired*. There is a sinister American consul, who uses his power to issue visas to gain sexual access to teenage Haitian girls, while other relationships feature two black characters or two white ones, and not all of the attraction is heterosexual. The text is disciplined and not at all didactic (and is translated by Wayne Grady rather than David Homel). Laferrière, rather than comment once again on how he should be read, offers a vivid depiction of Haiti during the 1970s, when North American and European tourists flocked to the country as a sexual playground.

Especially powerful is the story "Heading South," which was the primary basis of the film. Three of its four narrators are white women who have come to Haiti to hook up with beach boys: fit young men who lavish them with attention, sexual and otherwise, in exchange for "gifts," and other rewards. Two of the women are obsessed with Legba, an especially fine beach boy who is named after a god of Haitian Vodou. A fourth narrator, the Haitian barman at the resort where the women are staying, initially appears to be an enforcer of propriety by discouraging the women from approaching Legba. It turns out that he has his own crush on Legba and is their sexual rival. The narrators all address an investigator who is looking into Legba's death. Laferrière is again a Japanese writer insofar as the story has a Rashomon structure: Each narrator offers a different account of how Legba died, more than one of which revolves around the jealously of this or that tourist suitor.

One of the tourists is encouraged by her otherwise sexually dull husband to indulge her lust for Legba so that he can watch. It occurs when they are on a secluded beach, where Legba is lying beside them with his eyes closed: "My husband took my hand and guided it toward Legba's torso. When he let go, my hand fell on his chest and I kept it there. Legba briefly opened his eyes then shut them again…. It was as though he was making me a gift of his body." The sexually explicit scene that follows ends with the narrator breaking down in tears of gratitude after Legba gives her, at the age of fifty-five, her first orgasm.

Legba's precise age depends on which narrator one trusts. According to the American woman who mounts him on the beach, "he didn't look like he was more than fifteen." "Heading South" draws attention to Haiti's occupation by the United States from 1915 to 1934, and the woman's indifference to any question of age of consent seems to place her in a long line of colonial occupiers with a sense of entitlement to local flesh. As Mills aptly observes, "in [Laferrière's] work we see that Empire, in the end, not only played out in the macroeconomic sphere and in the realm of state policy... It also reached deep inside the self, constructing itself and working out its regimes of power in the most intimate sphere of all, sex" (my discussion of Laferrière throughout this chapter owes a debt to Mills' work).

Criticizing colonialism is of course a common theme in modern fiction. What makes Laferrière's writing distinctive is how it manages to do so while avoiding a simplistic dichotomy between colonialist white sex tourists and innocent Haitian victims. Legba is most often described as seventeen, which is above the age of consent in both Haiti and the United States. If we accept that Legba is seventeen then the encounter, which also causes him to orgasm, is at least consensual, whatever else it might be. But the fact that Legba's age is unsettled means that the coupling on the beach is more ambiguous than a straightforward crime or joyful sexual awakening: neither understanding quite rules out the other. The women who come to Haiti to have sex with beach boys also have their own complexity that distinguishes them from traditional colonizers. They are seeking to escape social scripts that categorize them as too old or too fat to be sexual, which seems a more forgivable reason to summer in Port-au-Prince than, say, deposing the Haitian president.

At one point, a female Haitian character observes the American consul as he chats up a waitress: "[He] is flirting with the little tramp. That's the problem with whites, you have to watch them all the time. They can't seem to get it into their heads that there is also a social hierarchy among blacks. Waitress, heiress, it's all the same to them. An all-inclusive racism." What she describes is indeed a form of racism. But her contempt for "tramps" and waitresses is also a type of prejudice, one that does not seem anodyne even after we recognize that she has less power than the consul. In this way, she is typical of the book's Haitian characters, who share many of the same flaws and drives and dreams as the white characters with whom they interact. A triumph of the book is the skill with which it presents recognizably human characters from vastly different social spheres.

Laferrière once told an interviewer that moving to Quebec gave him a new appreciation of Haiti's status as a republic. "It's interesting coming to a land of white people where everyone complains about being crushed by English colonists. Haiti has nothing but its independence, whereas Quebec has everything but its independence. Rich people here say they have only a morsel of bread; whereas Haitians all believe they own a bakery."

Heading South also offers a view of Quebec informed by its differences with Haiti. While *How to Make Love* saw a major social divide between Anglos and Francophones, the middle-aged Quebecois women in *Heading South* are no different from the Americans with whom they compete for beach boys' attention. In this way, Laferrière adds nuance to the 1970s sovereigntist view of

Francophones as essentially oppressed. If they are underdogs inside Canada, outside of it they are members of the global overclass.

Since 2019, Laferrière has lived in Paris in order to participate in weekly meetings of the Académie Français. In one of the ceremonies marking his induction he noted the extent to which his fiction has been shaped by the village in Haiti where he grew up and other places he has lived. "For those who have often heard me tell these stories, I would say in my defense that there are only two or three stories in life that we can tell from the gut. For me it's childhood in Petit-Goâve, adolescence in Port-au-Prince and the years of factory work and writing in Montreal." He went on to recount how migrating was what made it possible for him to write, not only about Quebec and Haiti, but anything. "For me Montreal is not an intellectual branch of Paris, but a place of incubation." There are worse legacies for a city to have than enabling a writer on the run from Duvalier to escape into immortality.

CHAPTER 10

A SPECK OF FASCISM

When Mavis Gallant was in her early twenties, she worked as a feature writer for the *Montreal Standard*. One day in the spring of 1945, the newspaper's art director called her into his office to look at some photos for an upcoming supplement. In the era before television, lavish picture sections were a staple of weeklies like the *Standard*. No prior supplement, however, prepared Gallant for what she saw. Spread across the art director's desk were the first images of concentration camps taken by British and American army photographers. They showed mounds of bodies alongside prisoners so numb and emaciated, it was impossible to distinguish the living from the dead.

"One thing you truly cannot imagine was what the first concentration camp pictures were for someone my age," Gallant told an interviewer years later. "That's something you can't imagine because you've seen them all your life." Unlike those born after the war, members of Gallant's generation had to assimilate their knowledge of the camps into their existing conception of Germany. In Gallant's case, while she was staunchly anti-fascist, "there was hardly a culture or a civilization I would have placed as high as the German." Now she was handed the pictures and given a perfectly impossible assignment: write the photo captions and an accompanying essay, on deadline and in less than 750 words.

Gallant resolved not to discuss the grisly visual details. In her mind they were not the pictures' most important aspect. They forced the viewer to ask not *what* had happened but *why*. How did the country of Bach and Goethe become the country of Bergen-Belsen? Why had German culture, religion, and art all failed to function as a restraint? Gallant dutifully handed in an essay focusing on these questions. Her editors killed it and ran a story lingering over the images of corpses instead. When Gallant asked why, one of them blew up at her. "Culture! Our readers never went to high school and you're talking about culture? All the Germans are bastards and that's that."

Gallant's experience at *The Standard* highlights the historical context that shaped her work. That context was one in which the catastrophe of fascism was central. As she told her interviewer, for members of her generation, it cried out for explanation at a level deeper than proclaiming all Germans bastards. While countless non-fiction writers have sought to diagnose the reasons for fascism's rise, less noted has been Gallant's engagement with this question and, using the less programmatic and more indirect tools of fiction, offering her own answer.

Nowhere is this truer than in "Speck's Idea." First published in *The New Yorker* in 1979 and since anthologized many times, it is Gallant's most widely published story. Funny, sad, and beautiful, it is arguably Gallant's masterpiece, the one story that most warrants re-reading in the wake of her death. Critics have often interpreted it as a cautionary tale about the commodification of art. To read the story carefully, however, is to note an abiding preoccupation with far-right extremism. Set in Paris in the 1970s, its title character seems to slowly embrace fascism. Yet there are also details in the story that seem to undermine his association with fascist ideology. A conspicuous feature of the character in question is that he is introduced in a sympathetic way—the opposite of a bastard. The result is a riddling and enigmatic text, with evidence both supporting and undermining a straightforwardly fascist interpretation of its central figure. A major interpretive challenge the story poses is to make legible the politics of its protagonist.

The best answer to that challenge is one that ultimately marks him as a fascist, but of a particular, non-ideological type. In the 1970s France was finally reckoning with the full legacy of World War II. Historians and documentarians were calling the country to admit that its encounter with fascism had not been defined by valiant resistance alone but also included many different forms of collaboration. Gallant's story is informed by this debate. This is obvious in its references to French writers and artists who enthusiastically supported fascism. But another important feature of the story is its dramatization of how a segment of the French population, which its central figure represents, could tolerate and condone fascism for reasons other than attraction to fascist ideas. These include indifference and self-interest. Gallant's protagonist ultimately illustrates how fascism drew not merely on ideological, but also on opportunistic motivations.

Gallant's focus is not just backward looking. Her story also depicts pitfalls of understanding particular to our post-fascist age, such as the distortion of historical truth. This is often accomplished by suppressing or whitewashing events from the fascist period, but Gallant also has in mind more insidious failures of understanding. They include explanations of fascism that emphasize the uniquely monstrous character of its adherents, or denunciations of the work of fascist intellectuals that are so indiscriminate and prejudicial that they take a step toward fascism in the very moment of opposing it. Gallant's story does not locate fascism's allure in the warped character of national groups that embraced it, but in routine habits of mind. Among these is credulity toward historical narratives that perpetuate false and exclusionary national identities. In this way, Gallant provokes reflection on the unfinished project of constructing maximally inclusive conceptions of belonging.

Sandor Speck runs an art gallery in Paris that specializes in the work of undistinguished and little-known artists. Early in the story, Speck's wife divorces him while shouting "Fascist! Fascist! Fascist!" The story ends shortly after Speck hurls the same insult at another character. The action of the story takes place between these symmetrically placed denunciations, and revolves around Speck's attempt to mount a show by an obscure French painter who turns out to have supported the Nazis during the war. When Speck discovers that his painter was pro-fascist, he appears comfortable with this information. This and other details suggest that Speck is not entirely opposed to fascism himself.

One incriminating detail involves a bookstore across the street from Speck's gallery that specializes in the writing of Mussolini and other far-right authors. The store's political orientation makes it a regular target of left-wing commandos who smash its windows and beat its customers with iron bars. Speck is accustomed to the sound of violent clashes on his street, "the hoarse imprecation of the Left and shriller keening of the Right." But whenever the police come around to ask him and his gallery assistant if they have seen anything, both refuse to get involved. Speck's assistant justifies staying silent on the comically ludicrous grounds that he is Swiss. In Speck's case, his justification for quietism is that "the commerce of art is without bias."

Speck is more directly associated with fascism during a scene in his gallery in which he angrily demands that his assistant remove a Turkey carpet. "Speck raised his voice to the Right Wing pitch heard during street fights: 'Get it out! Get it out of my gallery!... I won't have my gallery stuffed with filth.'" Speck's tone associates him with the fascists who patronize the bookstore. That the object of his ire is culturally foreign and his use of the term "filth," the rhetorical power of which the Nazis well understood, only reinforce the dark associations of Speck's outburst. The end result of this and other incidents involving Speck, as critic Danielle Schaub has aptly observed, is that "the reader feels that [Speck] rather agrees with fascist ideas, especially in the light of the insult proffered by his wife."

And yet other details in the story complicate Speck's fascism. Chief among these is his use of "fascist" as a term of abuse. The obscure far-right painter whose work Speck hopes to show is named Hubert Cruche, and the character whom Speck denounces is Cruche's widow. Much of the story's rich comedy and drama consists in Speck's delicate but determined campaign to obtain permission for his show from the obstinate old woman. Eventually, she outsmarts Speck and arranges for another dealer to display Cruche's work on more lucrative terms. This means the other dealer will have the glory. Speck responds by unsuccessfully pleading with the Widow not to go through with it. His plan is undone.

In a daze, Speck makes his way to a bus stop where he reflects on the scope of his failure. He hears someone calling out to him. It is the Widow Cruche, "her raincoat open and flying, waving a battered black umbrella, [bearing] down on him out of the dark." In a moving scene, the widow tells the broken and defeated Speck that he can have his show after all. Her manner now is tender, as though they will soon be not just partners but lovers. Speck agrees to go through with the show. But because the Widow has made it known she could work with another dealer, she can now negotiate more favorable arrangements from Speck. Any retrospective of her husband's work will be on her terms, even though such a retrospective was Speck's idea, as the story's title denotes. Just as his bus is pulling away Speck is overcome with frustration at having been outfoxed. He brings his face up to the window and yells: "Fascist! Fascist! Fascist!" While doing so he pauses to note how satisfying the denunciation feels: "It was amazing how it cleared the mind, tearing out weeds and tree stumps, flattening the live stuff along with the dead. 'Fascist' advanced like a regiment of tanks."

An analysis of Speck must explain how, if he is a fascist, he can use "fascist" as an insult. It should also explain something else. After Speck gets off the bus a young man presses a pamphlet into his hand, bearing a strange political message:

FRENCHMEN!
FOR THE SAKE OF EUROPE, FIGHT
THE GERMANO-AMERICANO-ISRAELO
HEGEMONY!
Germans in Germany!
Americans in America!
Jews in Israel!
For a True Europe, for One Europe,
Death to the Anti-European Hegemony!

As Speck reads the confusing message he wonders what it means: "Was it a [fascist] statement or an anti-[fascist] plea? There was no way of knowing." Fascism was an international movement, but insofar as the pamphlet expresses a coherent political thought, it would appear to be the rabidly nationalist one that France must be uncontaminated by foreign influence of any kind. The story ends with Speck turning the pamphlet over and writing catalog copy for his show, which he has resolved will go on. This suggests an association between Speck and the strange politics of the pamphlet.

The reader is ultimately left with a puzzle. Who is Sandor Speck, and what exactly does he represent?

If Speck is associated in a complex way with fascism, he has a more straightforward association with France. In order to clarify his relationship with fascism, it is helpful to first note his specifically French attributes. These attributes do much to associate Speck with France not only of the 1970s but of the 1930s and 1940s as well. The story's opening paragraph sets in motion several thematic preoccupations that each link Speck with a different aspect of French identity:

Sandor Speck's first art gallery in Paris was on the Right Bank, near the Church of St. Elisabeth, on a street too narrow for cars. When his block was wiped off the map to make way for a five-story garage, Speck crossed the Seine to the shadow of Saint-Julien-le-Pauvre, where he set up shop in a picturesque slum protected by law from demolition. When this gallery was blown up by Basque separatists, who had mistaken it for a travel agency exploiting the beauty of their coast, he collected his insurance money and moved to the Faubourg Saint-Germain.

Speck is introduced as a hapless and vulnerable figure, scrambling from one gallery to the next, at the mercy of social forces more powerful than himself. This is in keeping with many details associating Speck with smallness. They include not only his name, Sandor Speck, which evokes grains of sand and dust, but also the fact that Speck is small on a professional level. A small-time dealer in terms of gallery size, he also specializes in minor artists, a professional niche that has "earned him the admiration given the devoted miniaturist who is no threat to anyone."

The story's opening suggests that Speck is conservative. This is evident in his decision to finally locate his gallery in the Faubourg Saint-Germain. This Left Bank neighborhood has long been associated with the French aristocracy. Not only was it their traditional home before the revolution, in the early nineteenth century it became home to conservatives bent on restoring the monarchy. As historian Stephen Kale notes, "the term *le faubourg Saint-Germain*, or simply *le faubourg*, became political shorthand for organized ultra-royalist.... The public knew by instinct that the term referred not just to the concrete reality of a predominantly aristocratic neighbourhood but 'to all those who wanted to revive prerevolutionary France.'"

The suggestion of conservatism contained in Speck's choice of neighborhood is reinforced throughout the story. His gallery occupies a decaying and subdivided *hôtel particulier*, as the grand urban homes of the nobility were called. The other tenants are down-at-the-heels aristocrats whose failings Speck forgives "for the sake of being the Count of this and the Prince of that." Similarly, when Speck gazes out at the right-wing bookstore, he finds himself admiring it because it is painted royal blue, "a conservative color he found reassuring."

Speck's attraction to aristocracy has strong political overtones. Within France, the French Revolution is normally seen as a great breakthrough that not only brought France into the modern world but created the modern world itself. Speck's indifference to it and his attraction to France's old order is one of many personal traits that align his values with the French right, whose chauvinist nationalism he shares: "French education had left him with the certainty that he was a logical, fair minded person imbued with a culture from which every other Western nation was obliged to take its bearings. French was his first language; he did not really approve of any other."

Finally, in addition to smallness and conservatism, the story's opening foreshadows a thematic preoccupation with left-wing radicalism. This is suggested by the Basque separatists who destroy Speck's second gallery. At the time of the story's publication the Basque group most responsible for terrorism was Basque Homeland and Freedom, known by its Spanish acronym ETA. That the ETA was historically a Marxist-Leninist organization means that Gallant's opening can be taken to contain the first of many references to communism. Speck's gallery in the Saint-Germain shares a street with three "Marxist embassies," while his ex-wife is described as a book critic for an uncompromising political weekly. One of her articles, "A Marxist Considers Sweets," attacked sugar on ideological grounds (and suggests a less than sunny personality).

In each of his dimensions, Speck typifies France during the 1970s. The country was in decline. In the 1870s, France had been the center of a colonial empire, second in size to only Britain's. During the 1960s, France lost the Algerian war and saw all of its major colonies declare independence, so that by the 1970s, it was left with only French Guiana and scattered remote island territories, the so-called confetti of empire. As the country's political importance shrank, so did its cultural significance. Speck works in the art market, which Paris once dominated, both artistically and economically. By the 1970s the rise of New York as the new center of the art world, a process that began in the 1940s, was complete, a transformation to which Gallant's story draws attention with mentions of New York as the place where French dealers and artists now dream of making a fortune.

The political polarization of Speck's marriage thus mirrors a longstanding feature of French politics, which for decades lacked a strong liberal or centrist party. As intellectual historian Mark Lilla observes, the French Revolution left European societies deeply divided over its legacy. In each one there sprang up "a counterrevolutionary party defending Church and Crown and hoping to restore their authority; opposing them was an equally determined party wishing more radical forms of democracy to accomplish what the French Revolution had already begun. As time passed the two parties shared little apart from their hostility to liberalism." French politics during the 1970s still followed this broad pattern with the Socialist party competing for power with the Republicans and other right-wing parties representing a form of conservatism that, while it no longer sought to undo the Revolution, left little space for moderation.

Viewed against the backdrop of his Frenchness, Speck's drift to fascism represented not just the political impulses of one individual, but the larger career of French right-wing extremism. The year 1972 saw the birth of the National Front (NF), whose leader, Jean-Marie Le Pen, would become an enduring force in French politics, making countless xenophobic statements about immigrants, gays, and Muslims. France in the early 1970s also underwent a major policy change on immigration. During the post-war period, it had actively encouraged permanent immigration. Following the 1973 oil crisis, it not only discouraged immigration but, in a move that Le Pen would have appreciated, encouraged immigrants to leave as well. Although that particular policy came to naught, the shift in focus endured to the point that, as French immigration analyst Virginie Guiraudon observed in 2001, "since 1973 immigration [debate] in France has focused on stemming and deterring migration." If there are far-right groups doing battle in Speck's street, it is because their membership rolls, like that of the NF in 1970s France or Golden Dawn in Greece today, have historically swelled in periods of economic decline, a phenomenon that the economically insecure and culturally intolerant Speck typifies.

The story also intervenes in another French debate of the 1970s, this one about its wartime past. Prior to this time, discussion of the war had exaggerated French resistance and downplayed collaboration—hence the famous scandal of *The Sorrow and the Pity* (1969), which documented French collaboration, not being shown on French television for years after its production. Finally, by the end of the 1970s, a wide-ranging debate broke out among historians, some of whom sought to give an honest accounting of France's Vichy period.

When Speck discovers that Hubert Cruche was far right, he reflects on what this means, and why it may not be a barrier to his planned retrospective. Speck's ruminations do much to clarify how Speck himself should be seen:

Nowadays the Paris intelligentsia drew new lines across the past, separating coarse collaborators from fine-drawn intellectual Fascists. One could no longer lump together young hotheads whose passionate belief in Europe had led them straight to the Charlemagne division of the Waffen-S.S. and the soft middle class that had stayed behind to make money on the black market. Speck could not quite remember why *pure* Fascism had been better for civilization than the other kind, but somewhere on the safe side of the barrier there was bound to be a slot for Cruche.

Members of the Charlemagne division were French volunteers who fought for Germany. Profiteers who stayed in France after the occupation did so because of the economic opportunity it represented. Speck's reflection is in keeping with one of the story's central preoccupations, which is to draw attention to the multiple motivations on which French support for Fascism drew, both explicitly ideological and crudely opportunistic.

Gallant highlights both motivations in an important scene recounting a vision. "Though he appreciated style," Gallant writes of Speck, "he craved stability even more." Speck's yearning for stability causes him to grow concerned about the violence outside the bookstore. While walking by it one night he imagines the patrons of the shop lying beaten in the street, only to get up and storm his gallery, "determined to make Speck pay for injuries inflicted on them by total strangers." In Speck's anxious vision, he sees his "only early Chagall (quite likely authentic) ripped from its frame," by right-wing thugs who scream "Down with foreign art!" When the imaginary thugs attack Speck's assistant with a set of books they turn out to be "the complete Charles Maurras, fourteen volumes, full morocco."

The historical figures conjured in Speck's vision have unmistakable associations. Chagall has been called the quintessential Jewish artist of the twentieth century. It is no surprise that right-wing hooligans would tear out his painting. Nor is it an accident that they would use the works of Charles Maurras as a bludgeon. Maurras, in addition to being a critic and poet, was the founder of the far-right group *Action Français* and a hysterical anti-Semite. When French authorities introduced a law in 1940 depriving Jews of citizenship and sending them to internment camps, his only criticism was that the law did not go far enough.

Speck's vision of the marauding right-wing thugs depicts them as a menace, yet what disturbs him is not their political motivations but their potential to disrupt the local order. His concern is less political than prudential. This is in keeping with the attitude toward fascism that Speck displays throughout most of the story. At one point, he daydreams about inventing a wartime artist and showing the paintings of this imaginary painter alongside correspondence and ephemera of famous figures to suggest they knew him. The correspondence Speck envisions mounting for display "straddle[s] half a century, from Degas to Cocteau. The scrawl posted by Drieu la Rochelle just before his suicide would be particularly effective on black. Céline was good; all that crowd was back in vogue now."

After the Dreyfus affair, Degas broke off all friendship with Jews and refused to use any model who might be Jewish. The novelists Drieu la Rochelle and Céline were both enthusiastic collaborators. In the wake of the liberation, Drieu la Rochelle had to go into hiding before killing himself; Céline wrote pamphlets denouncing the "international Jewish conspiracy" and grew so closely identified with the Vichy government that after its fall he would join the surviving members in exile in Germany. The vogue crowd Speck has in mind is composed of French fascists of the pure kind.

Yet Speck does not imagine decorating his gallery exclusively with the spittle of Nazis. "There would be word from the Left, too," in the form of postcards from communist poets and left-wing political leaders. It is thus not because he is attracted to Nazism on ideological grounds that Speck wants to display letters by Céline and his sinister cohort; it is because they are in vogue. For the same reason Speck is happy to throw in some communist scribblings. Speck, as ever, takes a pragmatic view, eager to appeal to both forms of extremism that do battle in his street.

This aspect of Speck's character would appear to explain his ex-wife's denunciation. Right before calling him a fascist, she made it known that "Speck appraising an artist's work made her think of a real estate loan officer examining Chartres cathedral for leaks." Her insult expresses her revulsion at Speck's pragmatic view of art. This again highlights the manner in which Speck approaches not only his fictional art show, but more or less everything. At one point he decides to attend a Masonic lodge ceremony on the grounds that the Grand Architect of the Universe and his well-connected Masonic worshipers could potentially be of benefit to him. A similar thought causes him to want his assistant to join the Communist party, which could also benefit the gallery. If Speck is open to fascism, he is equally open to Masonry, Communism, or any other worldview that might be good for business. Whatever is good for business is good for Speck.

Speck's particular brand of fascism should now be clear. If at first glance it appears puzzling, it is because it grows out of more banal and familiar motives. Speck reconciles himself to fascism due to a desire to get ahead, which is a desire most of us share.

This makes it harder to view him and the dark political ideas he tolerates, and at times embodies, as entirely alien. Gallant's story offers the salutary reminder that fascism could find support in traditionally liberal democratic states such as France, the birthplace of the Rights of Man, due to its ability to satisfy the psychic needs not of historically unique monsters but of ordinary men and women.

This is worth recalling given some characterizations of fascism since Gallant's story was published. Daniel Goldhagen's 1996 book *Hitler's Willing Executioners* emphasizes annihilationist anti-Semitism as the fundamental motivation behind the Holocaust. This view attracts criticism, not because anyone believes anti-Semitism played no role in support for fascism, but because other factors were also involved. In the words of Hitler's biographer Ian Kershaw, "The road to Auschwitz was built by hate, but paved with indifference." According to Kershaw and other historians, while the Nazi leadership was ruthlessly anti-Jewish, the general population, by and large, was indifferent to the fate of the Jews.

Indifference, like pragmatism, is a trait that did not disappear with the fall of the Third Reich. In calling it to mind, we come to see supporters of fascism and its projects less as inhumane freaks and more as people similar to ourselves. Goldhagen's view downplays this disturbing affinity, which some critics have suggested is the reason why his book became a best-seller, particularly in Germany. Says Ruth Bettina Birn, former chief of Canada's war-crimes unit, "It's a vision which is palatable for North American and German readers fifty years after the fact... If it's just these evil guys, hallucinatory demonological anti-Semites, why should I be bothered?"

Gallant's story delivers the opposite message. Speck tolerates and at times embraces fascist symbols and ideas, not because he is demonic, but because he is normal. Rather than cartoonishly evil, he is appealingly vulnerable. Gallant at one point movingly describes him closing up his art gallery on a wet night, reflecting on the break-up of his marriage: "The faint, floating sadness he always felt while locking up had to do with the time. In his experience, love affairs and marriages perished between seven and eight o'clock, the hour of rain and no taxis." Speck's emotional state here and elsewhere is finely drawn. Like the best fictional characters, he is relatable. It is a sign of the power of the story that this lingers even after we realize that he is politically sinister.

It is no accident that Speck is both emotionally wounded and politically extreme. In linking these two aspects of his character, Gallant recalls something of Hannah Arendt's remark that totalitarianism "bases itself on loneliness, on the experience of not belonging to the world at all, which is one of the most radical and desperate experiences of man." Arendt had in mind a political conception of loneliness. In her view, the atomizing forces of modern life deprived us of the experience of deep belonging, which created an opening that collectivist authoritarianism could exploit. The more personal form of loneliness Gallant depicts in Speck is not quite the same. Yet it, too, makes individuals susceptible to the false lure of fascist community. Speck serves as a reminder of the way fascism takes advantage of our yearning for fellowship and other vital human needs. In rooting its appeal not merely in hate-driven ideology but also in this and other aspects of our communal nature, Gallant's story offers a historical explanation more subtle than Goldhagen's, a scholarly and intellectual version of "all Germans are bastards."

The overall portrait of Speck we are left with is the embodiment of a kind of indirect and loosely-worn fascism. Indirect, because it grows out of more ultimate motives that are not themselves inherently sinister. Loosely worn, because Speck is at times just as happy to embrace anti-fascist beliefs and symbols when doing so is to his advantage. His outburst concerning the Turkey carpet suggests that he does not always keep fascist modes of thought entirely at arm's length. After a certain point, the boundary between pragmatic and pure fascism will blur. Nevertheless, Speck most often manages to stay on the "safe side of the barrier" separating the two.

"Speck's Idea" frequently suggests affinities between sharply opposing political ideologies. This is evident in the description of the violence outside the bookstore, which involves left-wing commandos. If their right-wing opponents are "shriller," this suggests they are the worse form of extremism. The leftist street fighters' tendency to violence is nonetheless something they share with their far-right counterparts.

A similar affinity between left and right is suggested when Speck first decides to mount his show. He is motivated by newspaper articles calling for something new in the art world. These calls are "poignant and patriotic on the right, neo-nationalist and pugnacious on the left," suggesting a nationalistic overlap between the two viewpoints. Speck is especially influenced by an article in *Le Monde* under the headline "Redemption Through Art—Last Hope for the West?," which describes the contemporary cultural scene in apocalyptic terms: "Must the flowering gardens of Western European culture wilt and die along with the decadent political systems, the exhausted parliaments, the shambling elections, the tired liberal impulses?" Whether the author's message comes from the left or the right is not stated. What is clear is the hostility to liberalism associated by Lilla with both poles of French politics.

The pamphlet Speck receives is in keeping with the story's suggestion that, while right-wing illiberalism is ultimately in a class of its own, the Stalinist segment of French communism bears similarities to it. In addition to a mutual antipathy to liberalism, both are happy to appropriate nationalism. In the communist case, this is evident in the exhibition Speck's gallery is showing on the night he locks up in a melancholy mood: "Paris and Its Influence on the Tirana School, 1931–2." Before the fall of the Berlin Wall, tiny Albania was often depicted as offering a humane form of communism. A show depicting Paris's influence on painters in the Albanian capital would thus flatter France's superiority complex, but in a way that would also appeal to politically correct Parisians such as Speck's ex-wife. (The ridiculousness of a retrospective devoted to a two-year period also brings out Speck's small-mindedness with a comic flourish.) Speck receives the pamphlet because he inhabits a political universe in which the far right and far left are often indistinguishable.

Similarly, Speck's use of "fascist" as an insult is in keeping with the thematic preoccupation with seemingly opposed ideologies that blur and overlap. The widow was married to a fascist artist toward whom she still feels protective. The problem with Speck's insult is thus not that it misidentifies her—she likely is a fascist. It is rather the way Speck delivers it. His denunciation moves forward "like a regiment of tanks." The military image highlights the insult's function as an offensive act. Speck may be denouncing someone as a fascist, but in so doing he himself employs a rhetoric of assault, one that favors verbal violence over dialogue and negotiation. This serves as a reminder that anti-fascism is more than a matter of finding the right words. It is also a question of conducting oneself in the right way. Here again, the story speaks to debates about the fascist period that have occurred since the story was published.

As we have seen, a possible pitfall of the post-fascist age, illustrated by Goldhagen, is to depict fascism entirely as an ideology of inhumane monsters. But another pitfall is to think that because fascism was so obviously a moral disaster, and because it warrants violent opposition the moment it becomes armed and organized we can never be too adamant and uncompromising in our opposition to fascists and all their artistic and intellectual work. Gallant's story has bearing on recent debates over the work of fascist intellectuals that have called this simplistic idea into question.

In recent decades, we have become familiar with exposés of prominent intellectuals who lived through the fascist period. Years later, long after achieving international prominence, lost or suppressed writings emerge betraying their support for National Socialism. Martin Heidegger and Paul de Man are well-known examples. In such cases, after the thinkers in question are exposed, there are debates about how their work should be read.

One answer to this question is to view the thinker's entire corpus as fatally compromised. Such a view is taken by French philosopher Emmanuel Faye, author of a 2005 book on Heidegger's fascism. Faye concludes that Heidegger's complete works represent "a collection of texts containing principles that are racist, eugenic, and radically deleterious to the existence of human reason. Such a work cannot continue to be placed in the philosophy section of libraries; its place is rather in the historical archives of Nazism and Hitlerism." In Faye's view, no matter how abstract Heidegger's writings at times become, and no matter how far they stray from political questions, they are to be viewed without exception as Nazi documents.

There is an alternative approach. It is exemplified by the Jewish-Romanian novelist Norman Manea. Like Faye, Manea has exposed the far-right sympathies of a well-known intellectual. In Manea's case it was fellow Romanian Mircea Eliade. Affiliated for many years with the University of Chicago, Eliade was perhaps best known for his three-volume work *A History of Religious Ideas* (1978–85). After Eliade's death in 1986, Manea published a widely discussed article documenting Eliade's previously unknown support for the Iron Guard, Romania's fascist party. Manea unearthed passages from Eliade's writings of the 1930s that praised the "discipline" and "dignity" of the Guard; characterized the "liquidation of democracy" in positive terms; and lamented that "Jews have overrun" Romanian villages and cities.

Manea's exposé of Eliade was unflinching. But while his opposition to Eliade's politics was total, Manea was nonetheless careful not to suggest that all of Eliade's writings were compromised by his political views. As Manea put it in a thought-provoking passage, "To draw a connection between his scholarship and his 'fascist' period, to cast an inquisitorial eye on 'suspect' details in his many learned studies, would be to provide a perfect example of totalitarian methodology."

This is the danger Speck falls victim to in denouncing the Widow. Like Manea, Gallant alerts us to the danger of "fascist anti-fascism." In Speck's case, it occurs when he treats the widow as an enemy worthy of full-throated hate. His stance is toward a body of writings rather than a person, yet it is in its own way a form of intolerance. Such a stance needs to be transcended if our opposition to fascism is to be complete.

Looking back from the 1970s, Speck is not especially concerned with getting the details of France's past correct, let alone reckoning with its disturbing elements. He will portray Cruche as an ideological or opportunistic fascist, depending on which version turns out to be more acceptable. Speck is thus a kind of meta-pragmatist, willing to employ the distinction between pragmatic and non-pragmatic fascists in whichever way proves most useful. In this way, Speck exhibits a tendency to construct a false account of the past driven by the needs of the present.

Charles Maurras famously saw modern France as defined by decadence and lost grandeur. The enlightenment, the Revolution, and what Maurras termed "anti-France," made up of the "four confederate states" of Protestants, Jews, Freemasons, and foreigners, were all negative forces responsible for France's decline. Maurras thus invented a tradition of continuity between his vision of France and a purported lost golden age. Gallant's story suggests that the invention of tradition is not confined to fascists. It is also undertaken by other ideologues who seek to define a political community in narrow or exclusionary terms. Subtle details in the story suggest an alternative, more inclusive conception of society, one that is better able to avoid mythologizing the past.

At one point the widow Cruche informs Speck that she is a Japhethite, an offshoot of the obscure British Israelite religious movement. Named after Noah's son Japheth, her religion posits an alternative history in which Western Europeans are descended from the lost tribes of Israel. "Japheth's people settled in Scotland," the widow informs Speck. "Present-day Jews are imposters." The notion of British Israelism, which arose in the seventeenth century, is strongly contradicted by modern genetic and other evidence. Nevertheless, it attracted adherents for several hundred years and retains a few stray congregations today. Critics have suggested that the movement's appeal is based on a prejudicial view of history. It offers a segregated view of human ancestry, according to which white Europeans can claim their own line of descent, separate from that of non-white races, who are envisioned as ancestors of Noah's other sons. It thus reassures Anglo-Saxons that they have a glorious genealogical past and come from racially superior stock.

Speck's approach to political history mirrors the Widow's religion. Before he happened upon Cruche, he would have been happy to show the work of a wartime artist with a made-up biography. Here again Speck seems emblematic of a segment of the larger society in which he resides. Gallant's story mentions, for example, a minor character who authored a book about Vietnam called *When France Was at the Helm*, which is a perennial bestseller. The book's popularity suggests that it contains a pleasing message that, rather than ask troubling questions about French intervention in Indo-China, reassures its readers that French colonialism was benevolent. Somewhat similarly, a virus going around Paris is described as the Warsaw Flu, suggesting that Gallant's Parisians cannot admit that disease can originate within France (thereby exhibiting a form of prejudice historians have wryly dubbed "the foreignness of germs"). French national identity is constructed so as to filter out unpleasant details.

Importantly, the self-understanding represented by both Speck and the wider society is depicted as inaccurate. Speck is a chauvinist who views himself as monolithically French. Yet Speck's family background is not French. He rather descends from "generations of highly intellectual Central European agnostics and freethinkers." There is a moment when the reader wonders if Speck might be Jewish. When Speck exhibits a sense of Gallic imperialism, it is characterized as a moment of "second generation distress," suggesting that his chauvinism may be compensation for feeling less than purely French himself.

Speck's self-understanding as absolutely French, despite biographical details suggesting a more complicated identity, recalls the influential strand of French nationalism known as republicanism. A notion with no real equivalent in English-speaking countries, it has been described by Lilla as "the least precise and most widely invoked concept in the French political lexicon." Whereas republicanism originally referred to a belief in the Revolution and its ideals, during the nineteenth century, it became associated with the project of building the French nation, a project that has historically mixed progressive and exclusive elements. As Lilla details them, they include a commitment to secularism and a strong public school system. At the same time, republicanism also became associated with "a highly centralized, majoritarian government; a homogenous culture, achieved through national education but also through a slow war of attrition against signs of diversity (for example, the campaigns against regional French dialects). In short, republicanism was a syncretic mix of political principles, some universal and some chauvinistic."

Speck's view of himself as purely French mirrors the republican understanding of France's identity. But that Speck has a more mixed identity also reflects something about France. No country is culturally homogenous. Even in France, there have always been polyglot groups that undermine the monolithic view of the nation. This, again, is evident from the beginning of Gallant's story. Basque separatists are French (and Spanish) citizens without wanting to be, simultaneously inside and outside the imagined community of France. Something similar is true of the two churches mentioned in Gallant's opening paragraph. Saint-Julien-le-Pauvre, built in the thirteenth century, is one of the oldest churches in Paris, an enduring icon of France's Catholic heritage. But in the nineteenth century it was given to a congregation of Melkites, Byzantine-Rite Catholics from the Eastern Mediterranean, making the same church an emblem of France's mixed cultural identity. The church of St. Elisabeth also recalls France's pre-revolutionary past, having been built in the seventeenth century. Its full name, however, is the Church of St. Elisabeth of Hungary, making it simultaneously a foreign symbol. Speck, whose first name, Sandor, is also Hungarian, is similar to both churches in that his arch-French exterior masks a more complex inner reality. For Speck, as for France, a multicultural identity is submerged beneath a republican facade.

There is a moment in "Speck's Idea" when a more inclusive understanding of national and personal identity briefly comes into view. It occurs when Cruche's widow informs Speck that she is from Saskatchewan. In the context of the story, her Canadian nationality allows her to represent the Anglo-Saxon cultural hegemony that Speck resents, while also being anti-American, a quality she shares with her fascist husband. Speck is so ignorant of Canada that he has to look up Saskatchewan in an atlas. For anyone less ignorant, however, it will not escape notice that during the 1970s, the same decade in which the story takes places (and long after the widow left), Canada became the first society to embrace official multiculturalism—the opposite approach to community advanced by republicanism and nationalism, let alone Japhetism and fascism.

Canadians, of course, have long debated what precise form multiculturalism should take, and it would be simplistic to think that with multiculturalism all problems of historical understanding and belonging will disappear. Nevertheless, Gallant's story serves as an indirect reminder of multiculturalism's appeal. It replaces false myths of national homogeneity with an open acceptance of difference. A multicultural conception of belonging suggests an avenue of escape from the false traditions of cultural purity that hold Speck so firmly in their grip.

Events in France since the publication of "Speck's Idea" suggest that its themes remain all too relevant. The National Front has continued to peddle imaginary traditions of the kind Gallant's story debunks. In 1991 Jean Marie Le Pen said that the NF represented "the French people born with the baptism of Clovis in 496, who have carried this inextinguishable flame, which is the soul of a people, for almost one thousand five hundred years." In reality, were Clovis to return today, he would find French culture and politics deeply alien, not least because he did not speak French.

The majority of French people reject the vision of France Le Pen so long represented before finally resigning his party's leadership in 2011. After the National Front scored a breakthrough in the 2002 election, more than 900,000 people marched against the party in the then-largest street demonstrations in France since the Liberation. But if Le Pen's extreme view never captured French reality, neither can it be said that France's self-understanding is as open to immigration and pluralism as it could be. While there have been times in France's history when it has taken in more immigrants per capita than the United States, France still does not see immigration as central to its identity. This is one reason the country has banned Muslim head scarves and called for further limits on immigration. The disconnect between immigration as a fact of national life, but not of national self-understanding, has caused France to be grouped with other

Western European states as "reluctant countries of immigration." Gallant's story remains as pertinent as ever in understanding the specifically French version of that reluctance.

Yet the story's deepest thematic concern is universal. Speck denounces the widow as a fascist because she outwitted him in a business deal. Speck is a sharp operator who is willing to cut corners with the truth to get what he wants, an aspect of his character that eventually undermines the reader's sympathy. Now it turns out the Widow is more cunning still. She asserts her interests at the expense of his. Hence the deep symmetry with his wife's earlier use of the same insult to denounce him and his loan-officer approach to art. In both instances, the fascist epithet is hurled at a character who is prudential to a fault.

Wheeling and dealing in order to advance one's interests are not small aspects of modern life. We burnish our résumés, wheedle, negotiate, and press our advantages in a thousand small ways. The motivations that drive Sandor Speck are the motivations behind transactions we engage in every day—hence the economic universe in which we live, in which "entrepreneurial," "competitive," and other terms valorize the pursuit of self-interest. Gallant's story reminds us that it is possible to be a little too enamored of our species' prudential motivation. For in a different place and time, the same motive enabled the spread of political evil. In forcing us to recognize this aspect of fascism's support, the story issues the salutary instruction that we should not be too quick to conceive of fascism's adherents as aliens or monsters. Millions of people reconciled themselves to it for reasons of prudence rather than philosophy. The dangers of unprincipled pragmatism and quietism are not limited to a particular place and time. There is a speck of Sandor in us all.

AFTERWORD

The preceding chapters have taken a political approach to their subjects, variously teasing out and analyzing an author's political claims or implications, or outlining how their work relates to the wider historical context it treats or was written in. But I have tried not to let politics drive all my conclusions. Good writing, particularly good fiction, must uphold other virtues. So while I am sympathetic, for example, with Laferrière's desire not to be read simply as "black writer" or an "immigrant writer," I criticize the didacticism with which he expresses this idea in his fiction. Similarly, if agreement on language and cultural policy were all that mattered, I would have no criticisms of Charles Taylor's philosophy. It's rather the poor quality of his argument for those policies that I am trying to draw attention to. Conversely, I find much to value in John Metcalf's literary criticism, even though it is less consciously political than mine and more concerned with elucidating literary style on a molecular level.

If I have often been critical, I hope to at least have been fair. I once reviewed a book by a literary critic who was scathing about everything. A desire to be relentlessly negative seemed to explain his approach to choosing what books to review, which were disproportionately works by mid-list authors working outside of their usual genre. So he would gleefully assault a non-fiction author's first work of fiction, or a historical memoir by a novelist. I have tried to take a different approach. Not only are the writers I am most critical of generally well established, I attempt to meet them on their own terrain. Although Atwood is primarily a writer of fiction and poetry, for example, these are not her only output. She has written over half a dozen books of literary criticism, including the most influential one ever written about Canadian literature. If I am critical of Atwood's criticism, or Taylor's philosophy, or Frum's writing about American politics, or Black's popular history, it is because in each case they are prominent voices in the domain in question.

In focusing on authors who have achieved some level of prominence, my discussion has inevitably been slightly backward looking. As noted in my chapter on Kymlicka, for example, Quebec's recent legal measures restricting the ability of civil servants to wear turbans, hijabs, crosses, and other religious symbols go beyond anything Kymlicka (or Taylor, for that matter) has defended. Likewise, although cultural nationalism has informed recent proposals to require online platforms such as Netflix and YouTube to subsidize Canadian content, a nationalist approach to culture is not the force it once was.

But looking back at recent history allows us to see long-term cultural and intellectual trends in a way that is not possible when we are caught up in the immediacy of current controversies. Boyden's case has bearing on a similar one that occurred in 2019, when a group of Inuit musicians boycotted the Indigenous Music Awards to protest the nomination of Connie LeGrande, a Cree performer, whom they accused of culturally appropriating throat singing. If particular subjects and styles are the property of the cultures in which they originated, then such a charge would seem the logical culmination of criticism directed at Boyden and just as misplaced. Similarly, Laferrière's work can help us make sense of the legislation

Quebec introduced in 2022, which aimed to protect professors' ability to use or mention whatever words they consider necessary to make an academic point. The law was in part a response to a scandal at the University of Ottawa, in which a professor was suspended for mentioning the n-word as an example of a slur that has been reclaimed by social groups who experience racism. The thinking behind the legal measure recalls Laferrière's view that the unflinching mention of racist terms can be a step toward nullifying their power.

Many of the writers examined here have been active in debates over nationalism and liberalism, both of which continue to inform intellectual life in Canada. We will be in a better sense to make sense of future debates over these and related subjects if we have an understanding of how they began and how they have, and have not, changed over time.

ACKNOWLEDGMENTS

Several chapters originally appeared in a slightly different form as articles:

Chapter One first appeared as "The Wacousta Syndrome," *The New Republic*, June 24, 1996.

Chapter Two first appeared as "Conrad Black's Rise to Greatness Is an Ambitious, If Flawed, Chronicle of Our Country," *The Globe and Mail*, November 14, 2014.

Chapter Three first appeared as "Critical Un-Favourite," *Literary Review of Canada*, March, 2017.

Chapter Six first appeared as "Francophonia Forever," *Times Literary Supplement*, July 23, 1999.

Chapter Seven first appeared as "David Frum's Trump Card," *Literary Review of Canada*, January 2018.

Chapter Ten first appeared as "French Fascism and History in 'Speck's Idea'," *Studies in Canadian Literature* 40/2 2015.

I'm grateful to the editors who first thought these articles were worth publishing. I'm even more grateful to Ken Whyte for commissioning this book, improving the entire manuscript with his editorial suggestions, and helping me come up with a title. I also owe a debt of gratitude to Sarmishta Subramanian, who originally commissioned two chapters as articles for the *Literary Review of Canada* and then gave me invaluable feedback on the new chapters. Finally, I am thankful to Noah Jerge for helping assemble the notes.

NOTES

Introduction: Literary Nationalism Rides Again

p. ix *"Lamey's passion for his"* Val Ross, "Magazines," *The Globe and Mail*, June 24, 1996.

Chapter 1: The Wacousta Syndrome

p. 1 *"local color"* Jorge Borges, "The Argentine Writer and Tradition," *Labyrinths: Selected Stories and Other Writings* (New York: New Directions Publishing Corporation, 1964), p. 179.

p. 2 *"If we surrender ourselves to that voluntary dream"* Borges, *Labyrinths*, p. 185.

p. 2 *"we have listened too long to the courtly muses of Europe"* Ralph Waldo Emerson, "The American Scholar," *The Portable Emerson*. Carl Bode and Malcolm Cowly, eds. (New York: Viking, 1981), p. 70.

p. 3 *"for a generation we have been the thank-Gods of America"* Andrew Macphail, quoted in Carl Klinck, Alfred Bailey, Claude Bissell, Roy Daniells, Northrop Frye, and Desmond Pacey, eds. *Literary History of Canada: Canadian Literature in English Volume III*. Second Edition. (Toronto: University of Toronto, 1976), p. ix.

p. 4 *"the human activity that takes the fullest and most precise account"* Lionel Trilling, *The Liberal Imagination: Essays on Literature and Society* (New York: Doubleday, 1950), p. 10.

p. 4 *"'good writing' or 'good style' or 'literary excellence'"* Margaret Atwood, *Survival: A Thematic Guide to Canadian Literature* (Toronto: House of Anansi Press Limited, 1972), p. 12.

p. 4 *"Canada is a collective victim"* Atwood, *Survival*, p. 36.

p. 4 *"victim positions"* Atwood, *Survival*, p. 36.

p. 4 *"Position one: To deny the fact that you are a victim"* Atwood, *Survival*, p. 36, 38.

p. 4 *"animal victims"* Atwood, *Survival*, p. 69.

Notes

p. 4 *"starting points for those who would like to know more"* Atwood, *Survival,* p. 253.

p. 4 *"If these are carefully studied"* Atwood, *Survival,* p. 253.

p. 5 *"Here Nature holds her Carnival of Isles"* Charles Sangster, quoted in Atwood, *Survival,* p. 52.

p. 5 *"diffuse, vague, and ridiculously inflated in diction"* Desmond Pacey, *Ten Canadian Poets* (Toronto: Ryerson Press, 1958), p. 23.

p. 5 *"in any other country this kind of unexplained inconsistency of image"* Atwood, *Survival,* p. 52.

p. 5 *"I repeat once again that the mainstream of Canadian literature"* Ronald Southerland, "The Mainstream," *Canadian Literature No. 53,* Summer 1972, p. 38.

p. 6 *"only a consciously nationalist criticism will"* T.D. Maclulich, "Thematic Criticism, Literary Nationalism and the Critic's New Clothes," *Essays on Canadian Writing* Winter 1987, Issue 35, p. 17.

p. 6 *"the development of the Letter to the Editor"* David Arnason, quoted in John Metcalf, *What is a Canadian Literature?* (Guelph: Red Kite, 1988), p. 68.

p. 6 *"rejection of the Canadian tradition"* Robin Mathews, *Canadian Literature: Surrender or Revolution* (Toronto: Steel Rail Educational Publishing, 1978), p. 150.

p. 6 *"At one level they have found in U.S. poetry"* Mathews, *Canadian Literature,* p. 152.

p. 6 *"private and wayward pleasure"* John Metcalf, *What is a Canadian Literature?,* p. 95.

p. 7 *"rooted in local soil"* John Metcalf, *What is a Canadian Literature?,* p. 95.

p. 7 *"The division he is trying to create"* Metcalf, *What is a Canadian Literature?,* p. 96.

p. 7 *"It would be difficult to imagine a book more rooted in local soil"* Metcalf, *What is a Canadian Literature?,* p. 96.

p. 7 *"Other literatures do have 'victims:'"* Margaret Atwood, *Second Words: Selected Critical Prose* (Boston: Beacon Press, 1984), p. 132.

p. 8 *"these key patterns, taken together, constitute"* Atwood, *Survival,* p. 13.

p. 8 *"uncertain of themselves"* Edmund Wilson, *O Canada: An American's Notes on Canadian Culture* (New York: Farrar, Straus and Giroux, 1965), p. 105.

p. 8 *"in Canadian proportions"* Frye, quoted in Wilson, *O Canada*, p. 109.

p. 9 *"it seems to me dangerous to talk about 'Canadian' patterns"* Atwood, *Second Words*, p. 142.

p. 9 *"none of these women grew up in Canada"* Margaret Atwood, *Strange Things: The Malevolent North in Canadian Literature* (Oxford: Clarendon Press, 1995), p. 96.

p. 10 *"surely the search for the Canadian identity"* Atwood, *Strange* Things, p. 8.

p. 10 *"These lectures depart from the position"* Atwood, *Strange Things*, p. 11.

p. 11 *"The Windigo"* Atwood, *Strange Things*, p. 78.

p. 11 *"Beeg feller, always watchin'"* William Henry Drummond, *Dr. W. H. Drummond's Complete Poems* (Toronto: McClelland & Stewart, 1926), p. 178-9.

p. 12 *"the bad thing that happens to"* Atwood, *Strange Things*, p. 78.

p. 12 *"one of the first laws of late twentieth-century Canadian literature"* Atwood, *Strange Things*, p. 83.

p. 12 *"the malevolent North"* Atwood, *Strange Things*, p. iii.

p. 12 *"the literature of urban life"* Atwood, *Strange Things*, p. 5.

p. 12 *"For Ethel Wilson, as for Gwen MacEwen"* Atwood, *Strange Things*, p. 103.

p. 13 *"abridged by some 15,000 words"* Douglas Cronk, "Bibliography." In James Reaney, *Wacousta! A Melodrama in Three Acts with a Description of its Development in Workshops* (Toronto: Press Porcépic, 1979), p. 161.

p. 13 *"not more than one twentieth of the Canadian people"* John Richardson, quoted in Douglas Cronk, "Editor's Introduction," in John Richardson, *Wacousta, or, The Prophecy* (Montreal-Kingston: McGill-Queen's University Press, 1987), p. xxxvi.

p. 13 *"the vast difference of the reception"* John Richardson, *Eight Years in Canada* (Montreal: H. H. Cunningham, 1847), p. 172.

p. 14 *"is now out of print, and copies of it are now"* James Bain, editorial note accompanying "Wacousta, A Canadian tale of the time of Pontiac, by Major

Notes

Richardson," *The News Magazine* (part of the *Evening News*) Toronto, Vol. 2 Issue 13, March 22, 1902. Quoted in William Morley, *A Bibliographic Study of Major John Richardson* (Toronto: Bibliographical Society of Canada, 1973), p. 84).

p. 14 *"master works of Canadian authors"* Douglas Cronk, "Editor's Introduction," in John Richardson, *Wacousta, or, The Prophecy* (Montreal-Kingston: McGill-Queen's University Press, 1987), xlii. For the 1920s interest of the Radisson Society in Wacousta, see Margery Fee, English-Canadian Literary Criticism 1890–1950: Defining and Establishing a National Literature. PhD Thesis, University of Toronto, 1981.

p. 14 *"Wrote abominably"* Claude Bissell, quoted in A.J.M. Smith, "Introduction." *Masks of Fiction: Canadian Critics on Canadian Prose* (Toronto: McClelland and Stewart, 1961), p. vii.

p. 14 *"the worst (which we therefore here ignore)"* A.J.M. Smith, "Introduction." *Masks of Fiction*, p. ix.

p. 14 *"it is difficult to understand how"* John Charles Dent, *The Last Thirty Years: Canada Since the Union of 1841* v. 2 (Toronto: George Virtue, 1881), p. 547.

p. 14 *"His novels are deficient in interest"* D. Appleton and Company, *Appleton's Cyclopedia of American Biography* v. 5, James Grant Wilson and John Fiske, eds. (New York: D. Appleton and Company, 1888), p. 242.

p. 14 *"An internationally famous romance"* Reaney, *Wacousta!*, jacket copy.

p. 14 *"Seminal"* Douglas Cronk, "Editor's Preface," in John Richardson, *Wacousta*, p. xiii.

p. 14 *"Fresh and exciting"* David Beasley, *The Canadian Don Quixote: The Life and Works of Major John Richardson, Canada's First Novelist* (Simco, On. and Buffalo, New York: Davus, 2004 [1977]), p. 284.

p. 14 *"the foundation stone of Canadian literature"* Beasley, *The Canadian Don Quixote*, p. 284.

p. 15 *"at the centre of the Canadian imagination"* Robin Mathews, *Canadian Literature: Surrender or Revolution* (Toronto: Steel Rail Educational Publishing, 1978), p. 13.

p. 15 *"father of Canadian literature"* James Reaney, quoted in Michael Hurley, *The Borders of Nightmare: The Fiction of John Richardson* (Toronto: University of Toronto Press), p. 3.

p. 15 *"Canadian culture as a whole"* Gaile McGregor, *The Wacousta Syndrome: Explorations in the Canadian Langscape* [sic] (Toronto: University of Toronto Press, 1987), p. 10.

p. 15 *"explores Richardson's influence on"* Michael Hurley, *The Borders of Nightmare,* jacket copy.

p. 15 *"the new ancestors"* John Metcalf, *Freedom From Culture: Selected Essays 1982-92* (Toronto: ECW Press, 1994), p. 71. This phrase was originally the title of a novel by Dave Godfrey.

p. 15 *"the first major novel written by a writer born"* Mathews, *Canadian Literature,* p. 13. Since Mathews wrote, *St. Ursula's Convent* (1824), by Julia Catherine Beckwith, has come to be credited as the first Canadian novel.

p. 16 *"now, with over 40,000 words cut"* Douglas Cronk, Bibliography. In Reaney, *Wacousta!,* 162.

p. 16 *"The officers never ventured out unless"* John Richardson, *Wacousta,* abridged edition. Carl Klinck, ed. (Toronto: McClelland and Stewart, 1967), p. 19.

p. 16 *"going Indian"* Atwood, *Strange Things,* p. 42.

p. 16 *"two essentially nineteenth century writers"* Atwood, *Strange Things,* p. 42.

p. 16 *"it was phenomenally popular"* Atwood, *Strange Things,* p. 42.

p. 17 *"Wacousta was recently given a resurrection"* Atwood, *Strange Things,* p. 43.

p. 17 *"Although I had the rare privilege"* James Reaney, *Wacousta!,* 7-8.

p. 17 *"rural areas… it is simply laughable"* Patricia Ludwick. "One Actor's Journey with James Reaney," *Essays on Canadian Writing,* Winter82/Spring83, Issue 24/25, p. 137.

p. 17 *"waves"* Atwood, *Strange Things,* p. 95.

p. 17 *"and the 'second wave', women"* Atwood, *Strange Things,* p. 95.

p. 18 *"three patterns: the tourist, the coper, and"* Atwood, *Strange Things,* p. 97.

p. 18 *"it's the Catharine Parr Traill model"* Atwood, *Strange Things,* p. 99.

Notes

p. 18 *"literary ancestress"* adapted from Atwood, *Strange Things*, p. 89.

p. 18 *"Traill's book,* The Canadian Settler's Guide" Atwood, *Strange Things*, p. 96.

p. 19 *"The famous Canadian problem of identity . . . But it is with human beings"* Northrop Frye *The Bush Garden* (Toronto: Anansi 1995 [1971]), p. xxi.

Chapter 2: The Black Book of Canada

p. 21 *"Good land have we reached"* Eirik the Red's Saga: A Translation. J. Sephton, Trans. https://www.gutenberg.org/files/17946/17946-h/17946-h.htm

p. 22 *"cunning and unsentimental observer"* Conrad Black, *Rise to Greatness: The History of Canada from the Vikings to the Present* (Toronto: McClelland & Stewart, 2014), p. 594.

p. 22 *"the tactical sense to try"* Black, *Rise to Greatness*, p. 369.

p. 23 *"Canada, unlike the United States"* Frederick Schauer, "The Politics and Incentives of Legal Transplantation." CID Working Paper Series 2000.44, Harvard University, Cambridge, MA, April 2000, p. 12.

p. 24 *"complicated"* Black, *Rise to Greatness*, p. 616.

p. 24 *"strange"* Black, *Rise to Greatness*, p. 705.

p. 24 *"eccentric mystic"* Black, *Rise to Greatness*, p. 701.

p. 24 *"'a gentleman's agreement' limiting"* Black, *Rise to Greatness*, p. 442-3.

p. 25 *"there was only an economic reason"* Black, *Rise to Greatness*, p. 208-9.

p. 25 *"It was absurd that such a measure"* Black, *Rise to Greatness*, p. 934.

p. 25 *"If it had not been for the Native Americans"* Jared Diamond, *Collapse: How Societies Choose to Fail or Succeed*. Revised Edition (New York: Penguin, 2011), p. 210.

p. 25 *"Stone Age"* Black, *Rise to Greatness*, p. 8.

p. 26 *"Thank God the reviewer"* Hayden King, November 16, 2014, https://twitter.com/Hayden_King/status/534002083788505088.

p. 25 *"What's worse, Black calling"* Hayden King, November 16, 2014, https://twitter.com/Hayden_King/status/534003397784256512.

p. 27 Reservations about non-Natives writing about indigenous history. See King's remark about "exhaustion with non-Native writers." Hayden King, November 17, 2014, https://twitter.com/Hayden_King/status/534350988355072000.

p. 27 *"Black is obviously worse"* Hayden King, November 17, 2014, https://twitter.com/Hayden_King/status/534351485455589376.

p. 28 *"Seriously absurd pretexts"* Conrad Black, "A word of reply to my critics." *National Post*, December 6, 2014.

p. 28 *"Stone Age"* Conrad Black, "A word of reply to my critics," *National Post*.

p. 28 *"John A. Macdonald really was"* Conrad Black, *National Post*.

Chapter 3: The Importance of Being Metcalf

p. 29 *"out of firm disagreement with John Metcalf"* Leon Rooke, *The Second Macmillan Anthology* (Toronto: Macmillan of Canada, 1989). p. 192.

p. 29 *"I did not doubt that what"* John Metcalf, *An Aesthetic Underground* (Toronto: Thomas Allen, 2003), p. 146.

p. 30 *"She had been astonished by the hostility"* Mordecai Richler, quoted in John Metcalf *Shut Up He Explained: A Literary Memoir Vol. II* (Windsor: Biblioasis, 2007), p. 288.

p. 31 *"dangerous to talk about 'Canadian' patterns"* Margaret Atwood, *Second Words: Selected Critical Prose* (Boston: Beacon Press, 1984), p. 132.

p. 31 *"If the foreign critics are described properly"* Mathews, *Canadian Literature*, p. 45.

p. 31 *"for more than a decade, I have"* John Metcalf, *Freedom From Culture: Selected Essays 1982–92* (Toronto: ECW Press, 1994), p. 127.

p. 32 *"Tell them that the book that"* Alice Munro, in Metcalf, *Freedom From Culture*, p. 105.

p. 32 *"An expert should be able to tell"* Cyril Connolly, quoted in Metcalf, *Freedom From Culture*, p. 199.

p. 32 *"This sentence changed the way I"* John Metcalf, *Freedom From Culture*, p. 199.

Notes

p. 33 *"a prose narrative of some length that"* Randall Jarrell, in Metcalf, *The Canadian Short Story*, p. 159.

p. 34 *"Our present 'culture' is a subsidized"* John Metcalf, *Kicking Against the Pricks* (Downsview, Ont. : ECW Press, 1982), p. 61.

p. 34 *"Agree or disagree with it, you must"* Sam Solecki, "Some Kicks Against the Prick," in Sam Solecki, John Metcalf, and W. J. Keith, *Volleys: Critical Directions* (Erin: The Porcupine's Quill, 1990), p. 14.

p. 35 *"was described in the by-line as"* Metcalf, *Freedom From Culture*, p. 42.

p. 36 *"Squat, unblinking, ready to engulf"* Metcalf, *Kicking Against the Pricks*, p. 159.

p. 36 *"Canada remains so very much"* Metcalf, *Kicking Against the Pricks*, p. 53.

p. 36 *"While I would describe myself as"* Metcalf, *Kicking Against the Pricks*, p. 156.

p. 37 *"heavy on the Brits"* David Eddie, *Chump Change* (Toronto: Random House of Canada Limited, 1996), p. 48.

p. 37 *"there's such a problem in Canada"* Philip Marchand, "Can Lit Comes out of the Wilderness," *Toronto Star*, June 8, 1991.

p. 38 *"Metcalf is a nationalist who"* Robert Lecker, *Keepers of the Code* (Toronto: University of Toronto Press, 2013), p. 297.

p. 40 *"this would suggest either that"* Metcalf, *Freedom from Culture*, p. 211.

p. 40 *"What a squalid little mind"* John Metcalf, *An Aesthetic Underground* (Toronto: Thomas Allen Publishers, 2003), p. 256.

p. 41 *"banishes the urbane, charming Master"* Metcalf, *The Canadian Short Story*, p. 23.

p. 42 *"dim lands of peace . . . it dulls the image"* Ezra Pound, "A Few Don'ts by an Imagiste," *Poetry*, March 2013. https://www.poetryfoundation.org/poetrymagazine/articles/58900/a-few-donts-by-an-imagiste.

p. 42 *"familiarity, conventional diction"* Metcalf, *The Canadian Short Story*, p. 37.

p. 42 *"neatly delivered little packages"* Metcalf, *The Canadian Short Story*, p. 130.

p. 43 *"Similes usually clog up the works"* Metcalf, *The Canadian Short Story*, p. 65.

p. 44 *"the starting point for a literary discussion"* Metcalf, *The Canadian Short Story*, p. 159.

p. 44 "*big house publishers, bleating media savants*" Metcalf, *The Canadian Short Story*, p. 2.

p. 45 "*not for me logic-chopping*" Metcalf, *Shut Up*, p. 161.

p. 46 "*all about the thrill of destruction*" Lisa Ruddick, "When Nothing is Cool" *The Point*, December 7, 2015.

p. 46 "*After a few years in the profession*" Ruddick, "When Nothing is Cool."

p. 47 "*Canada's pre-eminent literary press*" Roy MacSkimming, *The Perilous Trade* (Toronto: McClelland & Stewart, 2007), p. 260.

Chapter 4: The Liberalism of Difference

p. 49 "*global guru*" G. Pascal Zachary, "A Philosopher in Red Sneakers Gains Influence as Global Guru," *The Wall Street Journal*, March 28, 2000.

p. 49 *The Kathmandu Post*, editorialized. "Living with self-determination," *The Kathmandu Post*, December 15, 2011.

p. 49 Kymlicka was called in to address Bolivia's president, Canadian Forces Join Multicultural Experts to Help Bolivia, Canada.ca, September 4, 2004.

p. 49 The United Nations sponsored a workshop on African multiculturalism, Richard Werbner, "Introduction: Challenging Minorities, Difference and Tribal Citizenship in Botswana," *Journal of Southern African Studies* 28/4 (2002), p. 672.

p. 52 "*Man is bound*" Andy Stark, "Tongue Tied," *The New Republic*, April 23, 1990, p. 18.

p. 52 "*when these insular people*" quoted in Stark, "Tongue Tied," p. 18.

p. 53 "*cognitive or physiological*" Stark, "Tongue Tied," p. 18.

p. 53 "*needs community to survive*" Stark, "Tongue Tied," p. 19.

p. 53 "*embodies an awareness of*" Stark, "Tongue Tied," p. 19.

p. 53 "*I am someone's son*" Alasdair MacIntyre, *After Virtue: A Study in Moral Theory*. Second Edition (Notre Dame, Ind.: University of Notre Dame Press, 1981), p. 220.

Notes

p. 54 *"Hugely impressed"* "A Conversation with Will Kymlicka on the Challenges of Multiculturalism," Carnegie Council Transcripts and Articles, November 12, 2014, p. 2.

p. 54 *"Enable the Indian people"* "Statement of the Government of Canada on Indian Policy 1969," in Dale Turner, *This is Not a Peace Pipe: Towards a Critical Indigenous Philosophy* (Toronto: University of Toronto Press, 2006), p. 123.

p. 54 *"A thinly disguised program"* Harold Cardinal, *The Unjust Society: The Tragedy of Canada's Indians*, Edmonton: M.G. Hurtig, 1969), p. 1.

p. 55 *"Canadians could never endorse"* Conversation with Will Kymlicka," Carnegie Council Transcripts and Articles, p. 2.

p. 55 *"I was even more disturbed"* "Conversation with Will Kymlicka," Carnegie Council Transcripts and Articles, p. 2.

p. 56 *"This decision is always"* Will Kymlicka, *Liberalism, Community and Culture* (Oxford: Oxford University Press, 1989), p. 164.

p. 56 *"Our language and history"* Kymlicka, *Liberalism, Community and Culture*, p. 165.

p. 58 *"Intolerance, indignation and disgust"* Patrick Devlin, *The Enforcement of Morals* (Oxford: Oxford University Press, 1965), p. 17.

p. 59 *"The Americanization of political philosophy"* Will Kymlicka, "The Americanization of Political Philosophy in Canada," *Oxford Literary Review* 28/1, 2006, p. 80.

p. 60 *"Ethnic Pandemonium"* Daniel Moynihan, quoted in Will Kymlicka, "Liberalism, Community and Culture Twenty-five Years On: Philosophical Inquiries and Political Claims," *Two Homelands* 44 (2016), 67.

p. 60 *"Confronted by this pandemonium"* Kymlicka, "Liberalism, Community and Culture Twenty-five Years On," p. 67.

p. 61 *"does not entail that"* MacIntyre, *After Virtue*, p. 201.

p. 62 *"celebrates hybridity, impurity, intermingling"* Salman Rushdie, *Imaginary Homelands: Essays and Criticism 1981–1991* (London: Granta Books, 1991), p. 394.

p. 63 *"refuses to think of himself... Though he may live"* Jeremy Waldron, "Minority Cultures and the Cosmopolitan Alternative," *University of Michigan Journal of Law Reform,* 25/3&4, p. 754.

p. 63 *"Meaningful options may come"* Waldron, "Minority Cultures and the Cosmopolitan Alternative," p. 783.

p. 65 *" So the unavoidable"* Will Kymlicka, *Multicultural Citizenship: A Liberal Theory of Minority Rights* (Oxford: Oxford University Press, 1995), p. 105.

p. 66 *"Societal culture . . . territorially concentrated"* Kymlicka, *Multicultural Citizenship,* p. 76.

p. 66 *"anchor for [their] self-identification"* Avishai Margalit and Joseph Raz, quoted in Kymlicka, *Multicultural Citizenship,* p. 89.

p. 67 *"They have uprooted themselves"* Kymlicka, *Multicultural Citizenship,* p. 96.

p. 67 *"the language of public schooling"* Kymlicka, *Multicultural Citizenship,* p. 111.

p. 70 Only 2.8 per cent of the global population was made up of immigrants, Charlotte Edmond, "Global migration, by the numbers: who migrates, where they go and why," World Economic Forum, https://www.weforum.org/agenda/2020/01/iom-global-migration-report-international-migrants-2020.

p. 71 *"Some people seem most... But most people"* Kymlicka, *Multicultural Citizenship,* p. 90.

p. 71 In 2020 it was 3.5 per cent, Edmond, "Global migration, by the numbers."

p. 72 Only 12.5 per cent of indigenous people, Statistics Canada, "The Aboriginal languages of First Nations people, Métis and Inuit," https://www12.statcan.gc.ca/census-recensement/2016/as-sa/98-200-x/2016022/98-200-x2016022-eng.cfm.

p. 73 *"To many of my American"* Alan Patten, *Equal Recognition: The Moral Foundations of Minority Rights* (Princeton: Princeton University Press, 2014, p. vii.

p. 73 *"by deprioritizing the claims"* Patten, *Equal Recognition,* p. 294.

p. 76 *"in most cases I'm happy"* Will Kymlicka, Liberal Multiculturalism as a Political Theory of State-Minority Relations," *Political Theory* 46/1 (2018), p. 82.

p. 76 *"Since most aboriginal communities . . . I take issue with"* Turner, *This is Not a Peace Pipe,* p. 57.

p. 77 *"Kymlicka's theory of minority rights"* Turner, *This is Not a Peace Pipe,* p. 70.

Chapter 5: The Orenda: A Defense

p. 78 *"Is Joseph Boyden actually"* IndigenousXca (Robert Jago), December 22, 2016, https://twitter.com/IndigenousXca/status/812116470712963072.

p. 78 *"variously claimed his family's"* Jorge Barrera, "Author Joseph Boden's shape-shifting Indigenous identity," *Aptnnews.ca,* December 23, 2016, https://www.aptnnews.ca/national-news/author-joseph-boydens-shape-shifting-indigenous-identity/.

p. 79 *"a byword for ethnic fraud"* Eric Andrew-Gee, "The making of Joseph Boyden," *The Globe and Mail,* August 4, 2017.

p. 79 *"I am not going to teach Joseph Boyden"* Accountable Panel, 29 March 2017. This account (@AccountablePanl) has since been deleted. The Tweet is on file with the author. The original tweet quoted Williamson stating "I am not going to teach Joseph Boyden[...] he takes up the space of indigenous writers." On April 19, 2017, Williamson tweeted, "What the ellipses say... 'as an Indigenous writer' - I don't believe in banning books from curriculum outright." https://twitter.com/jwilliambao/status/854724702060916736.

p. 79 *"If I were you"* Accountable Panel (@AccountablePanl), March 29, 2017. Tweet from deleted account on file with the author.

p. 79 *"Joseph Boyden should not be"* Dave Gaertner, September 3, 2020, https://twitter.com/davegaertner/status/1301599401618497536.

p. 81 *"authentically portraying the strength"* quoted in James Young, *Cultural Appropriation and the Arts* (Malden, MA: Wiley-Blackwell, 2008), p. 57.

p. 81 *"cultural appropriation is often defensible"* Young, *Cultural Appropriation and the Arts,* p. ix.

p. 82 *"I don't have time for it"* Tomson Highway Reading Q&A, Dalhousie University, fall 1990.

p. 82 *"Only women can understand"* Edward Said, *Culture and Imperialism* (New York: Vintage, 1993), p. 31.

p. 82 "*acknowledge the massively knotted*" Said, *Culture and Imperialism*, 32.

p. 83 "*The important European novelist*" Amit Chaudhuri, "*I* am Ramu," *N+1*, August 22, 2017, https://www.nplusonemag.com/online-only/online-only/i-am-ramu/.

p. 84 Had to learn their language, Bruce Trigger, *The Children of Aataentsic: A History of the Huron People to 1660* (Kingston: McGill-Queen's University Press 1987 [1976]), p. 65.

p. 85 "*the Indian and his culture*" quoted in Trigger, *The Children of Aataentsic*, p. 2.

p. 85 "*The Anishnaabe came down*" Joseph Boyden, *The Orenda* (Toronto: Penguin Canada, 2013), p. 22.

p. 85 By 500 A.D. indigenous trade networks had brought it to Ontario, Trigger, *The Children of Aataentsic*, p. 122–6.

p. 86 Fought with the Wendat over hunting and fishing grounds, Trigger, *The Children of Aataentsic*, p. 122.

p. 86 "*You know you can't*" Boyden, *The Orenda*, p. 57.

p. 87 "*no Knowledge of the face*" Thomas Hobbes, *Leviathan* (Hammondsworth: Penguin, 1968 [1651]), p. 186.

p. 87 "*For the savage people*" Hobbes, *Leviathan*, p. 187.

p. 88 "*shameless in their lack*" Boyden, *The Orenda*, p. 28.

p. 88 Did not require women to always cover their breasts, Trigger, *The Children of Aataentsic*, p. 37.

p. 88 Fine for both women and men to initiate sex . . . did not consider monogamy especially important, Trigger, *The Children of Aataentsic*, p. 49.

p. 88 This ruled out not only marriages between immediate relatives, Trigger, *The Children of Aataentsic*, p. 49.

p. 88 Took the form of a confederacy, Trigger, *The Children of Aataentsic*, p. 156–63.

p. 89 30,000 people at their height, Kathryn Magee Labelle, *Dispersed but Not Destroyed: A History of the Seventeenth-Century Wendat People* (Vancouver: UBC Press, 2013), p. 2.

p. 89 A plot detail that may strain plausibility, Trigger, *The Children of Aataentsic*, p. 39.

Notes

p. 89 *"What is the point of this torture"* Boyden, *The Orenda*, p. 135.

p. 90 *"For a time they were trustees"* Peter Newman, *Company of Adventurers: How the Hudson's Bay Empire Determined the Destiny of a Continent* (Toronto: Penguin Canada, 2005 [1985-91]), p 2.

p. 91 *"Great voice, he loves you"* Boyden, *The Orenda*, p. 55.

p. 91 *"Let us face it"* quoted in Michael Asch, *On Being Here to Stay: Treaties and Aboriginal Rights in Canada* (Toronto: University of Toronto Press, 2014), p. 3.

p. 91 *"What, beyond the fact"* Asch, *On Being Here to Stay*, p. 3.

p. 93 *"It is fair to say that"* Kathryn Magee Labelle, *The Orenda* by Joseph Boyden (review), *Canadian Historical Review* 96/3 (2015), p. 427.

p. 95 *"It's a game we play"* Boyden, *The Orenda*, p. 54.

p. 96 *"the violence is key"* "Canada Reads 2014: Panelists Wab and Stephen debate torture in 'The Orenda,'" CBC.ca, https://www.cbc.ca/player/play/2440227827.

p. 97 *"a comforting narrative for Canadians"* Hayden King, "Critical review of Joseph Boyden's 'The Orenda': A timeless classic colonial alibi," Muskrat Magazine, December 24, 2013, http://muskratmagazine.com/critical-review-of-joseph-boydens-the-orenda-a-timeless-classic-colonial-alibi/. King also states that the novel depicts the Haudenosaunee as terrifying villains, overlooking the sympathetic depiction of the Haudenosaunee narrator.

p. 97 *"It's unfair to blame only the crows"* Boyden, *The Orenda*, p. 153.

p. 97 *"because of the selfishness"* King, "Critical review of Joseph Boyden's 'The Orenda.'"

p. 98 *"the exclusive domain of the Indians"* King, "Critical Review of Joseph Boyden's 'The Orenda.'"

p. 98 *"splayed and tortured man"* Boyden, *The Orenda*, p. 264.

p. 99 *"for early explorers and settlers"* Margaret Atwood, *Survival: A Thematic Guide to Canadian Literature* (Toronto: Anansi, 1972), p. 32.

p. 99 *"Atwood even cites literature"* King, "Critical review of Joseph Boyden's 'The Orenda.'"

p. 99 *"Indians represent humanity"* Northrop Frye, quoted in Atwood, *Survival*, 93.

p. 100 *"not* nearly *as much blame"* Cam Terwilliger, "The Rumpus Interview with Joseph Boyden, *The Rumpus,* June 10, 2014, https://therumpus.net/2014/06 /the-rumpus-interview-with-joseph-boyden/.

p. 100 *"Among the Huron, men committed"* Trigger, *The Children of Aataentsic,* 78.

p. 101 *"gives voice to the indigenous"* "Canada Reads 2014: Day One," CBC.ca, https://www.cbc.ca/player/play/2440055574.

p. 102 *"in the name of upholding"* Jody Wilson-Raybould, "Address by the Honourable Jody Wilson-Raybould, PC, QC, MP to the BC Leaders Gathering (Premier, BC Cabinet, and Chiefs of BC)," Government of Canada, November 29, 2018, https://www.justice.gc.ca/eng/news-nouv/speech11292018.html.

p. 102 *"the heretics have ample evidence"* Hayden King, "Jody Wilson-Raybould and the paradox of reconciliation in Canada," *The Globe and Mail,* February 28, 2019.

p. 102 *"voting in or out unsupportive"* Hayden King and Sheri Pasternak, "Don't Call it a Comeback," *Literary Review of Canada,* January-February 2015.

p. 102 *"disengagement from and alternatives"* King and Pasternak, "Don't Call it a Comeback."

p. 102 *"can potentially lead to some gains"* King and Pasternak, "Don't Call it a Comeback."

p. 102 *"we do not believe in"* King and Pasternak, "Don't Call it a Comeback."

p. 103 *"I had to delete a tweet"* Hayden King, September 9, 2021, https:// twitter.com/Hayden_King/status/1436135110022242307.

p. 103 *"These voices, paradoxically"* Jody Wilson-Raybould, "Address by the Honourable Jody Wilson-Raybould."

p. 105 *"I don't mind him telling their story"* IndigenousXca (Robert Jago), December 22, 2016. https://twitter.com/IndigenousXca/status/812098058892808192.

p. 105 *"and everyone knows it's"* IndigenousXca (Robert Jago), December 22, https://twitter.com/IndigenousXca/status/812098469380947974.

p. 105 *"I've faced some hard days"* Joseph Boyden, "The Shortest Season," *Georgian Bay Today,* Fall 2019. The feeling Boyden describes may also have been due to the controversy over the so-called UBC Accountable affair, which revolved around a prominent public letter that Boyden helped organize. The letter said that the University of British Columbia failed to uphold procedural justice in its handling of sexual assault allegations against creative writing professor Steven Galloway. Critics characterized the letter as siding with Galloway over his accuser. For the original letter and a response to its critics, see http://www.ubcaccountable.com/.

p. 106 *"We're looking realistically at"* Sarah Viren, "The Native Scholar Who Wasn't," *The New York Times Magazine*, May 25, 2021.

p. 106 *"a tenuous genealogical relation"* Darryl Leroux, *Distorted Descent: White Claims to Indigenous Identity* (Winnipeg: University of Manitoba Press, 2019), p. 2.

p. 107 *"keepers of a number"* Jorge Barrera, "Author Joseph Boden's shape-shifting Indigenous identity."

Chapter 6: Mr. Taylor's Planet

p. 108 *"I welcome the chance . . . what has changed"* Bill Bantey, "Mount Royal: Solid Liberal Territory Since '40," *The Montreal Gazette*, November 3, 1965.

p. 110 *"I not only admire the historical"* Michael Walzer, in Charles Taylor, *Multiculturalism: Examining the Politics of Recognition* (Princeton: Princeton University Press, 1994), p. 99.

p. 111 *"fresh thinking . . . one of the liveliest, most readable"* Persky Stan, "Breathing new life into national debate," *The Globe and Mail*, June 24, 1995.

p. 111 *"the leading philosophers of our time"* David Miller, "What Holds us Together," *Times Literary Supplement*, December 15, 1995.

p. 111 *"turn on the need, sometimes the demand"* Taylor, *Multiculturalism*, p. 25.

p. 111 *"dialogical"* Taylor, *Multiculturalism*, p. 32.

p. 112 *"grievous wound"* Taylor, *Multiculturalism*, p. 26.

p. 112 *"vital human need"* Taylor, *Multiculturalism*, p. 26.

p. 112 *"true"* Taylor, *Multiculturalism*, p. 31.

p. 113 *"seminal idea"* Taylor, *Multiculturalism*, p. 31.

p. 113 *"crucial feature of the human condition"* Taylor, *Multiculturalism*, p. 32.

p. 113 *"of art, of gesture, of love"* Taylor, *Multiculturalism*, p. 32.

p. 114 *"the monological ideal"* Taylor, *Multiculturalism*, p. 33.

p. 114 *"negotiate it through dialogue"* Taylor, *Multiculturalism*, p. 34.

p. 114 *"the importance of recognition is now"* Taylor, *Multiculturalism*, p. 36.

p. 115 *"the unique identity of this individual"* Taylor, *Multiculturalism*, p. 38.

p. 115 *"It is precisely this distinctness that"* Taylor, *Multiculturalism*, p. 38.

p. 116 *"After all, if we're concerned with"* Taylor, *Multiculturalism*, p. 40.

p. 116 *"universalist"* Taylor, *Multiculturalism*, p. 38.

p. 116 *"recognition"* Taylor, *Multiculturalism*, p. 38.

p. 116 *"blind"* Taylor, *Multiculturalism*, p. 39.

p. 116 *"the supposedly fair and difference-blind"* Taylor, *Multiculturalism*, p. 43.

p. 116 *"guilty as charged by the proponents"* Taylor, *Multiculturalism*, p. 61.

p. 117 *"It is axiomatic for Quebec governments"* Taylor, *Multiculturalism*, p. 58.

p. 117 *"a society can be organized"* Taylor, *Multiculturalism*, p. 59.

p. 118 *"privileges and immunities"* Taylor, *Multiculturalism*, p. 59.

p. 118 *"live the life of diaspora"* Taylor, *Multiculturalism*, p. 63.

p. 118 *"our philosophical boundaries"* Taylor, *Multiculturalism*, p. 63.

p. 118 *"fusion of horizons"* Taylor, *Multiculturalism*, p. 67.

p. 119 *"that have, in other words, articulated"* Taylor, *Multiculturalism*, p. 72.

p. 119 *"our own limited part"* Taylor, *Multiculturalism*, p. 73.

p. 119 *"the culture of our ancestors"* Taylor, *Multiculturalism*, p. 58.

p. 119 *"fusion of horizons"* Taylor, *Multiculturalism*, p. 67.

p. 120 *"main locus of this debate"* Taylor, *Multiculturalism*, p. 65.

p. 120 *"through our developing"* Taylor, *Multiculturalism*, p. 67.

p. 121 *"inequality, exploitation and injustice"* Taylor, *Multiculturalism*, p. 64.

p. 121 *"actively seek to create members"* Taylor, *Multiculturalism*, p. 58–59.

p. 122 *"multicultural in the sense of"* Taylor, *Multiculturalism*, p. 61.

Notes

p. 122 *"live the life of diaspora"* Taylor, *Multiculturalism*, p. 63.

p. 123 *"monological"* Taylor, *Multiculturalism*, p. 32.

p. 123 Taylor, who has written brilliantly on many other topics. Works by Taylor that have influenced my own thinking include "What is Human Agency?," *Philosophical Papers Volume I* (Cambridge: Cambridge University Press, 1985), 15–44, and "What's Wrong with Negative Liberty?," *Philosophical Papers Volume II* (Cambridge: Cambridge University Press, 1985), 211–229.

Chapter 7: This American Gangrene

p. 124 *"The campaign's headquarters was"* David Frum, *What's Right* (Toronto: Random House Canada, 1996), p. 1.

p. 124 *"I devoted the resulting reading time"* Frum, *What's Right*, p. 1.

p. 125 *"one of the leading"* John McGinnis, "The Revolution that Wasn't," *The Wall Street Journal*, July 2, 1996.

p. 125 *"To demonstrate my distaste for"* David Frum, "The Conservative Case for Voting for Clinton," *The Atlantic*, November 2, 2016.

p. 125 *"Who mocks the disabled"* Frum, "The Conservative Case for Voting for Clinton," November 2, 2016.

p. 125 *"He has ripped the conscience out"* David Frum, *Trumpocracy: The Corruption of the American Republic* (New York: HarperCollins, 2018), pp. 207–8.

p. 126 *"sly Jew-baiting and his"* David Frum, "The Conservative Bully Boy," in *The American Spectator*, July 1991, p. 14.

p. 126 *"triviality and faddishness"* David Frum, *Dead Right* (New York: BasicBooks, 1994), p. 11.

p. 126 *"There are things only government"* David Frum, *Comeback: Conservatism That Can Win Again* (New York: Broadway Books, 2009), p. 19.

p. 127 *"one of the media's most effective"* Mark Oppenheimer, "The Prodigal Frum," *The Nation*, July 11, 2012.

p. 127 *"I believe in an American-led world"* Oppenheimer, "The Prodigal Frum," *The Nation*, July 11, 2012.

p. 128 *"It's very sad"* Frum, *Trumpocracy*, p 190.

p. 128 "*No American president in history*" Frum, *Trumpocracy*, p. 104.

p. 129 "*High among those dangers is*" Frum, *Trumpocracy*, p. 181.

p. 129 "*That outlook, good in its place*" Frum, *Trumpocracy*, p. 181.

p. 129 "*Tax disclosure refused for the first time*" Frum, *Trumpocracy*, p. 64–5.

p. 130 "*Just 13 percent described themselves*" Frum, *Trumpocracy*, p. 38.

p. 130 "*What set them apart from other Republicans*" Frum, *Trumpocracy*, p. 38.

p. 130 "*Donald Trump created in effect*" Frum, *Trumpocracy*, p. 217.

p. 130 "*distrusted flattery and flatterers*" Frum, *Trumpocracy*, p. 84.

p. 130 "*During his own tenure in the*" Frum, *Trumpocracy*, jacket copy.

p. 130 "*Modern political lies are so big*" Hannah Arendt, "Truth and Politics," *Between Past and Future: Eight Exercises in Political Thought* (New York: Viking, 1968), 253.

p. 131 "*the utter weakness and incompetence*" Dan Merica, "Trump joins the UN club he once derided," *CNN.com*, September 19, 2017.

p. 132 "*incidents of political interference*" Union of Concerned Scientists and the Government Accountability Project, Atmosphere of Pressure: Political Interference in Federal Climate Science. (Cambridge: UCS Publications, 2007), 6.

p. 132 "*The people of Alabama will do*" Donald Trump, Twitter (@realDonaldTrump), December 12, 2017, 6:09 AM.

p. 133 An egalitarian plateau, Will Kymlicka, *Contemporary Political Philosophy: An Introduction Second Edition* (Oxford: Oxford University Press, 2002), p. 4.

p. 134 "*need to prepare our children*" George W. Bush, State of the Union to the 107th Congress, Washington D.C., January 29, 2002.

p. 134 "*leaving the bodies of mothers*" Bush, State of the Union to the 107th Congress, January 29, 2002.

p. 135 "*When you get these terrorists*" Tom LoBianco, "Donald Trump on terrorists: 'Take out their families,'" *CNN.com*, December 3, 2015.

p. 135 "*It isn't just that you don't put up*" Aleksandr Solzhenitsyn, *The Gulag Archipelago 1918-1956: An Experiment in Literary Investigation. Volume I* (New York: HarperPerennial, 2007), p. 13.

Notes

p. 135 *"So why did I keep silent?"* Solzhenitsyn, *The Gulag Archipelago*, p. 17.

p. 135 *"I could easily have run away"* Mohamedou Ould Slahi, *Guantánamo Diary: Restored Edition* (New York: Back Bay Books, 2017), p. 138.

p. 135 *"I could at least have forcibly passed"* Slahi *Guantánamo Diary*, p. 138.

p. 136 *"from 2001 until at least 2004"* Slahi *Guantánamo Diary*, p. 155.

p. 136 *"Oh, very convenient!"* Slahi *Guantánamo Diary*, p. 154.

p. 136 *"We are not going to sweat to prove"* Solzhenitsyn, *The Gulag Archipelago*, p. 137.

p. 137 *"You know, you didn't make any mistake"* Slahi *Guantánamo Diary*, p. 26.

p. 137 *"tight"* Slahi *Guantánamo Diary*, p. 29.

p. 137 *"I kept saying, 'MP, Sir, I cannot breathe!"* Slahi *Guantánamo Diary*, p. 29.

p. 137 *"The torture squad was so well trained"* Slahi *Guantánamo Diary*, p. 242.

p. 138 *"The cell—better, the box"* Slahi *Guantánamo Diary*, p. 218.

p. 139 *"a great form of torture"* Solzhenitsyn, *The Gulag Archipelago*, p. 112.

p. 139 *"befogs the reason, undermines the will"* Solzhenitsyn, *The Gulag Archipelago*, p. 112.

p. 139 *"Communist Control Techniques"* Slahi *Guantánamo Diary*, p. 205–6.

p. 139 *"These methods do, of course, constitute"* Slahi *Guantánamo Diary*, p. 205–6.

p. 139 *"special interrogation plan"* Slahi, *Guantánamo Diary*, p. xiv.

p. 140 *"they also take things from us honestly"* Solzhenitsyn, *The Gulag Archipelago*, p. 544.

p. 140 *"When I was apprehended"* Murat Kurnaz with Helmut Kuhn, *Five Years of My Life: An Innocent Man in Guantánamo*, Trans. Jefferson Chase (New York: Palgrave MacMillan, 2008), p. 47.

p. 142 *"The evidence does show that"* Memorandum Order, *Mohamedou Ould Slahi v. Barack H. Obama*, No. 1:05-cv-00569-JR, 5, p. 30.

p. 142 *"Such support was sporadic"* Memorandum Order, *Mohamedou Ould Slahi v. Barack H. Obama*, No. 1:05-cv-00569-JR, 5, p. 30.

The Canadian Mind

p. 142 *"Rather, they tend to support Slahi's"* Memorandum Order, *Mohamedou Ould Slahi v. Barack H. Obama*, No. 1:05-cv-00569-JR, 5, p. 30.

p. 143 *"get a crack at the guys"* Slahi *Guantánamo Diary*, p. 393.

p. 143 *"It was at the end of this"* Slahi *Guantánamo Diary*, p. 395.

p. 146 One of them is physically weak. This example comes from Julia Driver, "Individual Consumption and Moral Complicity," *The Moral Complexities of Eating Meat.* Ben Bramble and Bob Fischer, eds. (Oxford, Oxford University Press, 2016), p. 71.

p. 146 *"As American forces advanced"* David Frum, *The Right Man* (New York: Random House Trade Paperbacks, 2003), p. 195.

p. 146 *"The left-wing British tabloid the* Mirror" Frum, *The Right Man*, p. 195.

p. 147 *"The transformation must begin with"* David Frum and Richard Perle, *An End to Evil: How to Win the War on Terror* (New York: Random House, 2004), p. 167.

p. 147 *"The FBI is essentially a police force"* Frum and Perle, *An End to Evil*, p. 168.

p. 147 *"inherently disabled"* Frum and Perle, *An End to Evil*, p. 168.

p. 147 *"Noncitizen terrorist suspects are not"* Frum and Perle, *An End to Evil*, p. 190.

p. 147 *"innocent goatherds and blameless wedding guests"* David Frum, "Letters from Guantanamo," *National Post*, November 11, 2006.

p. 148 *"those in the west who succumb"* David Frum, "Letters from Guantanamo," *National Post*, November 11, 2006.

p. 148 *"Maybe waterboarding was wrong"* David Frum, "Don't pretend this is a debate about 'torture,'" *National Post*, May 2, 2009.

p. 148 *"But make no mistake"* Frum, "Don't pretend this is a debate about 'torture.'"

p. 149 "la gangrene" Neil MacMaster, "Torture: From Algiers to Abu Ghraib," *Race and Class* 46/2 (2004), p. 12.

p. 149 *"was seen as a form of cancer"* MacMaster, "Torture: From Algiers to Abu Ghraib," p. 12.

p. 149 *"a total and complete shutdown"* Jenna Johnson, "Trump calls for a 'total and complete shutdown' of Muslims entering the United States," *The Washington Post*, December 7, 2015.

p. 149 *"immigrants and visitors from"* U.S. Commission on Civil Rights, "Redefining Rights in America: The Civil Rights Record of the George W. Bush Administration, 2001–2004," Draft Report for Commissioners' Review, September 2004, pp. ix–x.

Chapter 8: The Last Nationalist

p. 151 *"Novels are like movies now"* Russell Smith, *Noise* (Erin, Ont.: The Porcupine's Quill, 1998), 135. Quoted in *When Words Deny the World: The Reshaping of Canadian Writing* (Erin, Ont.: The Porqupine's Quill, 2002), p. 203.

p. 153 *"a pathetically provincial attitude"* When Words Deny the World, p. 171.

p. 153 *"TV-lobotomized, all-American"* When Words Deny the World, p. 174.

p. 153 *"These are people who"* When Words Deny the World, p. 170.

p. 154 *"It is one of the peculiarities"* When Words Deny the World, p. 34.

p. 154 *"leap to the sort of modernist"* When Words Deny the World, p. 36.

p. 154 *"If your reality is marginalized"* When Words Deny the World, p. 79.

p. 155 *"at the price of being packaged . . . In response to the demands . . . The mid-1980s has witnessed"* When Words Deny the World, p. 37.

p. 155 *"The collective idea of Canada"* When Words Deny the World, p. 99.

p. 156 *"superseded by a slick"* When Words Deny the World, pp. 99–100.

p. 156 *"globalization means Americanization"* When Words Deny the World, p. 134.

p. 156 *"irredeemably English . . . too Canadian . . . you can't sell . . . You've moved outside Canada"* When Words Deny the World, p. 91.

p. 157 *"It is easy to make fun"* When Words Deny the World, p. 138.

p. 157 *"flight from history into metaphor"* When Words Deny the World, p. 142.

p. 157 *"I thought I was going to"* Michael Ondatjee, *The English Patient* (New York: Vintage, 1993), 103. Quoted in *When Words Deny the World*, p. 141.

p. 157 *"North American troops"* The English Patient, 41. Quoted in *When Words Deny the World*, p. 143.

p. 157 *"North American"* The English Patient, 94. Quoted in *When Words Deny the World*, pp. 14344.

p. 158 *"shapeless showing off"* When Words Deny the World, p. 150.

p. 158 *"a city built in the bowl"* Anne Michaels, *Fugitive Pieces* (New York: Vintage, 1998 [1996]), 89. Quoted in *When Words Deny the World*, p. 147.

p. 158 *"She moves through history"* Anne Michaels, *Fugitive Pieces*, 176. Quoted in *When Words Deny the World*, pp. 153–4.

p. 159 "To anyone who has spent . . . this passage . . . her voluptuousness" *When Words Deny the World*, p. 154.

p. 159 *"the neon-lit glare"* Stephen Henighan, *A Report on the Afterlife of Culture* (Windsor: Biblioasis, 2008), p. 37.

p. 159 *"This 'mass' element pervades"* A Report on the Afterlife of Culture, p. 35.

p. 160 *"sloppy, fractured . . . intellectually malnourished"* A Report on the Afterlife of Culture, p. 35.

p. 160 *"ethnic fiction . . . the intensification of globalization"* A Report on the Afterlife of Culture, p. 309.

p. 160 *"hugely reprehensible"* A Report on the Afterlife of Culture, p. 329.

p. 161 *"in other countries"* When Words Deny the World, p. 243.

p. 161 *"Montreal is like the ocean"* Stephen Henighan, *The Streets of Winter* (Saskatoon: Thistledown, 2004), p. 147.

p. 162 *"critical and commercial attention"* A Report on the Afterlife of Culture, p. 243.

p. 163 *"mediocre fiction"* When Words Deny the World, p. 181.

p. 163 *"seems to be amassing"* When Words Deny the World, p. 96.

p. 163 *"the proven international salability"* When Words Deny the World, p. 170.

p. 164 *"a literature dominated by"* When Words Deny the World, p. 155.

p. 164 *The Favourite Game* and other Canadian poet's novels mentioned here are discussed in Ian Rae, *From Cohen to Carson: The Poet's Novel in Canada* (Kingston-Montreal: McGill-Queen's University Press, 2008).

p. 166 *"It was also fuelled . . . didn't just produce"* Nick Mount, *Arrival: The Story of CanLit* (Toronto: Anansi, 2017), p. 290.

Notes

p. 167 "*As long as they have*" Allan Bloom, *The Closing of the American Mind* (New York, Simon and Schuster, 1987), p. 81.

p. 167 "*the idea of historical*" *A Report on the Afterlife of Culture*, 47.

p. 169 For *The Handmaid's Tale's* influences, see Joshua Barajas, "Margaret Atwood on the dystopian novels that inspired her to write 'The Handmaid's Tale,'" *PBS.org*, September 9, 2019, https://www.pbs.org/newshour/arts/margaret-atwood-on-the-dystopian-novels-that-inspired-her-to-write-the-handmaids-tale.

p. 171 "*the boosterism inflating*" *When Words Deny the World*, p. 158.

p. 171 "*irrefutable . . . forge for Canada*" *When Words Deny the World*, p. 114.

p. 171 "*commitment to literary debate*" *When Words Deny the World*, p. 213.

p. 172 Munro's pioneering example may have contributed to the linked story cycle becoming popular among a later generation of Canadian writers. In a similar spirit, Nick Mount plausibly suggests that a tradition of Canadian writers drawing on the work of their predecessors begins in the 21st century. See his "Tradition and the Individual Canadian Talent," *Studia Anglica Posnaniesia* 55s2 (2020), 253–71.

p. 172 "*The new Canada . . . Dickens would require*" *When Words Deny the World*, p. 209.

p. 174 "*Underground Frailroad*" Margaret Atwood, *The Handmaid's Tale* (New York: Anchor Books, 1998 [1985]), 301. I say more about the novel in "Platonic Corruption in *The Handmaid's Tale*," *Fictional Worlds and the Political Imagination*. Garry Hagberg, ed. (Cham, Switzerland: Palgrave Macmillan, forthcoming).

p. 175 "*a strong girl, good muscles*" *The Handmaid's Tale*, p. 115.

p. 176 "*a major figure in*" This remark is quoted on the dustjacket of C.S. Giscombe, *Into and Out of Dislocation* (New York: Farrar, Strauss and Giroux, 2000).

p. 176 "*mined the Cariboo*" C.S. Giscombe, *Giscome Road* (Normal, Il.: Dalkey Archive Press, 1998), p. 7.

p. 176 "*to M. Atwood*" *Giscome Road*, p. 53.

p. 176 "*I am a place*" Margaret Atwood, *Surfacing* (New York: Anchor Books, 1988 [1972]), 187. Quoted in *Giscome Road*, p. 53.

p. 177 "*I'm wilderness . . . "I was/Africa and America"* Giscome Road, p. 53.

p. 177 "*Ms. Atwood's book . . . It was a teachable . . . [The novel] had an almost nauseating . . . had been talking"* Into and Out of Dislocation, p. 61.

Chapter 9: Immortal Laferrière

p. 181 "*She had a glass of whisky . . . She sang looking"* Dany Laferrière, "L'art de la Chronique," Gregor von Rezzori Prize - City of Florence, http://premiogregorvonrezzori.org/dany-Laferrière/?lang=en.

p. 181 "*[a] new and unprecedented"* Lee Skallerup Bessette, "Biography: Dany Laferrière," in *Dany Laferrière: Essays on His Works*, Lee Skallerup Bessette, ed. (Toronto: Guernica Editions, 2013), p. 181 (my translation).

p. 182 "*language is the nationality"* Vincent Destouches, "Académie française : Dany Laferrière, vu de France," *L'actualite*, December 12, 2013 (my translation).

p. 182 "*I don't just come"* Rachel Donadio, "Dany Laferrière, a Guardian of French, Joins the Académie Française," *The New York Times*, May 29, 2015.

p. 183 "*two blacks in a filthy apartment"* Laferrière, *How to Make Love to a Negro Without Getting Tired*, David Homel Trans. (Madeira Park, British Columbia: Douglas and McIntyre, 2010), pp. 29–30.

p. 184 "*you could hold a gun"* Laferrière, *How to Make Love*, p. 35.

p. 184 "*In the scale of Western values"* Laferrière, *How to Make Love*, p. 41.

p. 185 "*both of them were dogs . . I was laying in wait"* Laferrière, *How to Make Love*, pp. 150–1.

p. 185 A professor at Augsberg University, Colleen Flaherty, "Too Taboo for Class?," *Inside Higher Ed*, February 1, 2019.

p. 185 The same year another professor, Colleen Flaherty, "New School Drops N-Word Case," *Inside Higher Ed*, August 19, 2019.

p. 185 "*Like in China the common word"* Nina Agrawal, "Controversy over USC professor's use of Chinese word that sounds like racial slur in English," *Los Angeles Times*, September 5, 2020.

Notes

p. 186 A law professor at the University of Illinois Chicago, Stephanie Francis Ward, "In federal complaint, UIC law professor claims 'sensitivity training' violates his civil rights," *ABA Journal*, February 1, 2022.

p. 186 The same redacted term, "University of Illinois Chicago Training Materials," Foundation for Individual Rights and Expression, https://www.thefire.org/university-of-illinois-chicago-training-materials/, see PDF page 5.

p. 187 *"To us, enunciating slurs"* Randall Kennedy and Eugene Volk, "The New Taboo: Quoting Epithets in the Classroom and Beyond," *Capital University Law Review* 49/1 (2021), p. 9.

p. 187 *"Black [is] too free of stereotype . . . alternating when the occasion"* David Homel, "How to Make Love with the Reader . . . Slyly," in Dany Laferrriere, *How to Make Love*, p. 6.

p. 188 *"we no longer expect humor"* Lee Skallerup, *"How to Make Love to a Negro*: But What if I Get Tired? Transculturation and its (Partial) Negation in and Through Translation," *Interculturality and Translation International Review* 1 (2005), 90. Skallerup has added "Bessette" to her name since publishing this article.

p. 188 *"Don't worry about the translation"* quoted in Skallerup, "How to Make Love," p. 96.

p. 188 *"There is a manic, immigrant energy"* quoted in Skallerup, "How to Make Love," p. 96.

p. 189 *"On ne naît pas femme"* Simone de Beauvoir, *Le Deuxième Sexe* (Paris: Gallimard, 1949), pp. 285–6.

p. 189 *"One is not born"* Simone de Beauvoir, *The Second Sex*, Trans. and ed. H. M. Parshley (New York: Alfred A. Knopf, 1953), p. 301.

p. 189 *"just as the book appears"* Sean Mills, *A Place in the Sun: Haiti, Haitians and the Remaking of Quebec* (Kingston-Montreal: McGill-Queen's University Press, 2016), p. 214.

p. 189 *"A black person only exists"* quoted in Mills, *A Place in the Sun*, p. 213.

p. 189 *"I'd like to be one hundred"* Laferrière, *How to Make Love*, p. 42.

p. 192 *"the French language was dirty"* quoted in Mills, *A Place in the Sun*, p. 198.

p. 193 *"In the years I spent in Canada"* Bharatti Mukherjee, "Introduction," *Darkness* (New York: Penguin, 1985), p. 2.

p. 193 *"Pierre Vallières took five columns"* Laferrière, *How to Make Love*, p. 142.

p. 194 *"Quebecers are the irrefutable proof"* Jean Morisset, quoted in Mills, *A Place in the Sun*, p. 209.

p. 194 Relationships between Quebecois women and Haitian men were far more common, Mills, *A Place in the Sun*, p. 208.

p. 195 *"I could go ahead and write"* Dany Laferrière, *Why Must a Black Writer Write About Sex?*, Trans. David Homel (Toronto: Coach House Press, 1994), p. 105.

p. 195 *"Aren't you ashamed"* Laferrière, *Why Must a Black Writer*, p. 19.

p. 196 *"You give too much press"* Laferrière, *Why Must a Black Writer*, p. 95.

p. 196 *"I got what I wanted"* Laferrière, *Why Must a Black Writer*, p. 105.

p. 196 *"I'm not a black writer"* Laferrière, *Why Must a Black Writer*, p. 196.

p. 196 *"When I became a writer"* Dany Laferrière, *I am a Japanese Writer*, Trans. David Homel (Vancouver: Douglas and McIntyre, 2010), p. 14.

p. 197 *"I want to be taken"* quoted in Skallerup, "How to Make Love," 92 (my translation).

p. 197 *"that paternalistic attitude"* quoted in Skallerup, "How to Make Love," p. 93.

p. 198 *"In the international media"* Dany Laferrière, *The Return*, Trans. David Homel (Vancouver: Douglas and McIntyre, 2011), p. 96.

p. 213 *"[should] be seen as a movie novelization?"* Mark Harris, "Rueful Affirmative," *Canadian Literature* 192, Spring 2007, p. 191.

p. 200 *"My husband took my hand"* Dany Laferrière, *Heading South*, Trans. Wayne Grady (Vancouver: Douglas and McIntyre, 2009, p. 131.

p. 201 *"he didn't look like"* Laferrière, *Heading South*, pp. 128–9.

p. 201 *"in [Laferrière's] work we see"* Mills, *A Place in the Sun*, p. 223.

p. 202 *"[He] is flirting with"* Laferrière, *Heading South*, p. 203.

p. 202 *"It's interesting coming to a land"* Maya Jaggi, "Dany Laferrière: a life in books," *The Guardian*, February 1, 2013.

Notes

p. 203 *"For those who have often heard . . . For me Montreal"* Dany Laferrière, "Le discours de Dany Laferrière avant de recevoir son épée d'académicien," *Le Nouvelliste* (Port-au-Prince), June 1 2015 (my translation).

Chapter 10: A Speck of Fascism

p. 204 *"One thing you truly cannot imagine"* Geoff Hancock, "Mavis Gallant," *Canadian Writers at Work: Interviews with Geoff Hancock* (Toronto: Oxford University Press, 1987), p. 98.

p. 204 *"That's something you can't imagine"* Hancock, "Mavis Gallant," p. 98.

p. 204 *"there was hardly a culture"* Hancock, "Mavis Gallant," p. 99.

p. 205 *"Culture! Our readers never went to high school"* Hancock, "Mavis Gallant," p. 100.

p. 207 *"Fascist! Fascist! Fascist!"* Mavis Gallant, "Speck's Idea," *Overhead in a Balloon: Stories of Paris* (Toronto: Stoddart, 1997), p. 4.

p. 207 *"the hoarse imprecation of the Left"* Gallant, "Speck's Idea," p. 5.

p. 208 *"the commerce of art is without bias"* Gallant, "Speck's Idea," p. 5.

p. 208 *"Speck raised his voice to the Right Wing pitch"* Gallant, "Speck's Idea," p. 37.

p. 208 *"the reader feels that he rather agrees"* Danielle Schaube, *Mavis Gallant* (New York: Twayne, 1998), p. 133.

p. 208 *"her raincoat open and flying"* Gallant, "Speck's Idea," p. 44.

p. 207 *"Fascist! Fascist! Fascist!"* Gallant, "Speck's Idea," p. 45.

p. 209 *"It was amazing how it cleared the mind"* Gallant, "Speck's Idea," p. 45.

p. 209 *"FRENCHMEN! FOR THE SAKE OF EUROPE"* Gallant, "Speck's Idea," p. 47.

p. 210 *"Was it a"* Gallant, "Speck's Idea," p. 47.

p. 210 *"Sandor Speck's first art gallery in Paris"* Gallant, "Speck's Idea," p. 1.

p. 211 *"earned him the admiration"* Gallant, "Speck's Idea," p. 17.

p. 211 *"the term* le faubourg Saint-Germain" Stephen Kale, *French Salons: High Society and Political Sociability from the Old Regime to the Revolution of 1848* (Baltimore: Johns Hopkins University Press, 2005), p. 122.

p. 211 *"for the sake of being the"* Gallant, "Speck's Idea," p. 1.

The Canadian Mind

p. 211 "*a conservative color*" Gallant, "Speck's Idea," p. 2.

p. 212 "*French education had left him with*" Gallant, "Speck's Idea," p. 22.

p. 212 "*Marxist embassies*" Gallant, "Speck's Idea," p. 2.

p. 212 "*A Marxist Considers Sweets*" Gallant, "Speck's Idea," p. 18.

p. 213 "*a counterrevolutionary party*" Mark Lilla, "Introduction: The Legitimacy of the Liberal Age," *New French Thought: Political Philosophy*, Mark Lilla, ed. (Princeton: Princeton University Press, 1994), p. 9.

p. 214 "*since 1973 immigration*" Virginie Guiraudon, "Immigration Policy in France," *Brookings*. Brookings Institution, July 2001. Web. June 11, 2015.

p. 214 "*Nowadays the Paris intelligentsia drew new lines*" Gallant, "Speck's Idea," p. 35.

p. 215 "*Though he appreciated style*" Gallant, "Speck's Idea," p. 2.

p. 215 "*determined to make Speck pay*" Gallant, "Speck's Idea," p. 7.

p. 215 "*only early Chagall (quite likely authentic)*" Gallant, "Speck's Idea," p. 7.

p. 215 "*Down with foreign art!*" Gallant, "Speck's Idea," p. 7.

p. 215 "*the complete Charles Maurras*" Gallant, "Speck's Idea," p. 7.

p. 216 "*straddle[s] half a century*" Gallant, "Speck's Idea," p. 10.

p. 217 "*There would be word from the Left, too*" Gallant, "Speck's Idea," p. 10.

p. 217 "*Speck appraising an artist's work*" Gallant, "Speck's Idea," p. 29.

p. 218 "*The road to Auschwitz*" Ian Kershaw, *Hitler, the Germans, and the Final Solution* (New Haven: Yale University Press, 2008), p. 5.

p. 218 "*It's a vision which is palatable*" Sean Fine, "Nazi-Hunting Scholar Under Fire for View," *Globe and Mail* 26 Jan. 1998.

p. 219 "*The faint, floating sadness*" Gallant, "Speck's Idea," p. 3.

p. 219 "*bases itself on loneliness*" Hannah Arendt, *The Origins of Totalitarianism* (New York: Schocken, 2004), p. 612.

p. 220 "*safe side of the barrier*" Gallant, "Speck's Idea," pp. 35–6.

p. 220 "*shriller*" Gallant, "Speck's Idea," p. 5.

p. 220 "*poignant and patriotic on the right*" Gallant, "Speck's Idea," p. 7.

Notes

p. 220 *"Redemption Through Art"* Gallant, "Speck's Idea," p. 8.

p. 220 *"Must the flowering gardens"* Gallant, "Speck's Idea," p. 8.

p. 221 *"Paris and Its Influence"* Gallant, "Speck's Idea," p. 3.

p. 221 *"like a regiment of tanks"* Gallant, "Speck's Idea," p. 45.

p. 222 *"a collection of texts containing"* Emmanuel Faye, *Heidegger: The Introduction of Nazism into Philosophy in Light of the Unpublished Seminars of 1933–1935*, Trans. Michael B. Smith (New Haven: Yale University Press, 2009), p. 319.

p. 223 *"discipline"* Norman Manea, "Happy Guilt" in *The Fifth Impossibility: Essays on Exile and Language* (New Haven: Yale University Press, 2012), pp. 108–9.

p. 223 *"dignity"* Manea, "Happy Guilt," pp. 108–9.

p. 223 *"liquidation of democracy"* Manea, "Happy Guilt," pp. 108–9.

p. 223 *"Jews have overrun"* Manea, "Happy Guilt," pp. 108–9.

p. 223 *"To draw a connection between"* Manea, "Happy Guilt," p. 110.

p. 224 *"anti-France"* Timothy Baycroft, "Ethnicity and the Revolutionary Tradition," *What Is a Nation?: Europe 1789–1914*, Timothy Baycroft and Mark Hewitson, eds. (Oxford: Oxford University Press, 2006), p. 33.

p. 224 *"four confederate states"* Baycroft, "Ethnicity and the Revolutionary Tradition," p. 33.

p. 224 *"Japheth's people settled in Scotland"* Gallant, "Speck's Idea," p. 32.

p. 224 *"Present-day Jews are imposters"* Gallant, "Speck's Idea," p. 32.

p. 225 *"the foreignness of germs"* Howard Markel and Alexandra Minna Stern, "The Foreignness of Germs: The Persistent Association of Immigrants and Disease in American Society," *Milbank Quarterly* 80 (2002), p. 757.

p. 225 *"generations of highly intellectual"* Gallant, "Speck's Idea," p. 2.

p. 225 *"second generation distress"* Gallant, "Speck's Idea," p. 22.

p. 226 *"the least precise and most widely invoked"* Lilla, "Introduction: The Legitimacy of the Liberal Age," p. 9.

p. 226 *"a highly centralized, majoritarian government"* Lilla, "Introduction: The Legitimacy of the Liberal Age," p. 9.

p. 228 *"the French people born with"* Patrick Geary, *The Myth of Nations: The Medieval Origins of Europe* (Princeton: Princeton University Press, 2003), p. 9.

p. 229 *"reluctant countries of immigration"* Wayne Cornelius, Philip Martin, and James Hollifield, *Controlling Immigration: A Global Perspective*, Wayne Cornelius, Philip Martin, and James Hollifield, eds. (Stanford: Stanford University Press, 1994), p. v.

Afterword

p. 230 A literary critic who was scathing about everything. This was Dale Peck. See "The Art of the Bad Review," *The Walrus*, July–August, 2004.

p. 231 Boyden's case has bearing on a similar one. See Jolene Banning, "Amid calls of cultural appropriation, Tanya Tagaq and Inuit musicians boycott Indigenous Music Awards over Cree musician's throat singing," *The Globe and Mail*, May 19, 2019.

p. 231-2 Legislation Quebec introduced in 2022. See Joe Friesen, "Quebec bill on academic freedom says no words are off-limits in classrooms," *The Globe and Mail*, April 6, 2022.

INDEX

265

Index

election in, 108
generator of new norms, role as, 23
literary
  canon, 154
  history, 153
literature, 8, 154
  society, and, 12
poem of 1856, 4–5
political institutions, 101
short-story writing, 5–6
war-crimes unit, 218
writers, 6
written history of, 21
Canada First nationalist movement, 3
Canada Reads, 96
*The Canadian Don Quixote: The
  Life and Works of Major John
  Richardson, Canada's First
  Novelist*, 15
Canadianization, 39
*Canadian Literature: Surrender or
  Revolution*, 6, 31
The Canadian Settler's Guide, 18
The Canadian Short Story, 41, 44–48
Cardinal, Harold, 54
Carleton, Guy, 22
Catharine Parr Traill model, 18
Charter of Rights and Freedoms, 52
Chaudhuri, Amit, 83–84, 197
Central Intelligence Agency (CIA)
  Jordan's General Intelligence
    Department, proxy jailer for,
    136
  1956 report, 139
Childhood, 162

*The Children of Aataentsic: A History of
  the Huron People to 1660* (1976),
  93
Chong, Kevin, 162
Chump Change, 37
Civil Elegies, 167
Clarity Act, 23
Clark, Joe, 30
*Clearing the Plains: Disease, Politics
  of Starvation and the Loss of
  Aboriginal Life*, 27–28
The Closing of the American Mind, 167
Cohen, Leonard, 99, 256
The Favourite Game, 164
The Colony of Unrequired Dreams, 162,
  168
Comaneci, Nadia, 181
Coming Through Slaughter, 164
Communitarian, 53, 61
Company of Adventurers, 90
Connolly, Cyril, 32, 38, 240
  literary criticism, 32
Copeland, Ann, 44, 47
Couch, S.
  interview in *Guantánamo Diary*,
    143–144
  prosecutor assigned against Slahi, 143
Coupland, Douglas, 37, 162
Cranston, Toller, 36
Creelman, Libby, 47
Cross, Bill, 106
Cross, James, 193
Cultigen, 85
Cultural Appropriation and the Arts
  (2008), 80

Index

Index

271

Index

North American Free Trade Agreement
in 1994, 151
North American troops, 157–158

O

O Canada, 8
Oil crisis, 214
On Being Here to Stay (2014), 91
Ondaatje, Michael, 157–158, 164, 166
The English Patient, 165
Coming Through Slaughter, 164
One Hundred Years of Solitude, 155
Onigaming First Nation, 96
Orange Prize
Fugitive Pieces, 165
Larry's Party, 165
The Orenda (2013), 79–80, 84–85,
88–93, 95–97, 99–101, 103–104
Ottawa Citizen, 44
*The Oxford Book of Canadian Short
Stories in English*, 40

P

Parker, Gilbert Sir, 14
Parti Quebecois, 191–192
Patriot Act, 149
Patten, Alan, 73, 75
formulation, 74
subtle theory of culture, 76
theory, 73
Péloquin, Marjolaine, 192
Perpetual Motion, 10–11
Persky, Stan,
book critic, 111
multiculturalism, view on, 111
The Politics of Recognition, 49

Pound, Ezra, 42
Protestantism, 58
Proulx, Annie, 179
Pueblo people, 58
Pulitzer Prize
The Stone Diaries, 165
Purdy, Al, 19, 44
Pyper, Andrew, 163

Q

Quebec
character of, 59
collective rights, 55
colony at, 86
distinct society, 52
economy, 192
film from, 195
How to Make Love, sensation in,
191
indigenous people, 54, 60
journey to, 86–87
Laicity Act, 70
language laws, 116
liberalism, Taylor describes, 117
Taylor's argument on, 122
Law 101, 57–58
national assembly and other
institutions, 59
nationalists, 191–192
role for French, 57
separatism, 161–162
society, 192–193
unemployment rates, 192
Wendat to Catholicism, 85
Quiet Revolution, 24, 30, 192–194
Quill and Quire magazine, 44

Index

Index

cultural nationalism in Canada, 3
culture, 2
    traditional suspicion, 3–4
Unless, 162–163
Upper-class WASPs, 172
Urquhart, Jane, 153

V

Vallières, Pierre, 192
Volkh, Eugene, 187
Vollmann, William, 179
Voth, H. R., 82

W

Wacousta: or The Prophecy: A Tale of the Canadas, 12–14
The Wacousta Syndrome, 1, 15
Waldron, Jeremy, 62–63
    argument, 64
The Wall Street Journal, 49, 125
Walzer, Michael, 51
Ward, Bruce, 44
Weaver, Robert, 40
Wendat culture, 91
Wendat diet, 85
Wendat mythology, 97
Western films, history, 92
What Is a Canadian Literature?, 7, 31, 171
When France Was at the Helm, 225

When Words Deny the World: The Reshaping of Canadian Writing, 152–154, 157, 159, 165, 168, 171–172
White Niggers of America, 192
Why Must a Black Writer Write About Sex? (1994), 195–196, 198
Williamson, Janice, 79
Wilson, Edmund, 8, 20, 159, 234
    O Canada, 8
Wilson, Ethel, 12
Wilson-Raybould, Jody, 101
    indigenous reconciliation, 103
The Windigo, 11
Winesburg, Ohio, 32
Winnipeg General Strike, 24
Winter, Kathleen, 44
A Woman and Catholicism: My Break With the Roman Catholic Church, 35
The World is Moving Around Me: A Memoir of the Haitian Earthquake, 182
Wyndham, John, 169

Y

Young, James, 80
    book, 81–82
    framework, 81